D0090280

GOOD CHEAP FOOD

,75

ALSO BY MIRIAM UNGERER

The Too Hot to Cook Book

GOOD CHEAP FOOD

Miriam Ungerer

Illustrations by Dominique Strandquest

A WILLIAM COLE BOOK

The Viking Press / *New York*

Copyright © 1973 by Miriam Ungerer
All rights reserved
A William Cole Book
First published in 1973 in a hardbound and paperbound edition by
The Viking Press, Inc.
625 Madison Avenue, New York, N.Y. 10022
Published simultaneously in Canada by
The Macmillan Company of Canada Limited
SBN 670-34543-1 (hardbound)
670-01964-x (paperbound)
Library of Congress catalog card number: 72-81253
Printed in U.S.A.

M. Evans and Company, Inc.: "Tinga Poblana" from
The Complete Book of Mexican Cooking by Elisabeth Lambert Ortiz
Copyright © 1965 by The Conde Nast Publications Inc.

The Macmillan Company and Russell & Volkening, Inc.:
"Eggs in Hell" from Art of Eating: Five Gastronomical Works
by M. F. K. Fisher. Copyright 1942 by M. F. K. Fisher.

To W. S.

and

the late A. J. *Liebling, who wrote:*

"A man who is rich in his adolescence is almost doomed to be a dilettante. This is not because all millionaires are stupid but because they are not impelled to experiment."

CONTENTS

FOREWORD

This is the part that nobody reads, but it seems to be some kind of immutable tradition in publishing—so onward and downward.

First of all, the reason I wanted to write this book was a reaction to having worked incognito on an elaborate cookbook published by people who attributed to their readers the mentality of a gibbon and the inventiveness of an owl. Obviously, they were also assumed to be rich, since the recipes cost so much to make. Somewhere out there, I thought, must be an audience that is literate and poor who would like a cookbook. So, here it is—a book for skinflint gourmets.

The recipes should suit a variety of regional tastes, since they have been collected in South Carolina, North Carolina, Florida, Texas, Tennessee, Montana, California, Pennsylvania, New York, Germany, France, Italy, Switzerland, and some islands in the Caribbean. I've lived in most of these places and have good and sufficient reasons for all this hoboing and I'm keeping quiet about it.

To the frequently asked question "Did you make up all these recipes yourself"? the answer is "No." And neither does any other cookbook writer. Cooking is an evolutionary art proceeding simultaneously in many kitchens, and even when you do hit on something you think is original, chances are you'll find something very like it in the *Larousse Gastronomique*. I've invented some of the things in this book; others are my interpretation of classic dishes. In some instances I have adapted recipes for thrift, but never so much so that the character of the dish is ruined.

You can't fake a filet mignon, so why try? It's better to make a cassoulet instead. Cheap food is, alas, not often quick food (unless you consider frozen TV dinners to be *food*—in that case leave the room, please). Filet de Boeuf Wellington (filet mignon with truffles and *foie gras*) is pretty quick; Boeuf Bourguignonne (beef stew in red wine) is not. In very different ways one is as good as the other. The "other"—

cheap and good rather than priceless and good—is what you'll be seeing quite a lot of here.

To cook well and economically, you must know what to look for in food and how to make the best use of it.

M. U.

"*Economy is a distributive virtue, and consists not in saving but in selection. Parsimony requires no providence, no sagacity, no powers of combination, no comparison, no judgment.*"

—EDMUND BURKE, Letter to a Noble Lord (1796)

KITCHEN EQUIPMENT

Batterie de cuisine is the French for a set of cooking utensils, and it has a proud ring to it. It sounds like getting suited up for a major encounter with a solid roast or ragout—not just a minor skirmish with a TV dinner tray. People who feed off convenience foods hardly need any equipment at all, but this book is devoted to good, sound, money-saving, real food. It has to be cut, trussed, sometimes boned, molded, simmered, stirred, and cared for. Without at least the nucleus of a well-stocked *batterie de cuisine*, cooking is all pain and frustration and seldom successful.

Your hands are the best kitchen utensil there is. Use them for everything you possibly can: e.g., turning a salad, stuffing a chicken, mixing pastry ingredients. Spoons and spatulas slow you down and don't really do such a good job as your fingers. "Turn the roasting chicken over on its side, using two wooden spoons" is a piece of utter balderdash solemnly set down in many cookbooks. You are further admonished not to puncture the beast or tear its crispy skin—which the wooden spoons always do. So what *do* you do? Buy a pair of casserole mitts of thick cotton that can be easily washed with each use.

What is generally conceded to be basic cooking equipment might terrify you into "boil-a-bag" cookery for life. So I have pruned the list and include as many multi-purpose items as possible. First of all, don't buy "sets" of cookpots—even the sales of Le Creuset ware usually include some useless tiny pot or dumb frying pan. Look around in thrift shops, Goodwill Industries outlets, the Salvation Army stores, and keep out of department stores unless they're having an incredible sale of kitchenware that you know the true value of. Used cooking pans are often better than new ones, especially cast iron, which takes some time to season properly. I have found wonderful, smooth black iron pans in country junk shops.

As you become more involved with cooking, you find yourself mooning around hardware stores fondling French *poissonières* (fish kettles) and charlotte molds. Hardware stores are more likely to stock sensible, sturdy

round casserole

charlotte mold

roaster

oval casserole

cast-iron skillet

double boiler

frying pan

colander

saucepan

sauté pan

baking dish

gratin dish

utility baking
pan with rack

oval baking dish

stock pot

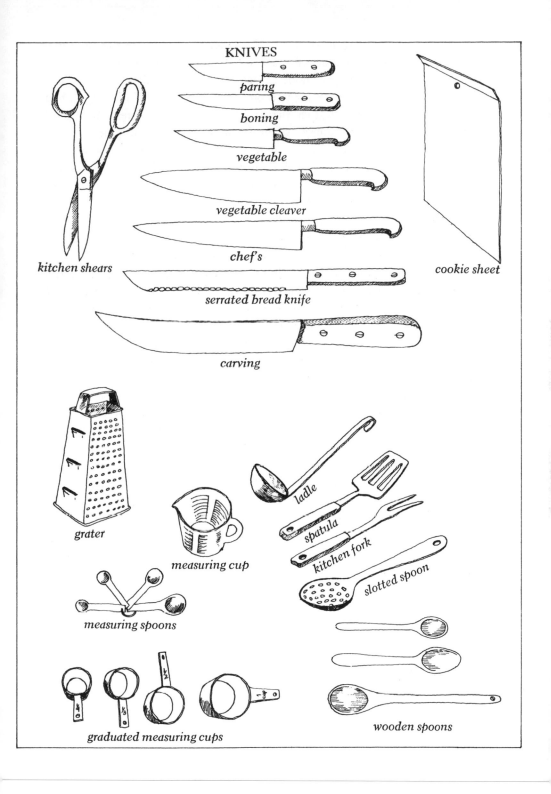

KNIVES

paring

boning

vegetable

vegetable cleaver

chef's

serrated bread knife

carving

kitchen shears

cookie sheet

grater

measuring cup

ladle

spatula

kitchen fork

slotted spoon

measuring spoons

graduated measuring cups

wooden spoons

kitchen equipment and leave the $150 copper fish kettles to the "gourmet corner" of department stores. For special things go to or write a real gourmet cookware store such as Dione Lucas, 226 East Fifty-first Street, or The Bridge Company, 212 East Fifty-second Street, in New York City. Their prices are fair, in fact cheaper than some department stores. Restaurant supply houses are good sources of professional cooking equipment at the lowest prices. "Lawn auctions," where the entire contents of a house are being disposed of, are a bargain-hunter's dream. Nobody is ever interested in the kitchen stuff, and you can pick up serviceable items, sometimes unusual and beautiful things no longer made.

French food would not look and taste the way it does if the French had not given more thought and care to the manufacture of kitchen equipment than anyone else in the world. We have multitudes of electrical gadgets gathering dust in our kitchens. (I have a blender, a toaster, and a coffee grinder that I use all the time and a big hulking electric mixer I never touch.) But the French have all sorts of cheap little hand tools that cut, scrape, grate, grind, core, scoop, and curl food. Those carbon steel Sabatier knives, the everlasting and beautiful Le Creuset enamel-lined iron casseroles, the warm sienna earthenware cooking pots made in Vallauris as they have been for a hundred years at least.

Good cookware is not an extravagance; it will outperform and outlast cheap pots and pans for generations if it's properly cared for. Build your collection of kitchen equipment slowly after the need for each piece has been established. Because I have the combined contents of a huge country kitchen and a fairly big city kitchen now sharing the same space, the superfluity nearly rivals Mrs. William Paley's clothes closet. Yet I continue collecting and finding things I positively cannot get on without. The things listed below, however, are so basic no serious cook should be without them. Try to keep everything within easy reach—on pegboard, overhead pot racks, open shelves. A kitchen needn't have its function concealed. Keep knives on a heavy steel magnet attached to the wall above the work counter.

Carbon steel knives of French or German manufacture:
   1 chef's knife with 10-inch triangular blade
   1 boning knife
   1 carving knife, 12-inch scimitar
   1 small paring knife, 4-inch triangular blade
   1 sharpening steel

Stainless steel:
  - 1 serrated bread knife
  - 1 vegetable knife, 6-inch blade
  - 1 Japanese vegetable cleaver or a good manual slicer

General equipment:
  - 1 colander
  - 1 fine-mesh strainer
  - 1 slotted spoon
  - 1 large ladle
  - 1 set measuring spoons
  - 2 sauce whisks (medium and large)
  - 1 swivel-bladed vegetable peeler
  - 3 wooden spoons, different sizes
  - 1 perforated spatula
  - 1 long 2-pronged kitchen fork
  - 1 2-cup measuring cup
  - 1 set metal measuring cups, graduated
  - 1 heavy rotary hand beater
  - 1 grater
  - 1 pepper mill
  - kitchen shears
  - 1 portable timer (1 minute to 1 hour)
  - 1 sifter
  - 1 saltbox
  - 1 long-handled wire mesh ladle
  - soft trussing string
  - pastry cloth and rolling pin with knit cover
  - 1 wooden mortar and pestle
  - 1 nutcracker
  - 1 nonelectric can-opener
  - 1 corkscrew
  - 1 chopping board
  - joined casserole mitts
  - pastry brush
  - glass jars for staple foods
  - stoneware crock, 6-quart
  - 1 meat grinder
  - 1 food mill   cheesecloth

poultry skewers
1 ice pick
1 bottle opener ("church-key")
3 funnels, graduated sizes
1 grooved carving board with well
potholders and tea towels
1 tea kettle
1 drip-type coffee pot, nonelectric
3 nested mixing bowls (heavy china)

Pots and pans:

1 enameled iron oval casserole with lid, 3-quart
1 enameled iron round casserole with lid, 2-quart
1 stainless steel double boiler (this can be improvised)
1 enamelware saucepan with lid, 3-quart (for boiling eggs and vegetables)
1 open utility baking pan (15 x 10 x 3 inches) with rack
1 enameled iron oval baking dish, 12 inches long
1 ovenproof porcelain gratin (oval) dish, 9 inches long
1 1½-quart tin charlotte mold (can be used for desserts and soufflés)
1 heavy-gauge aluminum sauté pan, straight-sided, 12-inch diameter
1 cast-iron skillet with cover, 12-inch diameter
1 Teflon-lined heavy-gauge aluminum frying pan, 8-inch slant-sided (for omelets and sautéing small amounts of food—does not have to be used only for omelets)
1 heavy steel Chinese wok, 12-inch diameter
1 cookie sheet
1 blue-speckled oval enamel roaster with deep cover, 12 inches long (can be used for braising, roasting, poaching fish, etc.)
assorted pie tins and baking tins
6–8 round ovenproof porcelain baking dishes, 4-inch diameter, 1 inch deep
1 heavy-gauge aluminum stock pot, tall, straight-sided, 8- to 10-quart (this is not the ideal material for a stock pot—but tinned copper or the old earthenware ones cost the moon and the enameled steel makers are practically out of business, so this very good type of stock pot is hard to find)
1 aluminum or, if you can find it, enameled steel ring mold

I do not by any means consider this list comprehensive, but many of the saucepans and casseroles are multi-purpose and capable of dealing with the scope of the average home cook. If you like to make bread, bake extensively, or have other special interests, such as pâtés and terrines, that equipment would have to be added. Aluminum-foil pans are ugly but useful for these purposes. French flame- and ovenproof earthenware casseroles are beautiful and excellent cookware, but require careful treatment.

An electric blender is to me the most useful of automatic kitchen tools. Perhaps if I had a better quality electric mixer, I might see more point to it—I can beat up four egg whites in my copper bowl using a hand whisk faster than the mixer. I think these machines are hardly worth having unless you can afford those designed for professional or restaurant use. Electric can-openers are ridiculous, and the knife sharpener attachment ruins good knives. Living in Manhattan, I have to face the possibility of a total power failure, but even so, a good cook should never be too reliant on automatic appliances. This includes electric stoves—when did you ever hear of a *gas* failure? Chiefly I find electric stoves impossible because the heat cannot be manipulated with the instantaneous speed of a gas range. Also, their timers are all right, but you can't carry them with you to another room like a simple, portable nonelectric timer. Finally, cooking with gas costs about one-third the price of electricity.

FATS AND THEIR USES

I am not willing to write "or margarine" after "butter" every place it turns up in this book. In the recipes where the butter flavor is essential, this is stated. When it comes to olive oil, I don't mean "or salad oil" unless specified, because the substitution would result in a fatal dullness. There are few things drearier than a vinaigrette dressing made with taste-less vegetable oils.

Margarine has improved enormously since the first noxious white block that looked like lard and tasted like Vaseline. Only the very poor used it in those days, but during World War II when all the butter went to war, everybody had to bear with it. I will never understand why we need more butter in wartime than in peacetime—the same men were eating before they put on uniforms. With the margarine, a little packet of orange powder was sometimes provided. A half-hour's mashing and blending could usually make the stuff look a little more edible, even though the streaky orange sunset effect hardly resembled butter.

Here is what *The Good Housekeeping Cook Book,* 1942 edition, has to say about it: "Margarine is made from either vegetable or animal fats or a blend of these, churned in a culture of skim milk to give it a flavor akin to butter. It has the same energy value as butter, and if 'fortified' or 'vitaminized' [writers began "izing" words that long ago] is as rich in vitamin A as butter. Children and adults may use it safely in place of butter."

Today margarine is usually made of corn or other vegetable oil, has vitamins A and D added, and is indistinguishable from butter to many palates. Alas, not to mine, but I find certain brands just dandy for general cooking. All this progress has been made in the teeth of a powerful dairy lobby which has forced legislation requiring margarine manufacturers to put everything but a skull and crossbones on their packaging. Wisconsin used to *prohibit* the sale of precolored margarine; now the state only *taxes* colored margarine but not the white stuff. Some states require restaurants who do so to post conspicuous signs declaring "Margarine Served Here."

At any rate, the butter lobby has made damn certain that margarine users know what they're getting and feel rather crummy about it too. Even during the Depression (the *other* one, in the thirties), a friend tells me, in working-class households margarine was associated with welfare and a great fuss was made about "not having fallen so low as to eat margarine."

Well, the old frump has come a long way toward respectability, if anybody still cares. I highly recommend the fresh, unsalted margarine for general use. Because it has no preservatives, it is found in the frozen-food bins and should be kept frozen at home except for the quarter being used. Sweet butter, as you are no doubt aware, costs more than salted butter—another example, like skimmed milk, of the dairy industry making you pay for leaving something out. Sweet margarine is almost undetectable in "herb butters." Tarragon, parsley, basil, and chive are the most useful ones to make. Soften the margarine, chop the herbs roughly, and whirl the mixture in a blender or just mash the things together with a fork. Store the herb butter in small jars (baby-food jars are useful) and keep them refrigerated. It is good on steaks, chops, hamburgers, baked potatoes, and many other things.

The hydrogenated vegetable shortenings (Crisco, Spry, etc.) are excellent for pastry and some cakes. Many cooks prefer them for frying, especially deep-fat frying. Corn or peanut oil is my choice for this purpose. Neither needs refrigerating even after opening unless you live near the equator or in San Antonio, Texas. Any oil or fat used for deep-fat frying is reusable if it is treated properly. It should be strained through several thicknesses of washed cheesecloth laid in a sieve. You can further eliminate any flavors it may have picked up by putting a few slices of potato into the cold oil or fat and bringing it slowly to the frying point. If, however, you have burnt food in the fat, or the fat itself, there's nothing for it but to throw it out.

Lard is pure hog fat rendered and refined to soft creaminess. It is the cheapest cooking fat and is widely used in the South and in Latin American cookery. Beef suet is wonderful for biscuits and the pastry for meat pies. Unfortunately I've never seen it put up in neat pound blocks the way it is sold in England and Ireland. You can make your own by saving the pure fat from a beef roast, straining it, and storing it in the icebox. It gives a delicious flavor to home-fries and smothered onions and makes nifty fried bread to eat with soups. Other kinds of "dripping" removed from broths and stews make tasty cooking fat. Never leave excess fat on broths or stews; this is one of the commonest reasons for the failure of a dish. Chill the dish and when the fat congeals you can easily lift it off.

Fat from a roast duck is copious and must be siphoned off as it accumulates so that it won't burn. It will have the flavor of herbs and onions which it imparts to the foods cooked in it. Bacon fat is also useful for lots of sautéing jobs, but too much should not be allowed to build up. A coffee can is too large and the fat in the bottom is usually rancid before it's half filled. Use frozen orange juice cans instead; keep them tightly covered and never keep more than one at a time.

If you live in a very hot climate, all fats and oils must be kept refrigerated. Under normal conditions, olive and vegetable oils and vegetable shortenings don't need refrigeration, but the cooked fats (drippings, bacon and duck fat, etc.) certainly do. You can also freeze them for longer storage.

With the exception of butter or margarine, deep-fat cooking oil, and olive oil for salads, you should have plenty of interesting and well-flavored cooking fats without having to buy anything. After all, the butcher has already charged you for them.

GOOD CHEAP FOOD

1

SOUPS AND CHOWDERS

"Soo—oop of the e—e—evening, beautiful, beautiful Soup!" the Mock Turtle crooned to Alice. As for me, I could take soup of the morning and soup of the noon as well. Some kind of soup is the usual breakfast of many European farmers, and at least one other eccentric American believes, with me, that it's a great idea.

In his diary-cum-cookbook, *The Haphazard Gourmet*, novelist-journalist Richard Gehman wrote of his bean soup, "A bowl of it will make anyone fit to do all his chores, take on new ones, settle the race crisis, or invent something more revolutionary than the wheel." I recommend Mr. Gehman, his book, and his bean soup to you most heartily. He once made a marathon bean soup that lived for three weeks by adding different bits of stuff each day which he ate daily at one meal or another. I too recommend this notion, which may be applied to *my* bean soup and a few others in this chapter. Once a soup base has been established, you can change its character again and again by adding leftover meats, stock, different vegetables, beans, or whatever strikes you as a good idea. This kind of perpetual pot is a good thing to have around if you, as I do, have people wandering in at odd hours for something to eat.

Because of changing eating (and drinking) patterns, most contemporary cookbooks begin with appetizers, but the old ones swung right into soups, which were an essential part of every cook's basic accomplishments. Eliza Acton's *Modern Cookery*, first published in England in 1845, lists over sixty soups. Since she was brought up in France, her knowledge of cookery was sound, and she had read up on nutrition, an embryo science few people knew much about.

Appalled at the carelessness and waste in English kitchens, the fastidious Miss Acton hectors her middle-class Victorians in Chapter I (Soups), "The art of preparing good, wholesome, palatable soups, *without great expense*, which is so well understood in France, and in other countries where they form part of the daily food of all classes of the people, has hitherto been very much neglected in England;* [the footnote is a pained Horrible Example] yet it really presents no difficulties which a little practice, and the most common degree of care, will not readily overcome; and we strongly recommend increased attention to it, not only on account of the loss and inconvenience which ignorance of it occasions in many households, but because a better knowledge of it will lead naturally to improvement in other branches of cookery connected with it in which our want of skill is now equally apparent." In this passage I would change only two words: "hitherto" to "lately" and "England" to "America."

Up until the Age of the Can-Opener, American cookbooks were filled with splendid soups, both staple and fancy, and there was certainly no question about the importance of soup in a family meal. I don't really expect that many people will be bothered to make their own stock, but if I can urge a *pot-au-feu* at least once every two weeks, your family will be deliciously fed and there will be, as well, the base of more "beautiful, beautiful Soup!"

POT-AU-FEU

About the closest thing we have to this mainstay of French home cookery is the New England Boiled Dinner—and that, more often than not, is several hectares away. Besides the soup, meat, and vegetables provided in the following one-pot meal (always described as "simple peasant fare" in French books), it should also furnish a couple of quarts of excellent stock for other cooking purposes. The stock from the salty corned beef of the New England dinner is good for nothing, although in every other way the dish can be comparable to a good *pot-au-feu*.

By "simple" I must assume that French cookery books mean "plain" fare, because the construction of a *pot-au-feu* is a damned big production. It cannot be made in small quantities (which would defeat its purpose anyway), and although I don't imagine any Frenchwoman would consider it appropriate, I serve *pot-au-feu* to dinner guests who seem delighted with its old-fashioned charms.

Serves 8–10

4 lbs. boneless beef pot roast (a well-shaped piece of top or bottom round or rump—not too lean)
3 lbs. beef shinbones and veal knuckle, mixed
1 4-lb. roasting chicken
1 whole kielbasy (round Polish sausage)
  pot vegetables:
    2 ribs celery, chopped
    1 peeled onion stuck with 2 cloves
    2 carrots, peeled and sliced
1 bouquet garni: 2–3 split cloves garlic, 8 peppercorns, 1 bay leaf, 3 sprigs parsley tied in a washed cheesecloth bag
16 carrots, peeled (cut in half, if large)
8 parsnips, peeled (ditto)
16–20 small white onions, skinned
8–10 cabbage wedges, tied in shape
4 quarts cold beef broth (canned or made with bouillon cubes)
salt and freshly milled black pepper
8–10 old potatoes, peeled and left whole
fresh parsley, minced

The French country cook is trying to extract the maximum flavor from the meat for the broth. However, if you prefer, as I do, to keep the meat as palatable as possible, the juices must be sealed in by boiling liquid. The beef roast should be neatly tied, the shin and veal knuckle cracked to give body and flavor to the broth. Even a sullen supermarket butcher should be willing to perform these simple tasks, but he probably won't truss the chicken for you. Do this yourself, first extracting the giblets from the cavity. The kielbasy isn't mandatory, but it's fairly cheap, and adds greatly to the appearance and feeding capacity of the *pot-au-feu*.

Tie a long heavy string to all the meats so that you can fasten them to the handles of your pot, enabling you to test the various components and remove them as they are done. The pot may be a problem: it should be very deep, not too wide, and with a heavy bottom. In other words, the traditional French stock pot, which few American kitchens possess. The best substitute is probably the large (10-quart) aluminum pot with

Pot au Feu

cover, which can be found in any housewares store. It is too wide but that's irremediable; to compensate for the too thin bottom, insulate it with an asbestos pad on top of the burner.

Put the shin and knucklebones into the pot with the cold bouillon. Bring it to the boil, skimming several times; then, after 10 or 15 minutes, put in the beef roast and, when the broth returns to the boil, reduce it to a simmer. Tie the "pot" vegetables (these are only to flavor the bouillon and will be discarded) and the bouquet garni into a cheesecloth bag and add to the pot, along with the chicken giblets, also tied in a bag. Set the lid slightly askew and simmer for two hours, then skim off as much fat as you can. Tie all the other vegetables in separate washed cheesecloth bags and leave them in a pot of cold water.

Next into the pot go the chicken and carrots. If you object to the look of white chicken, brown it first in some oil. The chicken will certainly be done in 45 minutes and *must* be removed or it will fall to bits—start testing after 35 minutes. The entire *pot-au-feu* should be done in a total of 3 hours. Add the remaining ingredients to coincide with this, following these cooking times: parsnips should be tender in about 30 minutes, the onions in 20 minutes, the potatoes also in 20 minutes. Kielbasy is wholly cooked and needs only 20 minutes simmering. Season with salt and pepper. The cabbage must be cooked separately or it will ruin the broth by imparting too cabbagy a flavor. Put the cabbage wedges, tied in shape with a string (no cheesecloth bag), into a saucepan, dip a couple of cups of broth out of the *pot-au-feu* to cook the cabbage in, and simmer until just tender, about 15 minutes.

All this sounds rather hectic, but remember, anything that is done may be removed quite easily—strings are tied to the meats and the vegetables are in separate bundles—and set aside with a little broth to keep them moist, then everything returned to the pot for heating up. Most French recipes simply put all the vegetables in at once and leave them for an hour, but this results in vegetables rather too mushy for American tastes. Admittedly my recipe's a bit fussy, but you'll like the veges as much as the meats.

You will need a heated platter of heroic proportions (and a couple of native bearers) to present the *pot-au-feu* at its most dramatic. Arrange the meats in the center of the platter with the vegetable garnish around them. Sprinkle liberally with fresh chopped parsley. Skim the bouillon; then strain it into a hot pitcher. At the table, let each person pour some over a piece of toasted garlic bread placed in the bottom of his soup bowl. While this is being eaten, carve the meats and serve on hot plates. Kosher (coarse) salt, a very hot mustard, and a horse-radish sauce are usually served in side dishes. An easy horse-radish sauce can be made with sour cream mixed with bottled white horse-radish (it should be fresh and bought from a refrigerated case in the store). The proportions are 1 cup sour cream to 1 4-oz. bottle of horse-radish, drained. Sauce rémoulade is also good with boiled beef.

Any leftover vegetables may be diced and served cold with a vinaigrette dressing; the beef and chicken can be used in sandwiches or made into salads.

POTATO AND LEEK SOUP

Some form of potato soup is the staff of peasant life in France, Germany, and many European countries. It is also the foundation of a number of classy soups such as watercress, spinach, sorrel, or broccoli, all delicious served hot or cold. And, as no doubt everybody has discovered, vichyssoise is just potato soup showing off.

3 Tbsp. butter

1 bunch leeks (or two large onions)

2 medium potatoes, peeled and diced (about 1½ cups)

3 cups chicken broth

½ pint light cream (milk is no disaster)

salt and white pepper to taste

minced fresh parsley or chives

Melt the butter in a heavy, enamel-lined casserole (plain iron will discolor this soup). Cut off most of the green tops of the leeks; split the leeks lengthwise almost through so that you can get at the sand lodged there. Wash thoroughly under cold running water and slice thinly. Simmer them slowly, covered, in the butter over a very low heat until transparent. Add potatoes and chicken broth and simmer about half an hour. Purée in a blender or food mill and return to heat. Season with salt and pepper and stir in cream. Serve hot or cold sprinkled with fresh herbs.

NOTE: All cold soups must be a bit more seasoned than hot ones because chilling blunts flavors; also remember that cold soup will be much thicker than hot soup.

VARIATIONS:

Watercress soup: Chop the stems off a bunch of watercress just above the string that binds it. Discard stems. Wash, drain, and coarsely chop the watercress and add it to the soup about 5 minutes before potatoes are done. Proceed with master recipe. Watercress soup really should be made with cream if it's to be served cold (a smoother texture is necessary in cold soups) and then thinned a bit with milk just before serving. The thinning is done when the soup is cold so that the consistency may be judged accurately.

Spinach soup: Wash 1 pound fresh spinach through several waters and tear out coarse stems and spines of big leaves. Blanch (throw it into boiling water) one minute, drain, and chop. Proceed with the recipe for Watercress Soup. Frozen chopped spinach (1 package) is a lot less work, though not as good. It should be thawed and drained of that evil-colored juice before being added to the soup.

Parsley soup: Substitute 1 cup fresh, chopped parsley for the watercress in that recipe.

Broccoli soup: Add leftover cooked broccoli to the potato soup just before puréeing. Or thaw a package of frozen broccoli, cut off and discard the coarser stems, and simmer the broccoli along with the potatoes in the master recipe. If the soup is to be served hot, enrich it with a couple of beaten egg yolks. To avoid curdling the yolks, do it this way: beat yolks with a wire whisk and slowly dribble in about ½ cup of hot soup, beating all the time. Then, off heat, beat this mixture back into the soup. *Do not boil.*

Cauliflower soup: Press excess water out of about 1½ cups freshly cooked cauliflower and add to the potato soup before puréeing. Here you cannot substitute frozen or leftover cauliflower; both are gray and ghastly as a rule. Enrich with egg yolks as in Broccoli Soup and serve hot.

Asparagus soup: Snap off and discard tough stems of ½ pound young green asparagus. Peel remaining stems up two inches. Cut off tips and simmer in a very little lightly salted water until tender. Reserve. Chop stalks and add to the soup along with the potatoes in the master recipe. Just before serving, stir the reserved asparagus tips and their juice into the hot soup. I've never served this cold, but I don't know why. Perhaps because there's never any left over.

There are other vegetables adaptable to the Potato and Leek Soup recipe. For instance, I've heard tell of a cream of turnip soup. I can't imagine it—but maybe you can. Each to his own taste and all that. . . .

SAVOURY SUMMER SOUP (ZUCCHINI)

When last summer's zucchini crop ran amok in the garden, this soup was created (along with a stuffed zucchini dish, zucchini pickles, zucchini salad, and a lot of other things until I finally decided to let the squashes grow to the size of watermelons and use them for outdoor footstools). Although it costs little to make (in season), I think this soup belongs in the grande luxe class because of its subtle flavor and opulent texture.

Serves 6 to 8

4 young, dark green zucchini (6 to 7 inches long)
1 green bell pepper
3 medium onions
2 large cloves garlic
4 Tbsp. butter
salt and white pepper

2 Tbsp. fresh thyme, chopped (skip this if the fresh herb is unavailable)
6 cups chicken broth
1 cup heavy cream
fresh chives or parsley, minced

Slice 3 zucchini, the pepper, and the onions. Mince the garlic. Sauté the vegetables in 3 tablespoons of the butter over very low heat in a heavy pot. Cook, stirring often, about 10 minutes, or until the vegetables are tender but have not browned at all. Add salt and pepper to taste and thyme, if available. Stir in the chicken broth and simmer, uncovered, for 15 minutes. Meanwhile, thinly slice (do not peel) the remaining zucchini and sauté it briefly in 1 tablespoon butter until barely tender and still bright green. This should take about 3 minutes—stir and watch closely that it doesn't overcook and go mushy. Immediately turn the sliced vegetable out onto a china plate to cool quickly. Reserve.

Cool the soup slightly and purée it in a blender (or a food mill). Stir in the cream and the sliced, cooked zucchini. Adjust the seasoning—the soup should be rather highly seasoned, as chilling vitiates flavors. Chill 24 hours and serve with a scattering of fresh herbs (chives or parsley).

HOT AND COLD ONION SOUP

A chilled and creamy soup of downright dazzling subtlety, this soup is the result of a love affair I had last summer with a nifty blender. We still have a beautiful relationship as we mellow into winter experiments.

Makes 1½ quarts

2 Tbsp. butter
1 tsp. cumin (powdered)
½ tsp. turmeric (saffron is nicer, but expensive)
½ tsp. white pepper or dried red flakes
1 cardamom pod (crushed)

3 large (4-inch) onions, sliced
1 large potato, diced
1 quart chicken broth
½ pint light cream (or milk)
salt to taste
minced fresh chives or parsley

Melt butter in an enamel-lined iron kettle. Add cumin, turmeric or saffron, white or red pepper, and cardamom. Stir and cook gently 5 minutes. Add the sliced onions, stir them around, cover, and cook until they are quite limp but not browned. Swirl the potato into the onions and spices and pour on hot chicken broth. Simmer, covered, 20 minutes. Cool about 10 minutes, then purée in a blender. Pour into a nonmetallic container, blend in the cream or milk, and taste for salt. Cold soups should always be slightly oversalted because chilling dulls the flavor, another reason why this seemingly spicy soup is so delicate cold. Chill overnight, if possible, or at least 4 hours. Serve in cold white china cups and sprinkle with minced fresh chives or parsley. Although it tastes sybaritic as is, when you get rich, serve the soup with a little dollop of black caviar adrift on the pale yellow cream.

NOTE: If you haven't got all these spices, substitute: ½ tsp. Italian crushed red pepper flakes, 1½ Tbsp. curry powder, and the juice of a quarter of a lemon. (But please don't do this!)

BLACK TURTLE SOUP

Turtle beans are another name for *frijoles negros*, or, in other words, plain black beans. You won't be needing any turtle. This soup was made up of stuff that happened to be in my icebox. One of these things isn't likely to be in yours: *chorizo*, a hard garlic sausage that I mush down to a special Mexican food store on Fourteenth Street to get at. You may substitute Italian pepperoni, which are easily available, with good effect.

Makes 1 quart

2 cups leftover cooked black beans (see recipe for Black Beans and Rice, page 46)
1 cup beef broth
¼ cup dry vermouth
1 clove garlic, minced
½ tsp. cumin
couple of whole coriander pods, crushed
½ small dried red pepper, crushed (optional)
1 *chorizo* (5 inches long), peeled and sliced in rounds
water to thin, if necessary

Put everything except the *chorizo* and water into the blender and purée until smooth. Scrape into a heavy pot (Teflon lining is especially good for this because the beans tend to stick terribly) and thin to desired consistency with water—it should be about like split-pea soup. Stir in the *chorizo* and heat carefully over low flame about 15 minutes, stirring often to prevent sticking. Decorate each serving with a thin round lemon slice, some chopped chives, or a little dollop of sour cream—or just eat it the way it is with some tortilla chips and beer.

WHITE BEAN SOUP

Rumor has it that a very special bean soup is served in the Congressional dining room. My congressman couldn't get me the recipe (but I forgive him; his voting record is excellent), so I made up this one.

3 quarts leftover beef tongue stock (see recipe, page 132) or 3 quarts cold water
1 ham hock
1 onion stuck with 4 cloves
2 cloves garlic, split

1 large carrot
1 bay leaf
1 Tbsp. coarsely ground black pepper
2 celery tops
1 lb. white pea or marrow beans

Bring all ingredients except beans to a boil, simmer for 1 hour, cool, skim off fat, and remove bay leaf, carrot, onion, garlic, and celery. Soak the beans overnight in cold water or wash and pick over beans, bring to a boil, turn off, cover, and let sit for 1 hour. Whichever method you use, drain the beans (discarding any really ugly ones) and put them in a heavy kettle with the ham hock and stock. Bring to a boil, skim off any scum that rises, cover, and simmer very gently about 3 hours, or until the beans are very tender. Remove ham hock; pick the meat from the bones and cut it into small pieces. (If you have used leftover tongue stock, you can substitute bits of unsightly leftover tongue for the ham hock). Purée about two-thirds of the soup along with a half cup of fresh parsley or watercress leaves. Return to soup pot, along with bits of meat. Stir and heat to boiling. Sprinkle with more minced parsley, and serve with rye bread and butter and beer or red wine.

NOTE: If you substitute red beans and add good chili powder to taste, then it becomes Louisiana Bean Soup.

LENTIL SOUP, CURRIED OR PLAIN

Curried lentil soup is a bit much for a whole meal, so it should be regarded as a first course. However, plain lentil soup makes a gorgeous meal, especially if served with a ring of cooked knockwurst slices floating around the edges. It was always served this way in the pigeonhole *Bierstube* where I often ate my lunches in Wiesbaden: lentil soup (*Linzensuppe*) on Monday and Thursday, oxtail (*Ochsenschwanzensuppe*) and split pea (*Erbsensuppe*) on other days, and omelets if you got sick of soup. But I never did.

½ lb. slab smoked bacon, cut in
   matchsticks
1 lb. brown lentils
1 cup chopped onion
2 cloves garlic, minced
2 Tbsp. curry powder (optional)
1 carrot, sliced
1 rib celery, chopped

bouquet garni: 1 bay leaf, ½
   tsp. thyme, 4–5 black peppercorns, tied up in washed
   cheesecloth bundle
fresh parsley
2 quarts chicken broth, canned
   or fresh
salt and pepper

Put the sliced bacon into a cold Dutch oven and slowly sauté until crisp. Remove, drain, and reserve. If you're using it, now is the time to stir in the curry and cook it briefly. Add the onion, garlic, carrot, and celery to the remaining bacon fat, cover, and simmer slowly until the vegetables are slightly browned and softening. Meanwhile, wash the lentils and pick them over. Sometimes there are bits of rock in them. Drain the lentils and add them to the Dutch oven along with the chicken broth. Throw in the bouquet garni and simmer the soup over low heat, covered, until the lentils are very tender. Nowadays most lentils are precooked, so this should not take longer than half an hour. When the soup is done, discard the bouquet garni, then purée the soup in a blender. Return to the Dutch oven and season to taste with salt and pepper. Serve in hot, huge soup plates with the aforesung knockwurst slices for a smashing winter supper. The curried version should be dusted with minced parsley (or plop a dab of sour cream on top) and served in rather small bowls or cups. In the curried version, you can fool around in the spice rack, adding a speck of mace or a touch of cumin, or maybe a dried red pepper if you like it really hot. Have a care with this, though, or you may find yourself eating alone—and this is quite a lot of lentil soup.

NOTE: Lentils have been a popular food since Biblical times (maybe that famous apple was really a bowl of lentil soup). Besides tasting good and growing in impossible places, lentils furnish more protein than lean beef, cost a fraction as much, and have twice the calories (this last being of no concern to your average starving person).

SPANISH BEAN SOUP (SOPA DE GARBANZOS)

A long time ago a Cuban restaurant in Tampa called The Columbia used to serve a Spanish baroque bean soup I've been trying to duplicate ever since. Do not expect to find anything like this in your usual run-of-the-paella Spanish restaurant. Their version barely makes it as a first course, but as you can see from the following list of ingredients, this garbanzo soup is meant to be all courses rolled into one.

Makes 4 quarts

1 lb. dried garbanzos (chick-peas)
3 quarts water
1 small chicken (fryer)
1½ lbs. good soup beef (shin)
½ lb. smoked ham, cubed (raw or cooked—it doesn't matter)
¼ lb. Spanish *chorizos* (sausages) (or Italian pepperoni)
¼ lb. slab bacon, cut in fine dice
2 cups sliced carrots
1 large onion, chopped

3 cloves garlic, crushed or minced
2 leeks, sliced (or ¾ cup yellow onions)
5 medium potatoes, peeled and cut in julienne strips (shoe-strings)
salt and cayenne pepper to taste
NOTE: A pinch of saffron should be in here, but as the world price is now about $24 the ounce, we'll let it go.

Soak the dried garbanzos in cold water to cover overnight. Drain, rinse lightly, and simmer in 3 quarts of water for about 30 minutes.

Get out a large heavy soup kettle or Dutch oven with cover. Heat some oil or bacon fat and sauté chicken and beef along with onion, garlic, and leeks. Add garbanzos with their cooking liquid to the sautéed meats and vegetables and simmer 30 minutes longer. Remove chicken and beef, discard skin and bones, cut into bite-size pieces, and return to soup.

Sauté the bacon until half-cooked and add it to the soup along with the ham and *chorizos*. Simmer, with lid askew, about an hour. Add carrots and cook 30 minutes longer. (This soup is especially fine for people who live in a one-room apartment or people who enjoy walking.) Taste for salt, stir in potatoes, and let it all bubble along for another half hour. Season to taste with cayenne pepper.

At last—a maddeningly aromatic, super soup worth every minute of its gestation. A salad of arugula, watercress, or sliced onions and oranges in a vinaigrette dressing are interesting, sharp flavors to enjoy with, or after, Spanish Bean Soup.

NOTE: Instead of dried chick-peas, you can use a 1 lb. 4 oz. can of cooked chick-peas, adding them in the last half hour of cooking.

CORN CHOWDER

An early American classic, corn chowder was probably designed to see a man through an afternoon of haying. Like most country fare, it is simple and filling. True, a lot of men will leave the house if you announce "soup for supper," anticipating canned soup and sandwiches with carrot eyes and pimiento mouths, but corn chowder is no sissy stuff. Cucumber and tomato salad makes a good taste and texture contrast, and both vegetables come to market cheaply, along with corn, in August.

Makes 1½ quarts

1 2-inch square lean salt pork (or bacon)
1 large onion, thinly sliced
2 medium "boiling" (old) potatoes, diced
2 cups chicken broth (fresh or canned)
1 can cream-style corn

¼ tsp. pepper (white looks best)
½ tsp. dried thyme leaves (or 1 Tbsp. fresh)
1 cup milk (light cream if splurging)
sprinkle of paprika
salt to taste

Wash the salt pork in hot water and drain and dry it. Cut it into sticks about one inch long and a quarter inch wide. Fry slowly in a big heavy pot (enamel-lined iron is ideal). Remove, drain on paper, and reserve. Sauté onion in the rendered dripping from the salt pork.

When the onion has melted, add the potatoes, chicken broth, pepper, and thyme and simmer, covered, about 30 minutes. Stir in the corn and milk and heat through. Taste for seasoning. Dish the chowder up in big heated bowls, dust with paprika, and sprinkle a bit of fried salt pork or bacon on top of each serving.

NOTE: This is, of course, even better made with fresh corn; in this case cream must be used instead of milk. To scrape fresh corn: slit the kernels, then grate them off the cob. The raw corn should cook in the soup 10 minutes before you add the cream.

SAUERKRAUT SOUP

When you make Choucroute Alsatian style (see recipe, page 190), it's unlikely you'll waste 4 hours making just a little bit. So undoubtedly you'll have the 2 leftover cups you will need to concoct this curious, warming, soothing soup. I think it was originally a Hungarian notion, but I first tasted it in Germany. I was told it is good for drunkenness, hangover, gastric gurglings, and just about everything except red hair (unpopular in Germany). But the main reason for eating Sauerkraut Suppe is that it's just wonderful.

Makes 1½ quarts

2 cups leftover *choucroute*
1 Tbsp. bacon dripping
½ medium onion, chopped
1 rib celery, finely diced
2 skinny carrots, thinly sliced
1 medium potato, cut in ½-inch dice

½ bottle beer
1 cup V-8 juice (or tomato juice)
2 cups water
salt and pepper

Heat bacon dripping in a heavy casserole with cover. Sauté onions and celery about 5 minutes. Add remaining ingredients, bring to a boil, lower heat, and simmer for about 1 hour. The soup improves with standing for about 1 hour before serving. Reheat it.

There's no point in making this with plain, canned sauerkraut—it would be lousy.

CREOLE FISH GUMBO

Christmas Eve often fills me with dismay at the thought of heaving around all those turkeys and pies the next day. So I plunder my geechee past for something that has nothing to do with all that and make this Creole stew. It's also a nice thing to have on the stove when people are dropping in or staying after a party.

Makes 1½ quarts

3 lbs. fresh cod fillet, cut in 1½-inch chunks (or thick fillets of haddock, striped bass, or sea bass)
2 cloves garlic, minced
⅛ tsp. turmeric mixed with ½ tsp. powdered cumin (or ¹⁄₁₆ tsp. saffron if you can afford it)
2 Tbsp. olive oil

1½ cups thinly sliced onion
1 cup fish stock (made from heads and trimmings)
1 cup dry white wine
⅛ tsp. thyme
½ bay leaf
1-inch dried red pepper, bled (or 2 tsp. crushed red pepper)

2 cups stewed tomatoes, slightly chopped	1 package frozen sliced okra, thawed
2 Tbsp. bourbon salt to taste	cooked white rice

Wash and dry the fish and cut it in chunks; rub the garlic and turmeric/cumin into them and refrigerate about 2 hours.

Heat olive oil in a large heavy casserole and sauté the onions. Add fish stock, wine, thyme, bay leaf, and red pepper, and simmer half an hour. Add tomatoes and bourbon, salt to taste, and simmer another 30 minutes. Add okra and fish chunks and simmer 10 minutes longer. Put a large spoonful of rice in each bowl and ladle the hot chowder over it. Sprinkle with parsley.

BRUNSWICK STEW

I always thought Georgia was the cradle of the one, true Brunswick Stew—that's what my Georgia relatives told me—but there are rumblings in some counties of North Carolina and Virginia that lay claim to its creation. Only one thing about this rich potpourri of meats and vegetables is certain: it is pure Southern roccoco. This humble country stew replaced the lavish barbecues of ante-bellum days—politicians ladled it out to skeptical voters at rallies from Reconstruction on. Since it can't be made in small quantities, nowadays it's a dish for family reunions, wakes, and other events where large numbers of relatives gather to quarrel. If nothing else, they will niggle over what *really* goes into a Brunswick Stew. Originally it had to contain squirrel or "it weren't no Brunswick Stew," but chicken is the principal meat now. Root around in the frozen poultry bin

Brunswick Stew

to find a stewing hen; it's cheaper, older, and tougher but has much more flavor than the young birds commonly marketed.

Serves 8–10

2 Tbsp. bacon fat
½ lb. onions, sliced
1 5-lb. stewing hen
2 lbs. shin beef (bone in)
1 lb. raw or leftover baked ham
3 quarts cold water
3 Tbsp. salt
  freshly ground black pepper
1 tsp. dried thyme (or 2 sprigs fresh)
1 whole dried red pepper pod, crushed
2 large (1½-lb. size) cans Italian plum or plain tomatoes

1 cup diced potatoes
2 cups fresh corn, scraped from the cob, or equivalent in canned whole-kernel corn
2 packages frozen Fordhook lima beans
2 packages frozen sliced okra
½ lb. fresh green beans, cut in 2-inch lengths (if fresh beans are not available, leave them out)
½ cup chopped parsley (optional)

You will need a very large, heavy kettle (preferably cast-iron) with a lid. Heat the bacon fat and brown the onions in it lightly. Cut the stewing hen in half and add it and the shin beef, turning the meats to brown slightly. Add the ham, cold water, salt, black and red pepper, and thyme. Simmer until the meat is falling off the bones (about 2 hours). Remove the meats from the broth, discard all skin and bones, and cut the chicken and beef into bite-size pieces and the ham into small cubes. Skim any excessive fat from the broth, return the meats to the kettle, and add all remaining ingredients *except* the okra, beans, and parsley. Simmer the stew 45 minutes; then add the okra and beans and continue cooking 15 minutes longer. As the stew is very thick, it should be watched and carefully stirred from time to time to prevent scorching. Sprinkle each serving with fresh parsley and pass around a bottle of Tabasco for those who like it hotter. Most Southerners take the fire out with iced tea, but I prefer beer or red wine with my Brunswick Stew.

DESPERATION SOUP

This is cheap, quick, healthy, and low-calorie—commendable attributes to nearly everyone but me. I invented it in desperation while on a dieting kick, and although it isn't great, it's passable. Certainly it's more satisfying than most diet junk.

Serves 2

1 package dried onion-soup mix	1 Tbsp. fresh parsley, minced
1 carrot	pepper to taste
1 onion	pinch of celery seed (optional)
large handful of sliced cabbage	

Prepare the soup according to basic directions. Peel and slice the carrot and onion thinly. Add them and all remaining ingredients, cover the pot, and simmer it slowly for about 10 minutes—15 if you aren't ravenous.

Unfortunately, this cooked salad has the Chinese-dinner syndrome, so something has to be done to quiet the nattering stomach. Cottage cheese *au naturel* nauseates me, but I learned to tolerate it this way:

As much cottage cheese as you can put up with
Scallions, minced
Cucumber, peeled and minced
Hot green tomato (or cherry) pickles, minced

Mix all these things together in the proportions you like and read something fascinating while you're eating it.

2

SALADS

Salad is great, salad is wonderful . . . it's just that it's served with such tedious regularity. American women embraced salad and permissive child-rearing with just about the same amount of enthusiasm and lack of discrimination. Nobody meant to suggest that salad should *totally* replace vegetables or that a few rags of green with some kind of drippy dressing was the whole romance-of-salad. The home-ec-nutritionists nearly did in American cooking in the thirties when the country became vitamin-conscious. A lot of half-raw vegetables converted Americans into salad-lovers out of desperation, but thirty years with the same greenery can get a little stale. There are good, cheap ways to vary this scene, and you can begin by forgetting about iceberg lettuce unless there is *nothing* else to buy (in times of war, drought, and famine). Instead, investigate the spectrum of colors, flavors, and textures in Boston lettuce, oakleaf and Bibb lettuce, spinach, watercress, arugula, Belgian endive, romaine and field lettuce. Escarole and chicory (also known as curly endive) are both of the daisy family and rather too bitter by themselves. (Restaurants love this twosome because they're cheap and resilient as bedsprings.)

GREEN SALAD

I know you probably know how to make this, but just in case it hasn't always been one-hundred-per-cent perfect we'll review this little turn. The single most important step in making a good salad is drying the leaves thoroughly after they're washed. If this isn't done, the dressing won't adhere and you'll wind up with limp salad greens and a well of watery dressing in the bottom of the bowl. After washing, shake the greens in a colander and then shake each leaf over the sink and lay it on a towel covered with a piece of paper towel (use a big thick bath towel if you're making a large quantity). The leaves should not be more than one layer deep. Roll this up like a poster (but loosely so you won't crush the greens) and put it in the refrigerator to crisp and dry out for about half an hour (or several hours if need be). Toss with dressing just before serving.

FRENCH DRESSING, OR SAUCE VINAIGRETTE

Nobody knows who blamed the French for that orangy guck we call French dressing (probably General Consolidated Amalgamated Foods, Inc.), but it really wouldn't be allowed to cross the French border. This again proves that almost nothing sold already prepared is either as good or as cheap as your own concoction. It's cheaper still if you cut the olive oil by about half with plain salad oil (Wesson or one of those vegetable oils). It isn't too good an idea to make more than a two-day supply of dressing because it can get rancid. Put it into a small screw-top jar.

Makes ¼ cup

3 Tbsp. olive oil (or half olive and half vegetable oil)
1 Tbsp. wine vinegar or lemon juice
⅛ tsp. salt
freshly ground black pepper

¼ tsp. dry mustard (optional)
minced or crushed half clove of garlic (optional, but don't leave it out)
minced fresh parsley, chives, basil, or tarragon (optional)

If you want the flavor of herbs and can't get any fresh ones, rub to powder any of the herbs listed in dried form. The flavor will develop in the oil and vinegar but just adds an unpleasant ashy texture if sprinkled on top of the salad greens. Shake everything up vigorously or beat it to an emulsion with a small wire whisk. Pour half the dressing on the salad and mix it gently with your hands (it's what chefs do and the only possible way to get the thing mixed well without mashing or bruising the leaves). Two tablespoons of dressing is usually enough for a small head of Boston lettuce. Most people drown their salads, which makes the greens flaccid. Be miserly—the salad will be better for it.

SOUTHERN WILTED LETTUCE

There are times when iceberg lettuce just has to be faced, one way or another. This is a rather better way than most; the hot bacon fat in the dressing wilts slightly the excessive hardness of this our native commercial lettuce. I can't imagine anyone actually raising it in a garden, but who knows? The French are importing the lousy stuff at great expense in preference to their own lovely butter-leafed *salade*.

Serves 4

1 small green head iceberg lettuce
8 slices bacon
2 Tbsp. wine or cider vinegar

¼ cup scallions, sliced thinly
black pepper
1 or 2 hard-cooked eggs, sliced

Wash, dry, and slice the lettuce into long shreds. Fry the bacon gently until just crisp, remove, and drain. Measure a scant quarter cup of bacon fat into a small saucepan, add the vinegar and pepper, and heat to bubbling. Pour the dressing over the shredded lettuce and mix well. Taste for salt (some bacon dripping is quite salty) and add more if you need it. Arrange the dressed lettuce in a salad bowl with the eggs in overlapping slices around the edge or in the center of the bowl. Crumble bacon over the top and sprinkle with the scallions. Present the salad at the table (it *must* be served at once) and mix again gently before serving.

BEAN, TOMATO, AND OLIVE SALAD

Unlike *Salade russe*, most of the mixed vegetables in this salad are uncooked. Also unlike *Salade russe*, it's low-calorie and has enough variety of tastes and textures to be a complete lunch, particularly if it is garnished with a couple of chilled hard-cooked eggs.

½ lb. cooked fresh whole green beans, cooled (You may use canned beans, but they must be the small, whole variety, which is much more expensive than the fresh.)

½ lb. ripe cherry tomatoes, halved
olive condite and 3 Tbsp. of the oil it is preserved in
½ cup scallions, minced
6–8 flat anchovy fillets

Olive condite is a mixed green-olive antipasto with bits of sweet pepper, capers, and whatnot packed in olive oil and flavored with vinegar. Italian food processors use up their broken olives in this highly seasoned and very tasty mix; therefore it's a great bargain. If you can't find olive condite in your supermarket, go to an Italian grocer, or soak some of our dull California olives (stoned and halved) in a good vinaigrette dressing of your own.

Just mix everything together gently—don't break the whole beans—and let it sit at room temperature for a half hour before serving. If you have them, throw in some pickled mushrooms or artichoke hearts. Garnish with anchovy fillets.

NOTE: Most vegetable salads look better if the serving bowl is first lined with fresh greenery—romaine, Boston lettuce, etc.

SPINACH, MUSHROOM, AND BACON SALAD

Although this rather odd combination has become somewhat more familiar in recent years, it's still passably exotic in some quarters. A very few New York restaurants serve it (always *à la carte*) at a mark-up of about 3000 per cent. Because it's unusual and heartier than most salads, and you have to buy that great big bag of spinach anyway, this is an excellent choice for a crowd.

Serves 6–8

1 1-lb. bag fresh spinach
½ lb. fresh white medium-size mushrooms
lemon juice

6 strips crisply fried bacon
salt and pepper to taste
3 Tbsp. vinaigrette dressing (or more)

Discard any very large or discolored spinach leaves and wash the remainder through two cold waters, lifting out the leaves each time.

Removing the stems is a bit tiresome but it really must be done: bend the leaf in half along the spine of the stem, and, holding the stem, pull it toward the center. Naturally, the very young, small leaves just need the stem ends pinched off. Roll the spinach up in a towel and put it in the refrigerator until just before serving time.

Clean and slice the mushrooms (caps only—chop the stems to use for filling omelets or for soup or something) and toss them in lemon juice diluted fifty per cent with water. Drain, blot lightly with paper towels, and toss with the spinach and just enough vinaigrette dressing to moisten. Add salt and pepper to taste, toss again, and scatter the crumbled bacon over the top. Serve at once.

BEAN SALAD VINAIGRETTE

Small white pea beans or marrow beans are most commonly used for this stand-by on the *hors d'oeuvre varié* platter. It might also be made with pinto or pink beans or a mixture of several varieties. I always think the *hors d'oeuvre varié* would make a dandy lunch, but I've never found the French restaurant that would let a customer get away with ordering only one course. We do have it at home, however, with the bean salad as the filler and some hard-boiled eggs, sardines, tuna, olives, pickled mushrooms, or whatever turns up in the icebox.

Serves 4–6

1 1-lb. box dried pea beans	½ cup chopped scallions
1 onion stuck with 2 cloves	½ cup minced parsley
bit of bay leaf	½ cup vinaigrette dressing
salt and pepper	

Wash and pick over the beans. Cover with cold water and soak overnight (or bring the beans to a boil, simmer slowly for a minute, turn off heat, and let the beans sit for 1 hour, uncovered). Drain, cover with fresh cold water, add the onion, bay leaf, about 1 tablespoon of salt, and a couple of grindings of the pepper mill. Simmer over low heat, partly covered, until beans are tender *but not mushy*. This may take anywhere from 1½ to 3 hours, depending on what the processor has done to them before you got hold of them. Drain the beans, discard the onion and bay leaf, and cool the beans to room temperature. Gently blend them with the scallions, parsley, and dressing.

FRENCH POTATO SALAD

Although I've covered this subject in another book and you will find a recipe for *Pommes de terre à l'huile* in any reliable cookbook, I'll repeat it, since this commendable dish still appears so seldom on American tables. Anyway, it is necessary to know this recipe in order to make the unusual Mussel and Potato Salad that follows.

Makes about 6 cups

8 to 10 medium all-purpose potatoes (do not use "baking" potatoes, as they crumble too easily)
3 Tbsp. hot beef bouillon mixed with 2 Tbsp. hot dry white wine

2 Tbsp. wine vinegar
½ tsp. salt
1 tsp. dry mustard
7 Tbsp. olive oil
6 scallions, minced
½ cup fresh parsley, minced

Scrub the potatoes and boil them in their jackets in salted water until just tender when pierced with a sharp fork. Drain and shake over low heat to dry. Peel them quickly and slice into eighth-inch rounds (or half-rounds, which is easier). As you put each layer of sliced warm potatoes into a big mixing bowl, sprinkle with some of the hot broth-wine mixture. Next whisk together the vinegar, salt, and mustard; then slowly beat in the oil. Toss the scallions and parsley into the potatoes and pour the dressing evenly over the top. Mix gently with your hands to avoid mashing the potatoes (which is almost impossible with a spoon). Taste for salt, then turn into a lettuce-lined shallow bowl and garnish with any or all of the following: sliced hard-cooked eggs, sardines, anchovy fillets, half-circles of hard salami, kosher dill gherkins, radish roses, ripe or green olives, drained tuna or smoked eel. The salad should be slightly warm, or at least room temperature. The full-dress version is considered an entire meal, but if the salad is to be merely a side dish, a few sliced pickles (*never* sweet ones, however—in fact never put sweet pickles into or around any food you respect) will do for garnish.

MUSSEL AND POTATO SALAD

I can't remember where I read about this peculiar notion, but I think it was in a novel or a story. At any rate, it's uncommonly good and I say hats off to the originator, whoever he or she may be.

1 recipe of French Potato Salad
1 quart fat fresh mussels
½ cup vinaigrette dressing
½ cup white wine and ½ cup water, mixed
    one small onion, minced

Prepare the mussels before starting the potato salad, as they will profit from an hour's rest in the dressing, whereas the potato salad derives no benefits at all from sitting around.

Scrub the mussels and put them into a heavy pot with a cover. Pour over them the white wine and water and throw in a little minced onion. In this broth steam the mussels open over medium heat. Do not over-cook: they are done when the shells open. Remove the mussels from their shells, turn them in the vinaigrette, and set them aside, covered, until the potato salad is completed. When the potatoes are arranged for serving (minus all the garnishes, of course), make a ring of mussels around the perimeter of the dish and serve.

MASHED POTATO SALAD

Do not despise the instant mashed potato. I know of a number of good cooks—some of them famous—who use them and find them, as I do, not only possible but quite acceptable. Instant potatoes do need a bit of touching up, however, and will never really duplicate the purity of flavor to be found in a creamy mound of freshly whipped just-cooked real potatoes. The instant product is undetectable in this concoction, and it is quick, cheap, and very good to know about when you've forgotten to buy potatoes.

Serves 4

1 package instant mashed pota-
    toes ("7 servings")
3 Tbsp. olive oil
2 Tbsp. wine vinegar

2 Tbsp. minced scallions
2 Tbsp. minced fresh parsley
    salt and pepper to taste

Make potatoes according to the package directions, substituting olive oil for the butter. Cool the potatoes about 15 minutes; then beat in the vinegar, scallions, and parsley, and season to taste with salt and pepper. Serve tepid, plain or garnished as in French Potato Salad.

CABBAGE SALAD

Cole slaw, or cabbage slaw, is a thing I like in direct inverse ratio to the amount of sugar used in its preparation—which is to say I like it hardly at all. Consequently, I have devised my own way of dressing raw cabbage that in no way resembles those noxious milky-sweet shreds dripping out of paper thimbles alongside every delicatessen sandwich.

4 large servings

½ small hard, green cabbage
4–5 Tbsp. vinaigrette dressing

Wash the cabbage in cold running water and dry it. Shred (*do not grate*) the cabbage with a sharp knife. To do this, halve the half head so that you are working with quarters. Lay it flat and make very thin slices across either cut side. Toss the shredded cabbage with the dressing about a half hour before serving and let it sit at room temperature (unless you live in a very hot zone, in which case you wouldn't have any cabbage anyway).

If there's any left over, store it, covered, in the refrigerator. It will wilt —some people prefer it this way—but it will still be delicious.

LENTIL SALAD

Although Arabs and Indians dote on them, and quite a few Europeans make a staple soup of them, lentils have never caught on too well with Anglo-Saxons and Celts. Mrs. Beeton, in her 1861 cookery book, speculates, "Although these vegetables are not much used in this country [England], yet in France, and other Catholic countries, from their peculiar constituent properties, they form an excellent substitute for animal food during Lent and *maigre* days. At the time of the prevalence of the Roman religion in this country, they were probably much more generally used than at present. As reformations are often carried beyond necessity, possibly lentils may have fallen into disuse, as an article of diet amongst Protestants, for fear the use of them might be considered a sign of popery."

This doesn't explain the Irish, but it may be a clue as to the almost total absence of lentil references in early American cookbooks. I've served this salad to a lot of Catholics and Jews and Protestants and atheists, who all found it good.

Serves 6

1 lb. dried lentils (approximately 2 cups)

1 peeled onion stuck with 2 cloves

1 bay leaf

1 Tbsp. salt

freshly milled pepper

1 tsp. cumin (ground)

½ cup garlicky vinaigrette dressing

2 hard-cooked eggs, sliced

1 Tbsp. parsley, minced

Wash and pick over the lentils. Put them in a pot with 1½ quarts cold water, the onion, bay leaf, salt, pepper, and cumin. Bring the beans to a boil, turn off the heat, and let stand 1 hour. Then simmer about 5 minutes, or until just tender. Lentils used to take hours to cook, but most of them are processed now and the problem is to avoid mushiness. If you accidentally overcook them, it is impossible to make salad of them but you can turn the disaster into a good soup or puréed vegetable.

Drain the lentils and discard the onion and bay leaf. After cooling to room temperature, dress them with the vinaigrette and garnish with the eggs and parsley.

NOTE: For Curried Lentil Salad, add 3 or 4 tablespoons good fresh hot curry powder to the cooking liquid.

SALADE ARGENTEUIL

Argenteuil, near Paris, is renowned for its asparagus—in fact, it *means* asparagus in French cookery. This one is a rather elaborate meld of cooked, chilled vegetables bound with mayonnaise and is more of a set piece for a buffet than a side dish. Along with a cold roast chicken, it is fancy enough for guests and cheap enough for a family meal on a late spring evening.

Serves 6

½ cup cooked green peas

½ cup cooked sliced carrots

½ cup cooked green beans (in 1-inch lengths)

½ cup cooked sliced celery

2 Tbsp. minced scallions

½ cup baked ham, diced or in strips

⅔ cup mayonnaise (see recipe, page 37)

salt and white pepper to taste

1½ lbs. fresh, green asparagus, cooked (see recipe, page 184)

4–5 hard-cooked eggs, quartered strips of canned pimiento

Cook all the vegetables separately, drain, and cool; all should have fresh, slightly crisp textures and individually identifiable flavors. Gently mix the peas, carrots, beans, celery, scallions, and ham with the mayonnaise, season to taste, and turn into a large round bowl, preferably glass. Using one quartered egg, standing upright, as the hub, make spokes of the asparagus, tips pointing outward and completely covering the vegetables underneath. Stand the remaining egg quarters around the inner edge of the bowl and garnish the asparagus with a few strips of pimiento. Cover tightly and chill before serving.

MACARONI AND TUNA SALAD

Another "composed" (i.e., made of mixed cooked things) salad, as naïve as Salade Argenteuil is sophisticated, brings together two American favorites. Children particularly like it and most adults find it tolerably good. Anyway, it's a workable compromise at cookouts with kids yammering for hot dogs and grown-ups yearning for grilled lobster.

Serves 6 generously

2 cups raw small elbow macaroni

3 Tbsp. salad oil

1 6-oz. can tuna, drained

4 scallions, minced

⅔ cup mayonnaise (see recipe, page 37)

salt and pepper to taste

2 Tbsp. chopped canned pimiento (optional, but pretty)

Cook the macaroni according to package directions, adding the salad oil to the boiling water during the last few minutes of cooking to prevent it sticking together. Drain and cool. Mix the macaroni with the tuna, scallions, and mayonnaise, and pimiento if you're using it; then season to taste with salt and pepper. Chill, and if you're taking this salad to a picnic, remember to pack it in an insulated hamper so that it will stay cold.

3

SAUCES

Sauces are associated in the American mind with extravagant French cooking. However, it must be remembered that thrift is the soul of French bourgeois cuisine (home cooking as opposed to complicated restaurant cooking), and some of the basic sauces are used with dazzling effect to elevate a simple dish or to transform leftovers. Anything called "gravy," no matter how dreary, seems to be acceptable to us, but the Anglo-Saxon attitude to "sauces" has been either Puritanical or primitively suspicious: "What's the point of mucking up a perfectly good boiled potato?" or "Damned French cooks, masking 'turned' goods in a fancy cover." Restaurants, with their heavy, sprawling sauces, must bear a good deal of the blame for the persistence of these musty old notions. Nothing can disguise spoiled food, and, at any rate, sauces are meant to enhance, not smother, other foods. It *is* true that a modest knowledge of sauce-making can vary and stretch rather smaller amounts of meat and fish than we are accustomed to serving per person.

Mayonnaise, hollandaise, and béarnaise are all quite simple to make in an electric blender. Some gourmets complain of a certain lack of delicacy of texture in blender-made sauces, but few people are that picky and will gratefully accept a golden, creamy hollandaise no questions asked. We are lucky to have quite decent factory-produced mayonnaise (in England and Ireland there is only a puzzlingly sweet vapid "salad cream" to buy if you can't make your own mayonnaise), but once you have tasted homemade mayonnaise, opening a jar of the commercial product is a rather wistful experience.

One may also buy criminally priced jars of hollandaise sauce (amalgamated, I suspect, with powdered eggs) if one has no respect for self or stomach. Some unfortunate attempts at dried hollandaise and béarnaise have been marketed and after testing them I conclude that there must surely be subtler ways of abusing the public.

Handmade sauces require a little practice and a good arm; blender sauces need only 115 volts of current and the ability to read. However you make them, sauces are bound to expand your enjoyment of cooking as well as your culinary repertoire. And the most unpretentious dishes—freshly boiled little new potatoes, a bit of poached flounder, even a hamburger sautéed in butter to a juicy pinkness— seem luxurious set off by a creamy hollandaise or béarnaise sauce.

CREAM SAUCES

One of the foundations of fine cooking is sauce béchamel, a cream sauce not terribly exciting in itself, but essential to a number of derivative sauces and a variety of dishes from soufflés to Lobster Cardinal. Béchamel and velouté sauces are used with eggs, fish, poultry, veal, and vegetables—in every course from hors d'oeuvre to savoury.

BASIC CREAM SAUCE (MEDIUM THICK)

If this sauce is made with chicken, veal, or fish broth, it is called a velouté; if with milk, it starts out as a sauce béchamel. Besides dressing vegetables, it is useful for combining leftovers and can be varied with herbs, spices, and cheeses. If a *thin sauce* is needed, use 1 tablespoon less flour; if a very *thick sauce* is wanted, use 1 tablespoon more flour and ½ tablespoon more butter than the recipe calls for.

2 Tbsp. butter or margarine	salt and white pepper to taste
3 Tbsp. flour	1 Tbsp. lemon juice
2 cups boiling liquid (broth or milk)	(*Continued*)

Optional Enrichment (to be added just before serving):
   1–2 Tbsp. softened butter

Melt the butter in a heavy-bottomed saucepan, either enamel, stainless steel, or lined with porcelain, as aluminum may discolor your sauce. Stir in the flour with a wooden spoon and cook, stirring over very low heat about 2 minutes to eradicate the raw flour taste. The *roux* (that's what you have now) should not color at all. Off heat, dump in the hot stock or milk and beat briskly with a wire whisk until the sauce is perfectly smooth. Beat in lemon juice and add salt and pepper to taste. You may continue cooking the sauce a little longer by setting the saucepan on an asbestos pad over low heat and stirring from time to time. This sauce used to be cooked for hours, but modern chefs cook the flour first, as indicated, thus obviating the need for long cooking. At any rate, further cooking won't hurt the sauce (unless you let it stick to the pan and get lumpy). You may keep the sauce warm for hours in an improvised *bain marie*—a pan of hot water with the saucepan set into it. If you choose to enrich your béchamel or velouté to a French lushness with egg yolk and cream and more butter, wait until serving time before doing so, as the butter tends to break down and separate if the sauce is kept hot too long. The extreme direct heat of a broiler has the same effect, so a sauce to be used in a gratin dish should not be enriched with more butter, although it is perfectly all right to add egg yolk and cream. For an herb sauce, just before serving beat in 3–4 tablespoons chopped fresh parsley, chive, tarragon, or chervil, or a mixture of these herbs. If dried herbs are used (although there is almost no excuse for dried parsley), decrease the amount to 1½ tablespoons and let the herb simmer in the sauce 5 minutes to develop its flavor.

Thick Cream Sauce

Make a thick béchamel using 3 tablespoons butter and 4 tablespoons flour. Stir in heavy whipping cream by spoonfuls until you have the consistency you want.

SAUCE PARISIENNE

This is often made with fish stock (a velouté) and served with fish fillets or shellfish.

HERB AND SPICE CHART

Basil

Sweet Bay

Cumin

Coriander

Dill

Fennel

Ginger

Marjoram

Mint

Parsley

Saffron

Sage

Savory

Tarragon

Thyme

Rosemary

  2 egg yolks
½ cup heavy cream
  2 cups medium-thick velouté or béchamel sauce
  3 Tbsp. softened butter

Beat the egg yolks and the cream together, then beat in a little of the hot sauce with a wire whisk (this will prevent the eggs scrambling) before beating the egg/cream mixture into the sauce. Last, beat in the butter spoon by spoon and use the sauce at once. (If necessary, you may hold the sauce in a double boiler or *bain marie* for an hour before adding the butter enrichment at the last moment.) For serving with fish, you might also add to this sauce *one* of the following:

  2 Tbsp. fresh dill weed, minced
  2 Tbsp. drained capers
2–4 Tbsp. minced, cooked white mushrooms (don't use old ones with dark gills, as they discolor the sauce)

SAUCE MORNAY

Restaurants invariably serve this cheesed sauce with cauliflower, which is very good, but the sauce has many other uses and is particularly suited to veal escalopes sautéed with mushrooms. Mornay sauce is pleasant mixed with egg noodles to serve with something on the dry side, like boiled chicken or plain roasts with no sauce of their own. Broccoli, small pearl onions, artichoke hearts, mushrooms, hard-boiled eggs, fish fillets, and shellfish are some other things one might serve in a sauce Mornay.

Makes 2½ cups

  2 cups basic (medium-thick) béchamel or velouté sauce
½ cup grated natural Swiss cheese (see note)
    pinch of nutmeg

Bring the base sauce to the simmer, then remove from heat and beat in the grated cheese with a wooden spoon. Add the nutmeg, then taste to decide if you'd like the spice a touch stronger. I'm very fond of this exotic nut from Jamaica and use it in mashed potatoes, creamed spinach, and béchamel sauce to be used with chicken, shellfish, or some vegetables. If used subtly, the aroma and flavor of nutmeg is mystifyingly piquant.

NOTE: Natural cheese is specified here and that's what I mean in any recipes where I have forgotten to specify; while those waxen leaves known as "process (cooked) cheese" are indeed cheap, the stuff is too revolting to be eaten out of hand, and too insipid to add anything but gluiness to a cooked dish.

BROWN SAUCES

As they occur in various dishes, I will include the appropriate brown sauces, but I don't think the average home cook needs or will bother with the traditional, long-simmered sauce espagnole. Unless you entertain lavishly, it's best to make up sauces as they are to be used because otherwise they just take up refrigerator space, finally spoil, and are no economy.

Just in case the sauce for your goose or turkey didn't make the celestial ratings last Thanksgiving, here are a few suggestions that may improve it.

1. A sauce can't be much if it doesn't start with a good stock made with wine and all the giblets (except the liver), neck, and wing tips. Put a carrot, an onion stuck with two cloves, a bay leaf, and a pinch of dried thyme into the wine, water, and chicken parts and simmer it all together while the bird roasts. You want to wind up with about 2 cups of concentrated, flavorful stock. Strain it and discard all the debris; the giblets have nothing left by now anyway. I usually reserve the liver, split it, sauté it in butter until medium pink, then chop it finely and add it to the finished gravy just before serving.

2. Cornstarch or arrowroot (the latter is expensive, but makes a limpid sauce) are better thickeners than flour because they react instantly, impart no "raw" flavor, and produce a translucent sauce with a lighter texture than a flour-thickened sauce. Also, there's no need for long simmering if your stock has been properly reduced. Cornstarch should be mixed to a thin paste with water, then beaten into the boiling stock.

3. Degreasing is crucial to any good gravy or sauce. Lazy cooks often omit this step and ruin whatever small chance they have of serving a good meal. From a turkey or chicken, pour off *all* the fat you can, leaving only the pan juices to boil up with your stock. There will be nothing *but* grease left from a goose. Pour it into a wide-

mouth jar and save it in the icebox; it makes splendid frying fat.

4. Finally, any gravy or béchamel-based sauce is meant to be still hot when it reaches the diner's mouth; sadly, it is rarely more than lukewarm, a condition that drains the pleasure out of the most carefully made sauce. Do have plates hot, sauceboat hot, and sauce almost at the boiling point before serving . . . and don't serve until the diners are strapped into their chairs.

On Packaged Gravies: Canned beef gravy, although I have seen it listed in cookbooks written by professionals, is no good. Canned beef bouillon, however, is very useful in making rich sauces and stews, and a few cans should be kept on hand unless you are in the habit of making your own (see *pot-au-feu* recipe, page 4). Dried gravy mixes are considerably more successful than the canned, but need half wine for the liquid and 30 minutes of low simmering to eradicate that dehydrated taste. Some brands are much superior to others (but sure as I name one, the company will be sold to a tire manufacturer who is diversifying, and the product will instantly deteriorate). When you find one, experiment with it adding fresh ingredients: a bit of sautéed onion, scallion, mushrooms, fresh herbs, the wine, or a splash of brandy, and you'll have a useful pick-me-up for quick dinners or leftovers the sauce has mysteriously disappeared from.

CREOLE SAUCE

Fish, shellfish, ham, and chicken may all benefit from a mingling with this old stand-by of New Orleans (and Charleston) cookery.

Makes 2 cups approximately

2 Tbsp. bacon fat or olive oil
2 cloves garlic, minced
1 medium onion, chopped (½ cup)
½ cup chopped green pepper
1½ cups canned tomatoes, drained and chopped
¼ cup dry (white) vermouth or white wine

pinch dried thyme (or 2 Tbsp. fresh, chopped)
pinch dried basil (optional)
salt and pepper to taste
crushed dried red pepper, cayenne pepper, or Tabasco sauce to taste (this is *not* optional— use one of these hot flavorings or you haven't got a Creole sauce at all)

Melt the bacon fat in a heavy skillet. Sauté the garlic, onion, and green pepper, stirring until tender. Add the tomatoes, white vermouth or wine, herbs, and seasonings, and simmer, uncovered, over low heat for about 30 minutes. Stir this thick sauce occasionally to prevent sticking. Add cooked fish or meat (see note) just long enough to heat through. Traditionally, this is served with white rice.

Should your icebox lack meat, fish, or shellfish, increase the onion and green pepper in the recipe and serve the sauce over rice and a couple of slices of bacon.

NOTE: If you use ham, cut it in cubes and brown with the onions and peppers.

EGG-LIAISON SAUCES

Enough balderdash has been written about these sauces—oil or butter in an egg yolk suspension—to scare off at least two generations of home cooks. Mayonnaise, hollandaise, and béarnaise can all be made with a wire whip (or even a heavy fork) and a bowl or pot. They may be made by hand or in an electric mixer or blender, and the latter methods are incontrovertibly labor-saving. However, as in learning to drive with a stick shift, I think one's understanding of how these sauces work is better if the hand method is mastered. Besides, what will you do if the power fails or you *do* get that long holiday on a remote island (or even deal with a European kitchen)? It is always a good idea to be as independent of mechanical help as you can before American kitchens get to look like Houston Control.

To the obvious "What's so economical about these sauces?" the answer is "Nothing," but they make a lot of cheap and unpretentious dishes wonderful, and, except for mayonnaise, no acceptable prepared sauces exist on the market. Things can go wrong, but they're not irremediable, so just relax, and with a clear brow and a fresh arm, take up your wire whisk.

MAYONNAISE

As I said at the beginning of the chapter, there are perfectly presentable commercial mayonnaises, certainly fine for sandwiches and the occasional quick dab on a solitary lunch. If you're in the mood for something special, and quite different, this homemade sauce is well worth the 10 minutes it takes to make it. Because it is made only with yolks (blender mayonnaise is made with a whole egg), a handwhipped sauce is yellower, richer, and stiffer than the commercial product. Very fresh eggs and good olive oil should be used because the flavor of both is quite pronounced. I like a mayonnaise made entirely with a light pure olive oil; however, in the interests of economy and the lighter flavor that may be preferred by some, I have substituted in this recipe plain salad oil for half of the olive oil normally used. A mayonnaise made solely with plain, unflavored salad oil would be quite tasteless—and pointless.

Have the eggs at room temperature and warm the oil to tepid (stand the can or bottle in a pan of warm water). Warm your bowl (round-bottomed and of 2- or 3-quart capacity) with hot water and dry it carefully. Get two dish towels to prop the bowl at a tilt so that you can beat properly and pour oil simultaneously. Some people hold the bowl between their knees, others press-gang relatives into holding it, but both are unreliable methods.

Makes about 1½ cups

2 egg yolks (U.S. Grade A "large")	scant Tbsp. lemon juice
½ tsp. dry mustard powder	¾ cup olive oil
½ tsp. salt	¾ plain salad oil
	2 Tbsp. hot water (maybe)

Tilt the bowl and make sure that it can't slip. (If your counter is slippery, wring out the towels in water.) Put the yolks, mustard, and salt into the bowl and whip the eggs a couple of minutes until they darken and get sticky, at which point they are ready to receive the oil. Put the tepid oil in a lipped jug or measuring cup and pour drop by drop, while beating the egg yolks steadily. You needn't flail your arm off—just steady as you go, and keep your eye on the droplets rather than the egg (although you do have to watch the egg somewhat to be sure the oil is amalgamating). After about ⅓ cup of oil has gone in, you may increase the droplets to a thin trickle, and as the mayonnaise gets thicker and thicker, you may even increase the flow a bit more, but remember: *too much oil too soon is what makes mayonnaise curdle.* The yolks won't be rushed; they balk, then collapse and release the oil. It's a mess, but can be fixed. Should this misery occur, put another egg yolk into another clean, warm bowl, beat it until sticky, then beat in the curdled sauce by table-spoonfuls until it is all reconstituted.

About halfway through, your mayonnaise will be quite stiff and should be thinned with the lemon juice. Continue slowly beating in the oil, and if gets too stiff again, beat in a bit of hot water. Some cooks say this stabilizes the mayonnaise—I don't know if it does or not, but it *does* make it a bit creamier, paler, and more opaque. Mayonnaise is made in various consistencies, depending upon what purpose you have in mind for it: e.g., as a sauce for fish or vegetables, a dip for raw vegetables, or in a composed salad.

Homemade mayonnaise keeps very well in a covered jar in the icebox for several days, but return it to room temperature before stirring it or it may separate. If it does, you can pull it together again using the method described above.

MAYONNAISE VERTE

Splendid on shrimp, crab, chicken, fish, boiled eggs, and things I've never thought of. Only fresh herbs will do—dried herbs make a *sauce grise*, not *verte*—and if parsley is all you can get, then so be it.

1½ **cups homemade or commercial mayonnaise**
2 **Tbsp. chopped parsley**
2 **Tbsp. chopped tarragon**
2 **Tbsp. chopped watercress leaves**
1 **Tbsp. chopped chives**

Blanch the watercress and herbs in boiling water for 2 minutes, drain thoroughly, squeeze dry, and pound to a paste in a mortar. If you haven't a mortar, just mince the herbs together as finely as you can. Mix into the mayonnaise.

SAUCE COLLIOURE

Waverly Root mentions this Catalan sauce in his classic *The Food of France*, which has left me many a night slathering my way through France in envy and an ecstasy of imagined delights. I don't think you need more than Mr. Root's description to make this sauce. He writes, "With cold fish, a good accompaniment is Collioure sauce. This is mayonnaise plus anchovy paste, chopped parsley, and grated garlic—except for the anchovy, much the same as the noted *aïoli* of Provence."

AÏOLI

Prodigious quantities of garlic (*ail*) go into this Provençal mayonnaise, traditionally served with *bourride*, a modest relation to the celebrated bouillabaisse of that region. It is also served on boiled fresh or salt cod, potatoes, and some cooked vegetables, and I have found it good with hot artichokes and as a dip for raw cauliflower, carrots, cucumbers, etc. *Aïoli* is easy to make in a blender although the texture is not authentic, and it holds up well under refrigeration (the garlic fumes would hold up a sagging gate). For a real *aïoli*, you will need a mortar and pestle.

Makes 1½ cups

1 slice day-old white bread, crustless
3 Tbsp. wine vinegar
6 small cloves garlic, chopped (or 4 large cloves; see note)
1 egg yolk

pinch of salt
1 to 1½ cups tepid olive oil
2 Tbsp. lemon juice (approximately)
3 Tbsp. boiling water

Soak the bread in the vinegar about 10 minutes. Remove and squeeze dry. Put the garlic and bread into a mortar and pound to a smooth paste. Pound in the egg yolk and salt. When it is thick and sticky, add the oil by droplets and after about ⅓ of it is incorporated, you may pour a little faster and use a small wire whisk to complete the beating. (A really cool hand with the mortar and pestle can pound up the finished *aïoli* without resorting to a whisk, but I find the pestle too clumsy for anything but brute work.) To keep the mortar from bouncing around, either wedge it into a pot with wet dish towels or grow another arm. Add some lemon juice when the sauce becomes very heavy. Continue thinning with the boiling water as necessary. *Aïoli* should be about the consistency of commercial sour cream, quite stiff. If it curdles, reconstitute it in the same manner as a regular mayonnaise (see recipe, page 37).

NOTE: Some things can be dumbed down for people with pussycat palates, but *aïoli* just isn't worth making for anyone who isn't a real garlic aficionado.

BLENDER AÏOLI

Makes 2 cups, approximately

1 crustless slice day-old white
   bread (home-style)
2 Tbsp. wine vinegar
4–6 cloves garlic, peeled and
   roughly chopped

3 egg yolks (U. S. "Large")
¼ tsp. salt
¼ tsp. white pepper
1½ cups tepid olive oil
2–3 Tbsp. boiling water

Whirl the slice of bread in the blender for a few seconds. You now have instant, painless, fresh bread crumbs. Add the vinegar and garlic and blend to a smooth paste at the highest speed. Add the egg yolks, salt, and pepper; blend at high speed until the mixture is quite thick and sticky. (Most blenders of recent vintage have a removable stopper in the center of the cover so that ingredients can be added without undue splatter. If yours hasn't this convenience, wear old clothes and a bathing cap.)

Running the blender at high speed, begin adding the olive oil by droplets directly into the center of the mixture. When about a third has been run in, you may pour the remainder in a thin stream. You will have to thin the mayonnaise with a tablespoon of the boiling water when you have added about half the oil. Add more when the machine starts to clog. When all the oil has been incorporated, you will have a very thick, pungent sauce which will be a pain in the neck to scrape out of the blender. But the mortar-and-pestle technique requires a certain degree of expertise and the forearms of a tennis pro. Before removing the sauce from the blender, taste for seasoning to be sure the amount of salt and pepper pleases you.

HOLLANDAISE SAUCE

Under the guise of hollandaise sauce, some truly weird concoctions have come my way, sometimes noxious, sometimes wanly pathetic, and occasionally unrecognizable. It is a somewhat tricky sauce to make by hand (although nothing could be simpler with an electric blender, and I usually do it that way), as the egg yolks can scramble, they can separate from the butter, or the sauce can simply refuse to thicken (when the butter is run in too fast). But if you avoid these pitfalls, a handmade sauce absorbs a good deal more butter than a blender sauce. There are many ways to arrive at this deservedly famous sauce and here are two I have found generally successful, though not infallible.

Blender Method

The only thing that has ever gone awry using this technique is when I have rushed the too hot butter into the yolks, causing the sauce not to thicken. As it is meant to be served tepid, there's no need to hassle yourself making it at the last minute.

Makes 1 cup

3 egg yolks (U.S. Grade A "large")
½ tsp. salt
dash Tabasco (3 or 4 drops) or sprinkle of white pepper

2 Tbsp. lemon juice (since this makes a slightly tarter hollandaise than the usual, you may like less lemon)
1½ sticks (6 oz.) unsalted butter very hot water

Put the eggs, salt, Tabasco, and lemon juice in the blender jar. Melt the butter over low heat, skim off the foam, and cool slightly. Blend the egg yolks at high speed for 3 or 4 seconds. Remove the center from the blender top (if your blender hasn't this kind of removable knob top, you're in trouble, but it's possible to rig up a dish towel, leaving a reasonably small hole at the top to pour the butter through). With the blender at high speed, *slowly* trickle in the melted butter. If the machine begins to clog, pour the butter a bit faster; if it still clogs, add a teaspoon of hot water to get it going. When the butter is in and the sauce thick (it should plop, not run weakly), taste for seasoning and add more salt, Tabasco, or lemon juice. Set the blender jar into a pan of tepid water, where it will keep well for half an hour or so. Serve the sauce in a warm sauceboat. If there's any left over, store it in a covered jar in the icebox. Before reusing, let it return to room temperature; the heat of the food it is served on will finish the warming.

Hollandaise by Hand

A double boiler would seem the ideal saucepan for this, but unfortunately the bottom of the top pot usually gets too hot and scrambles the egg yolks—the one fault you cannot undo. Use a heavy china bowl that will sit securely on a saucepan. This sauce is constructed over hot, but *never boiling*, water.

Makes ¾ cup

1 Tbsp. white wine vinegar (tarragon-flavored is nice) or 2 Tbsp. lemon juice
3 large egg yolks
4 oz. (1 stick) butter, softened and divided into 8 pieces (see note)
1–2 Tbsp. cold water (if necessary)
    dash white pepper (or few drops Tabasco)

Put the wine vinegar or lemon juice into the heavy china bowl and place it over a saucepan containing water kept hot over a very low flame. Beat the egg yolks and pour into the bowl, beating with a wire whip until they begin to thicken slightly. Whisk in the butter piece by piece. When this process is complete, the sauce should be as smooth and almost as thick as a mayonnaise. If the sauce seems very thick, whisk in the cold water to lighten the texture a bit, and season to taste. If you have used unsalted butter, the hollandaise will require some salt. If the sauce is not to be served immediately, set the bowl into a pan of tepid water and cover until it is needed, but it should not be held more than half an hour, as the sauce tends to lose its buoyancy.

NOTE: If the hollandaise won't thicken or if it separates (actually, 3 yolks will absorb much more butter than the amount given; the minimal quantity was given to reduce the chances of separation to almost nil), see the directions for reconstituting a turned mayonnaise. When it is a smooth cream again, beat in a couple of tablespoons of melted butter to finish it.

BÉARNAISE SAUCE

This sauce differs from hollandaise only in the flavoring—tarragon, wine vinegar, white wine, and shallots (or scallions) produce a strongly scented herbal sauce of considerable character. Thus it is more suitable with steaks, broiled chicken, roast lamb, fried fish, eggs mollet, etc., but the licorice flavor of tarragon is a bit overwhelming on most vegetables.

2 Tbsp. wine vinegar
4 Tbsp. dry white wine
1 Tbsp. minced shallots (or scallions)
black pepper
pinch of salt
1 Tbsp. minced fresh tarragon or ½ Tbsp. dried tarragon
1 Tbsp. minced fresh tarragon or parsley

In a small saucepan, combine all the ingredients except the last tablespoon of fresh tarragon or parsley. Reduce it over high heat to about 2 tablespoons. Cool to tepid. Strain this essence either into a heavy bowl or a blender jar and make a hollandaise according to one of the preceding recipes, omitting the flavorings. When the sauce is finished, taste and correct the seasoning with more salt or pepper if necessary, then stir in the final tablespoon of minced fresh tarragon or parsley. You may not substitute dried herbs here because they must always be cooked (or marinated) to release their flavor.

EGG SAUCE

There is no limit to what can be called "Egg Sauce," and indeed in nineteenth-century American and English cookbooks some strange specimens turn up. In general, egg sauce has fallen so far out of fashion as to seem quite new. It is good with cold sliced roast meat and hot or cold baked, broiled, or boiled fish.

1 Tbsp. minced shallot or scallion
1 Tbsp. chopped parsley
pinch of salt
freshly milled black pepper
3 Tbsp. olive oil, or half olive oil/half salad oil
1 Tbsp. red wine vinegar
½ tsp. prepared (Dijon-type) mustard
1 hard-boiled egg, chopped medium-fine
1 Tbsp. minced fresh chives, or green tops of scallions

Put all the ingredients together in a screw-top jar and shake well. You can also use this as a salad dressing.

VARIATION: Boil the egg only 3 minutes. Plunge it in cold water; then peel, cut off the top, and empty soft yolk into the vinegar and oil, beating all into a smooth emulsion with a wire whip. Beat in all other ingredients with a fork. Mince the egg white and add it to the sauce, along with a tablespoon of chopped capers.

4

BEANS, RICE, PASTA

BEANS

What we are discussing here are, obviously, dried beans, nourishment for the poor in nearly every country since man stopped grazing on wild berries. Dried beans and peas are fatless, bursting with protein, also bursting with calories, and possibly addictive. They satisfy the soul and the belly.

Although they should be eaten in moderation, there is absolutely no point in cooking a little bit of dried beans. The initial preparation is lengthy and there are many, many uses for leftover beans. Once they are boiled just tender, measure the amount required for the recipe you have chosen and stash away the rest in the refrigerator. Cold beans—white, black, pinto, red, or California pink—when dressed with a garlicky vinaigrette, surrounded with bits of canned tuna, anchovies, or corned beef, can make a splendid lunch or light supper.

Conflicting advice and often wildly inaccurate recipes are printed on boxes of dried beans, and many of the legumes that come in plastic bags simply leave you to shift for yourself. Possibly this is because the bean people know the housewife's basic fear of time and trouble, so they hope you won't notice what you're getting into until it's too late. Of course, beans *can* be cooked without soaking, but it takes forever. It's best to ignore the No Soaking Necessary signs (except for lentils) and proceed with this:

Wash the beans in cold water, drain in a colander, pick over for duds (shriveled, broken, or discolored beans); put them in a pot and cover with two inches of fresh cold water. Soak in a cool place overnight; they may ferment in a warm spot, so don't leave them on the back of the stove near a pilot light. If you forgot to do this the night before, there is still hope. Proceed as above, but bring the beans to a boil for 1 or 2 minutes. Turn off heat, cover, and let stand at least 1 hour before continuing with your recipe. This jazzed-up soaking system makes the beans take a bit longer to cook than those soaked overnight. But all dried beans, even those of the same variety, vary enormously in their cooking times. It's best to keep an eye on them as they bubble along lest they turn to mush. And if they do, they still have prospects: purée them, improvise on the seasonings, and you have soup.

BLACK BEANS AND RICE

Had I access to the pleasures of all the three-star restaurants of France in exchange for renouncing this dish, I don't know if I could bring myself to do it. Anyway, I'd probably end as lucklessly as all the other Faustian greedies; some demonic craving for beans and rice enters at birth the soul of every Southerner, Latin American, and West Indian. I like just about *any* kind of dried beans and rice, but this is my favorite.

Serves 6

1 lb. *frijoles negros* (turtle beans)
2 quarts water
1 Tbsp. salt
2 large onions, chopped
2 large cloves garlic, minced
1½ Tbsp. ground cumin
3 Tbsp. fresh chili powder (see note)
1 tsp. dried thyme
2–3 Tbsp. olive oil

1 lb. ground chuck beef
salt and dried red pepper (pequins or crushed Italian peppers) to taste
2 cups beef bouillon
boiling water if necessary
about 6 cups dry, fluffy cooked rice, white or yellowed by saffron (if you're rich today) or turmeric (if you're feeling poor)

Black beans take hours to cook, and although the packer says No Soak-ing Necessary, don't you believe it. Prepare the beans according to direc-tions at the beginning of this chapter. Add 1 tablespoon of salt to the water, which will now be a deep purplish black. Bring the beans to a boil and simmer 2 hours, leaving the lid slightly askew. Check occasionally to see that the beans don't cook dry, and add boiling water if at any time the beans aren't completely covered with liquid.

Meanwhile, heat the oil in a heavy skillet and sauté the onions, garlic, and ground beef about 5 minutes. Stir in thyme and spices and stir-fry a couple of minutes. Pour in bouillon, stir, simmer briefly, and set aside.

After 2 hours of simmering, the beans should be semi-tender but quite firm. Put them and their liquid into a rather deep earthenware casserole with a cover. Use a chopstick or the handle of a wooden spoon to stir the meat and onion mixture into the beans (a spoon tends to mash things up). The casserole should be full almost to the top, with about a half inch of liquid above the beans—if there isn't, add some boiling water. Set the casserole, covered, in the middle of a **preheated 325° oven** and bake until the beans are tender, usually about 2 hours, but sometimes more and sometimes less. Serve with the rice, beer, and a salad.

Note: I don't really use chili powder because in Manhattan one can buy fabulous dried whole Mexican chiles (peppers, in English). In place of the commercial powder, I use 6 *anchos*, stemmed, seeded, torn up, and soaked in 1 cup of hot water for 1 hour. The soaking water goes in too, along with a couple of tiny, red-hot chile pequins, crushed. Purée the chiles in a blender.

Dried peppers and such things as tortilla presses can be ordered from the Casa Moneo, 210 West Fourteenth Street, New York, N.Y.

CASSOULET

Cassoulet is French baked beans. Yards have been written about what does or does not make an honest-to-God cassoulet; the two constants generally agreed on are goose and white beans. In Toulouse the dish must contain the famous preserved goose, *confit d'oie*, of that region, but the Castelnaudry chefs say bosh to that: beans, garlic sausage, and any old goose will make a legitimate cassoulet. Well, you're not likely to stumble on any *confit d'oie* in this country, even if you could afford it. Frozen geese sometimes show up in supermarkets around Thanksgiving and

Christmas (once as tyrannically traditional as the turkey, goose fell from favor but seems to be coming out of retirement) and are more expensive than they should be. Duck is cheaper, readily available, and an excellent substitute.

There is no way of making a halfway authentic cassoulet for a small number of people, so, as it takes some time to build, reserve this cathedral of casseroles for a party. The dish derives its name from an obsolete clay cooking pot called a *cassole d'Issel*. Whatever combination of meats and beans goes into it, the cassoulet really should be cooked in an earthenware casserole. Not simply because the presentation at table is so richly beautiful, but because earthenware does not develop hot spots, never discolors food of any kind (important when many different things are combined), retains heat well, and thus is perfect for a buffet or for serving a lot of guests a dish that must be very hot.

Start the cassoulet a day before you plan to serve it, and if you keep your head, you will be rewarded with an imposing, authentic French country dish, wild praise, and an overblown reputation as a fine cook, even if you never master another dish.

Serves 8–10

2 lbs. dried white beans (Great Northern)

2 quarts cold water

2 tsp. salt

1 onion stuck with 2 cloves

1 carrot, peeled

1 bouquet garni: 2 cloves garlic, crushed, 1 tsp. dried thyme, 1 bay leaf, crumbled, and 2 sprigs parsley, tied in a washed cheesecloth bag

3 or 4 onions, chopped

2 cloves garlic, minced

3 ripe, fresh tomatoes, peeled and chopped, or equivalent of canned tomatoes

salt and freshly milled black pepper to taste

1 4–5 lb. duck

1½ lbs. lamb, boned and cubed

¼ lb. *lean* salt pork or bacon square (with rind)

1 ring of Kielbasy sausage (about 1 lb.) cut in 2-inch lengths or some other kind of smoked garlic sausage in a casing (e.g., German *Landjägers*)

1 cup white bread crumbs made from day-old bread

Soak beans as described on page 46. Drain, cover the beans with the two quarts of cold water, then throw in the salt, carrot, onion stuck with cloves, and the bouquet garni. Add the salt pork or bacon in one piece, and the rind cut into small squares. Cover and simmer slowly about 1½ hours or until beans are about three-quarters tender.

Meanwhile, roast the duck plainly (see page 113) in a **hot (375°) oven** for 1½ hours. Be sure to drain off the excellent fat as it accumulates and before it burns; store it in a screw-top jar in the icebox for frying other foods. Dredge the lamb lightly in flour, brown it in some of the duck fat, and then set aside. In the same skillet, sauté the onions and the minced garlic until transparent, then stir in the tomatoes and salt and pepper to taste. Cook over low heat, stirring often, until the tomatoes are quite soft. When the beans are nearly done, discard the onion, carrot, and bouquet garni. Drain beans but reserve their liquor. Add about 4 cups of it to the tomato-onion mixture and bring it to the simmer. Slice the bacon, then cut it into thick matchsticks—at this point, if the bacon seems on the fatty side it's a good idea to brown it in a small skillet and strain off the excess fat before mixing it back with the beans.

Spread a thin layer of beans and bacon in the bottom of a large (8–10 quart) earthenware casserole. Carve the duck into bite-size pieces, discarding the fat and skin, but reserve the legs and wings for garnish. Put the duck, lamb, and half of the sausage on the layer of beans, and spoon on the remaining beans. Pour the tomato and onion sauce over the whole construction and arrange an even layer of breadcrumbs over the top. Drizzle on some duck fat or melted butter. Bake the cassoulet, uncovered, in a **350° oven** for about 2 hours. Brown the rest of the sausage. During the last half hour of baking, punch into the crust the browned pieces of sausage and the reserved duck legs and wings. The beans should by now be creamy and tender, the meats steeped in heady flavors, the top a golden crust with trickles of juice bubbling through. Dazzling, that's what it is.

BLACK-EYED PEAS WITH BACON

Black-eyed peas (also known as cowpeas) are right in there with collard greens as number-one soul food, and since that subject has been flailed nearly to death, I suppose it's no longer necessary to explain what they are.

Jambalaya au Congri, which is New Orleans for Hoppin' John, is black-eyes cooked with a bit of ham or salt pork and afterward mixed with cooked white rice. This dish is similar, but the bacon is crisp and more palatable to modern taste than the old-fashioned boiled meats.

Serves 4–6

2 cups dried black-eyed peas
2 oz. lean slab bacon, cut in matchsticks
1 large onion, chopped
1 small pod hot red pepper salt and black pepper

2 Tbsp. wine or cider vinegar
2 cups cooked white rice
6 thick slices of lean bacon, broiled
2 Tbsp. fresh parsley, minced

Wash the peas and soak according to general directions in the beginning of this chapter. Drain, cover with fresh water, salt, and simmer until tender, usually 45 minutes to 1 hour. Fry the bacon cut in matchsticks, starting them off in a cold skillet. Drain on paper toweling. In the same skillet, sauté the onion in the bacon fat until tender and very lightly browned. If you have a fresh hot pepper, mince it and add to the onions —if, in all probability, you have a dried pepper, it should be chopped and soaked in a few tablespoons of hot water for about half an hour and added with its liquid to the onions.

Preheat oven to 350°. Broil the bacon and cook the rice while the peas are cooking. When the black-eyes are tender, drain, reserving ½ cup of the pot liquor. Mix together the peas, matchsticks of bacon, onion, red pepper, rice, and vinegar—this should be done with a delicate touch to avoid mashing the peas. Use a chopstick or the handle of a wooden spoon. Add salt and black pepper, if necessary. Turn into a buttered casserole, dribble over it the reserved pot liquor, lay the broiled bacon slices on top, and bake in preheated oven for about 20 minutes. Sprinkle with parsley and serve. Have a green salad with this dish and don't even think about the unrelieved starchiness of it—just give in and enjoy it.

LAMB NECK AND BEAN CASSEROLE

Lamb neck is normally used for stew. Bony but tasty, it's quite cheap; however, its lack of substance must be compensated for with something filling. I have chosen beans because they absorb so much flavor and therefore get the most mileage out of this not-so-meaty cut. Lamb neck isn't often on display in supermarket meat bins, but if you ask the butcher, he'll usually oblige.

Serves 6

1 lb. California pink beans or white marrow beans

1½ lbs. lamb neck (in small pieces)

¼ cup salad oil
salt and pepper

2 medium onions, sliced

2 cloves garlic, minced

1 medium can tomatoes, crushed

½ tsp. dried thyme

1 bay leaf

½ tsp. crushed red pepper (optional)

1 cup dry red wine

Pick over the beans and soak according to directions in the beginning of the chapter. Whichever soaking method you've used, drain the beans, cover again with fresh cold water, bring to a boil, throw in a tablespoon of salt, and simmer gently for about 2 hours. They should be whole and firm, not mushy—especially as they will be cooked another hour in the oven.

Preheat oven to 325°. Dry the lamb bits with paper towels. Heat the oil to nearly smoking in a heavy skillet. Toss in the lamb and brown the meat over medium heat, salt and pepper it lightly, and remove to an ovenproof casserole. Sauté the onions and garlic over low heat in the same skillet, stirring to scrape up the browned bits and juices of the lamb. Pour in the tomatoes, herbs, and wine and bring to a boil, stirring constantly. Simmer a few minutes.

Drain the beans and reserve the cooking liquor. Gently mix them into the lamb, and be careful not to mush up the beans. Pour the hot tomato and wine sauce over the casserole contents; if it does not cover the ingredients completely, add enough bean liquor to take care of that. Put a lid on the casserole or make one out of a double thickness of aluminum foil, sealing it tightly at the edges. Put it in the oven, and bake about 1 hour. In this time, the beans should absorb most of the liquid; if it seems too juicy (it shouldn't be dry either), uncover, **turn up the oven to 375°,** and bake until enough moisture evaporates.

While this dish takes quite a long time to make, it can be assembled in stages or made completely in advance and reheated. The casserole serves about six people, but even if there are only two of you, it keeps well and there's no pain in eating it a couple of times.

LENTILS AND HAM

In Elizabeth David's book *French Country Cooking*, she gives a recipe for a robust country supper dish of bacon and lentils. Unfortunately, the "farmhouse bacon" she specifies has little in common with American artificially smoke-flavored will o' the wisp strip bacon. Imported Irish bacon is the nearest thing to an earthy slab of lean bacon which has been hung for weeks in the coolish fireplace smoke of a French farmhouse kitchen. This adaptation of Mrs. David's recipe substitutes a cylindrical boneless smoked ham butt, which is to be found in any supermarket. Frierich's seems to me a fairly lean brand. The long, thin shapes are usually leaner than the stubby, rounded hams.

Serves 6

1 smoked boneless pork butt, weighing about 2 lbs.
2 Tbsp. bacon dripping
10 or 12 small white onions
1 carrot and a rib of celery, minced together
2 cloves garlic, crushed
1 bay leaf

½ tsp. dried thyme
1 lb. brown lentils
water to cover
salt and pepper to taste
butter
2 Tbsp. parsley, chopped
hard-cooked eggs, halved (optional)

Simmer the pork butt in water to cover for 1 hour. If it is wearing one of those stockinette covers, remove it after simmering. Peel the onions: this is quite simple if you drop them into boiling water for 30 seconds then immediately plunge them into cold water; the skins will slip off easily after you cut a thin slice off the root end. Melt the bacon dripping in a heavy casserole and roll the onions around in it until they brown lightly. Add the carrot and celery and stir about for a minute or so. Put in the cooked ham, the washed and drained lentils, the garlic, bay leaf, and thyme. Add water barely to cover (the casserole should be rather deep and narrow so that too much water will not be necessary). Bring to a boil, then cover and simmer very gently about 30 minutes. Check the lentils after 15 minutes, however, and every 5 minutes thereafter so they don't become overcooked. They should be perfectly tender but still round as the eye of a guinea hen.

Take out the ham and let it sit in a warm place for 5 minutes before slicing it rather thinly. Taste the lentils and add salt if necessary, then drain, butter, and grind some black pepper over all. Arrange them in the middle of a round hot platter and lay the ham, in overlapping slices, around the lentils. Garnish with egg halves. Sprinkle with parsley and serve very hot.

RICE

PILAF

Pilaf simply means rice cooked in broth rather than plainly boiled or steamed. We derived our word from the French *pilau*, which is a corruption of the Turkish *pilaw*, where it all began. It's good to serve with meat or chicken, especially if you haven't much of it. A cup of leftover meat or sea food added to the basic recipe makes the pilaf a main dish.

Serves 4

2 Tbsp. butter or salad oil
1 large onion, chopped
1 large clove garlic, minced
2 tsp. cumin powder
10–12 cherry tomatoes, quartered

1 tsp. salt
2 tiny dried red peppers, crushed, or cayenne pepper
1 cup raw rice
1¾ cups chicken broth

Use a heavy pot with a tight lid (a cast-iron skillet with lid will do very well). Heat butter to bubbling over medium flame and sauté onions, garlic, and cumin about 2 minutes. Add tomatoes and stir-cook 2–3 minutes. Stir in salt, pepper, and rice; then add chicken broth and bring to a boil. Cover tightly and simmer over very low heat 20 minutes. *Do not stir or peek*. The rice is done when tender and the liquid has evaporated. Fluff the rice lightly with a fork or a chopstick, put a paper towel between the pot and the lid, and leave it alone for 5–10 minutes to finish drying. (Or it can keep warm for 30 minutes in a 200° oven.)

LAMB PILAU

In the preceding recipe, the basic pilau, pilaf, or, in swamp dialect, "perlow," is described. However, most people really do expect a bit of meat, fish, or what-have-you in anything billed as a "pilau." Lamb shanks, scantily fleshed though they are, furnish enough flavor and substance to make a main dish of the pilaf.

4 meaty lamb shanks, well trimmed and cut short

2 Tbsp. oil or fat (butter or margarine)

salt and pepper

1 large onion, chopped

1 clove garlic, minced

1 cup water or chicken or beef broth

bouquet garni: 1 bay leaf, 4 whole cloves, ¼ tsp. ginger, ¼ tsp. cinnamon, 3 or 4 cracked cardamom seeds (or substitute an inch of lemon peel for this expensive spice), all tied together in a cheesecloth bag

1½ cups raw rice

2 Tbsp. chopped fresh parsley (optional)

Sear the lamb shanks in the oil or butter or a mixture of the two. Salt and pepper them as you turn them to brown. Remove the lamb while you sauté the onion and garlic in the same pan. When they are limp and golden, pour off any excess grease and return the lamb shanks to the pan. Add the water or broth and the spice bag, bring to a simmer, and braise slowly, covered, for about 3 hours, or until the meat is falling from the bones.

Remove the meat from the bones and cut it into small pieces. Discard the spice bag and pour the cooking liquid, along with the vegetables, into a bowl and cool it in the icebox while you are trimming the meat. Take off the congealed fat and discard it; then measure what remains and add enough water to make 3 cups of liquid. Put it in a clean, heavy pot with a lid, bring it to the boil, and add the rice and meat. Cook over low heat until the rice absorbs all the liquid—about 25 minutes. Fluff up the rice with a fork, distributing the meat evenly, turn the pilau onto a hot platter, and sprinkle with chopped parsley.

VARIATION: You may also serve this dish simply as braised lamb shanks, one to a customer, on a bed of plain, cooked white rice. However, it is still necessary to cool the braising liquid and degrease it.

PASTA

SAUSAGES AND SEA SHELLS

Maruzzelle are the smallish shells you'll be looking for among the spirals, bows, rings, and ruffled pastas to be found in almost any supermarket. If you can't find the shells, use some other pasta—for instance, *farfalle* (bows) or the little springs called *fusilli*.

Serves 4

6 Italian sweet or hot sausages
2 Tbsp. butter or olive oil
1 onion, chopped finely
1 clove garlic, minced
2 Tbsp. chopped parsley

2 fresh tomatoes, seeded and chopped
1 lb. *maruzzelle*
    additional chopped parsley (optional)
    grated Parmesan cheese

Prick the sausages with a sharp fork, cover with cold water, and bring to a boil. Simmer, uncovered, about 10 minutes, drain and dry, and slice in quarter-inch-thick rounds. Heat the butter or oil in a skillet and add the sausage, onion, garlic, and parsley. Cook, stirring often, until meat and vegetables are golden brown; then add tomatoes and simmer, covered, while you prepare the pasta. Cook the *maruzzelle* according to package directions. When its texture is *al dente*, drain in a colander but do not rinse. Mix the sausage and its sauce with the hot pasta, sprinkle with more parsley, and serve at once on hot plates. Pass the cheese at the table.

CAVATELLI WITH CHEESE

Cavatelli, a long, crinkle-edged shell, is a more interesting pasta than elbow macaroni (almost anything is). School cafeterias have so stigmatized macaroni and cheese that it's hard to convince anyone that it can be a good meal, either alone or in the company of roast or broiled meat. Anyway, *cavatelli* is prettier, holds its bite and shape well, and doesn't get soggy.

Serves 4

2 cups uncooked *cavatelli*
½ medium onion, chopped
½ stick butter
1 cup grated or shredded natural cheddar cheese

1 cup hot milk
½ cup grated Romano or Parmesan cheese

Preheat oven to 350°.

Bring 6 quarts of water to a full rolling boil. Add 2 tablespoons of salt and throw in the pasta. *Cavatelli* normally takes about 20 minutes to cook, but you will have to begin testing it (with your teeth) after about 10 minutes. Keep it boiling rapidly in a open pot, and meanwhile, back at the saucepan, sauté the onion in the butter until soft. Remove from heat. When the *cavatelli* is done, drain quickly and add to the onions along with the cheddar and hot milk. Mix lightly and carefully with a rubber spatula until the pasta is well coated. Turn into a buttered oven-proof dish, cover with the grated Romano or Parmesan, and bake for about 10 minutes. Serve an interesting green salad (perhaps romaine and arugula with a few bits of anchovy), and even if there's no meat course, you will still have a satisfying and healthy meal.

SPAGHETTINI CARBONARA

Word seems to be getting around in the United States that not all Italian food is red. Although pasta is undeniably omnipresent in Italian cookery, there are thousands of regional approaches to it. Of Roman origin, this bacon and egg concoction has no tomatoes and no garlic.

Serves 4

¼ lb. lean smoked bacon in one piece (or some thick-sliced lean bacon)
3 eggs, beaten
½ cup freshly grated Parmesan cheese
1 lb. spaghettini, linguine, fettucine, or whatever pasta you fancy
freshly milled black pepper

Since it isn't anything to begin with, those paper-thin slices of Incredible Shrinking American Bacon will add nothing to this dish. You will need a chunk of good, strong, smoked country bacon (or hog jowl) to give the spaghettini character. Cut a quarter pound of it into fat matchsticks and sauté them slowly in a heavy skillet that has been rubbed with fat. Drain on paper towels and set aside. Reserve the rendered fat in the skillet; add butter if you haven't 3 tablespoons left.

Cook the pasta *al dente* in at least 6 quarts of boiling salted water. Meanwhile mix together the beaten eggs, cheese, black pepper, and the bacon sticks. This mixture *must* be awaiting the freshly drained hot pasta or, simple as it seems, the dish will be a disaster. Drain the pasta well but quickly; then mix it by large forkfuls into the bacon-egg-cheese. Pour the warm reserved bacon fat over the spaghettini, toss quickly, and serve in hot soup plates with more cheese passed round. To my mind, a little freshly chopped parsley improves this dish, but then, to my mind a little chopped parsley improves almost any pasta dish.

SPAGHETTI WITH MEAT SAUCE

Tomato purée is used here instead of the usual Italian plum tomatoes because it doesn't need such long cooking to acquire the rich, thick texture that clings to the spaghetti strands. The sauce is guaranteed not to sink vapidly through the pasta and there is no cheating with flour to thicken it.

The Sauce   *Makes 6 cups*

1 lb. ground chuck beef
2 Tbsp. olive oil or bacon fat
2 medium onions, chopped
2 or 3 cloves garlic, minced
1 small carrot, minced
1 large can Italian tomato purée (about 3¾ cups)
NOTE: tomato *purée* is not the same as tomato *paste*

1¾ cups water
1 bay leaf
1 tsp. oregano or ½ tsp. oregano and ½ tsp. basil
¼ tsp. crushed red pepper
salt to taste

Brown the meat in the olive oil or drippings in a large heavy skillet, stirring occasionally to break up the meat and brown it evenly. If the meat renders excessive fat, drain off most of it. Add the onions, garlic, and carrot, and stir over medium-low heat until onions are wilted. Pour in the tomato purée; half-fill the empty can with water and stir that in. Blend in the seasonings, taking care not to oversalt. The sauce will concentrate during cooking. Simmer on the lowest heat (an asbestos pad under the pan prevents scorching), stirring from time to time and adding a bit more water if the sauce becomes too thick. Simmer, uncovered, for 45 minutes or up to 1½ hours, and don't forget to stir it often. Serve on very hot, cooked pasta.

NOTE: Naturally, this can be made in advance and it keeps well for four or five days in the refrigerator if tightly covered. Or you can freeze it in a plastic container with cover.

CHILI VARIATION: The approximate yield of this recipe is 1½ quarts, which could back you into a week of rather monotonous eating if you have no freezer space—ergo, this is how you convert it to chili.

2 cups (or more) leftover spaghetti sauce
1 cup beef broth
chili powder

cumin powder
1 can pinto or pink beans
cooked rice or frozen tortillas,
or both

Heat the sauce and stir in the beef broth to thin it. Add chili powder and cumin to taste (2 tablespoons chili powder and 2 teaspoons cumin make a temperate brew—you may use less, but the beans absorb a lot of flavor). Rinse the beans under cold running water, drain, and gently mix with sauce. Heat through about 15 minutes, but it's much tastier if the beans have a half hour to commune with all the flavors.

You *can* use kidney beans, but the canned ones tend to be so over-cooked they turn to mush at a touch of the spoon. You don't have to serve rice, but it stretches the chili. Tortillas to shovel up the chili are an especially messy, delicious way to eat it.

NOTE: Frozen tortillas disintegrate if you follow the package instructions. Instead, let the tortillas thaw at room temperature, separate carefully, then warm them in a dry skillet or fry crisp in oil.

FAKE CHINESE MEAL

Although Chinese cuisine requires rather elaborate chopping and slic-ing, the cooking techniques themselves are usually simple and some, like stir-frying, are very quick. Among the many charms of Oriental cookery is, to put it mildly, its lack of waste. Any interested beginner can get the basic principles of Chinese, Japanese, and Korean cookery from the ex-plicitly edited and illustrated *Oriental Cook Book*, a large but cheap paperback published by Sunset Books.

I had just begun my dalliance with Chinese cooking when it bailed me out of the Sunday-night supper dilemma of how to divide two pork chops among four people (hungry and impatient ones at that).

Serves 4

2 loin pork chops, 1-inch thick
(or buy 4 chops, ½-inch thick)
2 tsp. soy sauce
¼ tsp. powdered ginger (or
freshly grated ginger root)
½ cup sliced scallions

2 Tbsp. salad oil
1 (1 lb.) can bean sprouts,
drained
½ lb. fine egg noodles
dash of Tabasco (to substitute for Chinese hot oil)

Trim all bone and fat from the chops. If one inch thick, split them to half-inch thickness; then cut the meat in thin slivers, about two inches by an eighth inch. Marinate it in the soy sauce mixed with ginger while you slice the scallions, drain the bean sprouts, and cook the noodles in salted boiling water until just tender (about 4 minutes). Drain the noodles, mix them with a little oil so they won't tangle into a sticky lump, cover, and keep warm.

Heat the oil to smoking in either a wok or a heavy iron skillet, throw in the pork and scallions, and stir-fry (stir constantly with chopsticks or a wooden spoon over high heat about 1 minute—the meat will be browned and you will not get trichinosis because the finely cut pork cooks quite thoroughly in a few seconds. Add bean sprouts, lower heat a bit, and stir-fry ½ minute. Add fine noodles, stir-fry just to heat, sprinkle with Tabasco, and serve with or without plain white rice.

NOTE: A heavy steel wok with cover and ring base is by no means an extravagant investment; a wok may be used for quick sauté jobs (stir-frying), deep frying (less oil is needed because of the wok's spherical bottom), and steaming (with the addition of a round cake rack). As there are all sorts of tinny, ersatz woks on the market now, it would be safest to get the real thing in a Chinatown shop or, if you are unlucky enough to live in a city that has only one or two Chinese restaurants, ask the chef where he gets his cookware and ingredients.

CHICKEN AND NOODLES GRATIN

This dish is nothing to burble about, but it is simple, quick to make, and usually appealing to people who recoil from "foreign" dishes made with the cheaper, but less familiar, cuts of meat. Of course something has to give, and in this case the "plain eater" has to settle for a lot less meat and rather a lot of noodle. However, the finished dish looks rather fancy, and, Gael Greene, it will at least wow that ten-year-old niece from Cleveland.

Serves 3–4

1 large breast of chicken (both halves)
2 Tbsp. butter
1 medium onion, finely chopped
1 small (4-oz.) can mushroom stems and pieces

1 cup plain, unenriched medium-thick béchamel sauce (see recipe, page 31) made with milk
2 cups (uncooked) medium-width egg noodles
¼ cup grated Swiss cheese

BEANS, RICE, PASTA / 59

Preheat over to 350°.

Remove the skin and bone the raw chicken breast. It doesn't matter if you're not too neat about this operation, because the flesh should then be cut in small (half-inch) bite-size pieces. Melt the butter in a heavy skillet and brown the chicken, stirring constantly, about 2 minutes. Remove. In the same skillet (adding more butter if needed), sauté the onions until transparent. Drain the mushrooms and use their juices as part of the liquid in your béchamel sauce. Cook the noodles in boiling salted water about 4 minutes, or a minute less than the package directions indicate. Drain and rinse lightly in cold water to stop the cooking.

Butter a shallow, oval earthenware or Pyrex gratin dish. Mix together the chicken, onion, noodles, mushrooms, and sauce and turn them into the baking dish. Sprinkle the cheese over the top and bake until the sauce is bubbly and the cheese lightly browned. Do not overcook or the noodles will become hard and crusty. A tart green salad or some broccoli dressed with lemon butter is nice with the chicken gratin. Or you may feel you can serve both, having stretched one chicken breast beyond credibility.

5

EGGS

Consider the egg: both aesthetically and nutritionally, nature's triumph. Jewelers cut diamonds in its form; there are Venetian glass eggs and Roman marble eggs; and painting elaborate miniatures on real shells is a folk art in some Middle European countries. But besides being a Classic Beauty, the main thing about eggs is that they are so delicious and versatile and cheap.

Before we get into the recipes, there are some things about eggs confided to me by the United States Department of Agriculture that I think you ought to know. First of all, brown and white eggs are separate but equal: they contain exactly the same nutritional qualities and shell color does not affect flavor or grade. The breed of hen determines the color. Local or personal idiosyncrasy determines preferences and—sometimes—prices. In New York, white eggs usually fetch a higher price than brown eggs. In Boston, the reverse is true. So it goes.

HOW TO BUY EGGS

The U.S.D.A. grades eggs for farmers who request (and pay) for the service. The grade refers to the egg's freshness, and the size to its weight per dozen. The Grade AA (or Fresh Fancy) Extra Large egg is about the best one can do, short of keeping a henyard. This is the most expensive quality and size (except for Jumbo). Grade A is fine for most purposes and Grade B is generally used in baking and cooking, where beauty and absolute freshness are not important.

A really fresh egg should cover a small area when it is broken; the white should be thick and the yolk firm and high. Thin, watery whites and a flat yolk indicate staleness. Eggs should be bought only from refrigerated cases and stored immediately in the refrigerator. I have bought "farm-fresh" eggs (with no U.S.D.A. label) from picturesque roadside farmer's markets only to find them barely fit to mix with cat food. As a matter of fact, not fit, according to my cat Roger.

Remember, grade refers to freshness and is more important than size. There are six sizes ranging from Jumbo to Peewee (these are a little bigger than robins' eggs and are just great for Easter, when you want a lot of shells to color and not too much egg to waste). Grade A is usually excellent for just about anything except poaching. Poaching is the most rigid test and will surely disintegrate any but the freshest egg. Of course, if you poach eggs in an egg-poacher, the little round sections will hold together an egg of any age, but the French free-form method in simmering water instantly detects the middle-aged egg.

There are arguments against refrigerating eggs . . . mainly that the flavor is seriously impaired. As one who has tasted what used to be known as "cold-storage" eggs (which were held in warehouses some incredible length of time before being distributed to military messes and government institutions), I can vouch for the truth of this. However, I think that most poultry farmers are able to process and ship their eggs quite rapidly nowadays and that the objection to refrigeration is probably obsolete.

In case you're a real anti-machine-age nut or have relatives who are handing out free eggs, you can preserve eggs the way farm wives did before refrigerators came to pass. It might be useful if you're living in a remote commune or have staked out some acreage in Alaska. I have never tested this, but according to Monica Sheridan, author of *The Art of Irish Cooking*, who was raised on a farm in Ireland, this is one way of keeping eggs.

HOT BUTTERED EGGS

"Take the eggs fresh from the nest. Wipe lightly if they are stained, but do not wash. Smear your hands with butter and completely envelop each egg in a thin coating of butter. Store in papier maché egg trays with the narrow, pointed end of the egg down. The trays can be stacked one on top of another. These eggs take on the subtle flavor of the butter. Boiled or fried, they are superb."

Miss Sheridan cautions against storing eggs in the refrigerator and advises that they be kept in a "cool larder," which means a near-freezing room in an Irish or English farmhouse, a condition I doubt many American households could duplicate.

We'll assume you already know how to fry eggs. Most people don't do this very well, but they don't know it and like the result. Generally, this method of cooking eggs is accomplished over a roaring flame, which is wrong. With few exceptions (omelets) eggs became tough and leathery if they are not cooked over gentle heat.

The French never eat eggs at breakfast, but they certainly have put a lot of imagination into what they do with them at lunch and dinner. Poached eggs are used in a variety of main dishes, and, of course, the omelet is what every French housewife resorts to for a quick simple meal.

POACHED EGGS

Poaching is a little tricky and requires some practice, but since poached eggs are so versatile, it is an extremely valuable skill to master. If the egg isn't strictly fresh, though, nothing can shape it up and the ragged mess that cooks apart really isn't your fault. As I said, an egg-poacher resolves all this, but the whites tend to be a bit rubbery and there's just no satisfaction in mechanical cooking.

Fill a Teflon or stainless-steel saucepan with at least two inches of water. Add about 1 tablespoon of white vinegar to each pint of water used. Do not add salt because it counteracts the coagulating effect of the vinegar. Bring it to a simmer and place a small pan of warm water near the poaching pan. Also lay out a slotted spoon, which is absolutely essential.

Fold a couple of paper towels and put them nearby. Lower each egg (still in the shell) into the simmering water, count to 15, and remove. This helps the eggs to form neat rounds. Crack them and drop them into the simmering water as near to the surface as possible. Keep the water just trembling and lift out the first egg you put in after exactly 4 minutes, continuing with the others (never more than four at a time) in this manner:

Lift out the egg with a slotted spoon and lower it into the pan of warm water to wash off the vinegar. Quickly roll the spoon slightly over the paper towels to absorb the water and slip the egg onto a hot plate or a piece of toast. If you want to use the eggs later, put them directly into a bowl of cold water as you take them from the cooking water. They can be held, covered, in the refrigerator for a day or two for using in Eggs Benedict or Eggs Florentine (see below) or for decorating a mound of corned beef hash. To reheat them, warm them in a pan of very hot water for about a minute, drain in the spoon as described above, and serve.

A TV SUPPER

Two eggs on a piece of toast sounds dull, but a lot of familiar things are and we still like them. If the eggs are perfectly poached and drained and laid nicely on slices of French bread fried to a crispy gold in butter, it's a nifty quicky.

Fried bread was the precursor of toast and is still common in French cooking. Once you've tried it, the old electric toaster product will seem dreary indeed.

EGGS FLORENTINE

When you see the word "Florentine" appended to any item on a French menu, it means spinach lurks somewhere therein.

Serves 2

2 cups of creamed spinach (see recipe, page 196)
4 poached eggs, cooled
4 Tbsp. grated Swiss cheese

Preheat broiler.

Spread the hot creamed spinach in a shallow, flameproof casserole or pan. Lay the well-drained eggs in little nests you have made with the back of a spoon. Cover the eggs with the cheese and run under the broiler, about three inches from the heat, until the cheese starts to bubble.

This is perfect for lunch or a light supper. The casserole must go to the table and the dish looks nicer if it is cooked in individual pans because transferring it onto plates is a bit messy.

BAKED EGGS EN COCOTTE

These make a pleasant light supper dish (especially if it's Sunday and there doesn't seem to be much else in the refrigerator), or something rather different for Sunday breakfast. You will need either a small round flat baking dish or an old-fashioned china custard cup for each person; the flat dish for two eggs and the custard cup if they're getting only one. Baked custard seems to have gone out of style (pity!) and thrift shops are a good place to find those nice old cups.

1 or two eggs per person
1 Tbsp. cream per egg
  grated cheese (Parmesan, Swiss, or Romano, optional)
  parsley or tarragon, fresh and minced
  butter

Preheat the oven to 325°.
Butter the baking dishes or custard cups and set them on a cookie sheet or any flat pan so that you won't have to fool around with a lot of little red-hot dishes. Put them in the oven until they get hot and the butter melts. If you're doing more than 4 eggs or aren't too deft at cracking eggs, break them first into teacups so that you can get them all into the hot cups within a minute or two. Slide the eggs into the baking dishes, pour a little cream over each one, sprinkle with a bit of grated cheese, lay a large sheet of aluminum foil over all the dishes, and put them in the oven. They should be done in about 5 minutes, the whites set and the yolks soft, but it can take longer if you've fiddled with the cups too long. As residual heat continues to cook the eggs, it is wise to remove them a little underdone.

Strew the baked eggs lightly with the minced herb and serve at once.

VARIATIONS: Put a little hot, creamed spinach or asparagus in the bottom of the dish or cup before breaking in the eggs.

SCRAMBLED EGGS WITH —

Nearly everybody starts his culinary adventures with this dish. And whatever he does wrong may linger on for life. For instance, hard, dry eggs are usually preferred by the very young, and this unfortunate mistake is as hard to wean people from as well-done steak.

First of all, be sure that the white and yolk are completely amalgamated (I have seen men try to do this after the eggs are in the hot frying pan; it's too horrible to describe), then beat in ½ teaspoon of water, milk, or cream for each egg used. Sprinkle in salt and pepper and blend in any extra ingredient, such as cooked onions, herbs, cottage cheese, chipped beef, etc.

Put a generous amount of butter into the cold skillet (or lightly butter a Teflon pan) and set over medium heat. When the butter is hot and frothing (not browning or smoking), pour the eggs all at once into the center of the pan. Stir lazily in a circular motion with a fork until the eggs are semi-set but still moist. Serve on hot plates.

NOTE: Scrambled eggs used to be made (and still are in France, where they just don't seem to understand about scrambled eggs because there's no place for them in the French menu) in a double boiler. They were beaten with cream, turned into the top part of a double boiler with some melted butter in it, set over boiling water, and stirred constantly to, a relatively smooth mass. Few real Yankees admire the puddingy result of this method or the length of time it requires.

OMELETS

The chief difference between an omelet and scrambled eggs is that an omelet has charisma and scrambled eggs are sort of Hubert Humphrey. The best way to master the few little treacheries of omelets is to make one every day for a week. (Or you can go on an egg diet and make three a day for a couple of days, varying the fillings.)

Serves 1–2

   3 eggs
1½ tsp. water
   salt and pepper
   3 tsp. butter
   herbs or filling (optional)

Break the eggs into a bowl, add the water, salt, and pepper, and beat everything together thoroughly. Put the butter in a heavy, cold skillet and melt it over medium heat until frothing. Just as it settles down and begins to clear, pour the eggs directly into the middle of the pan, turn up the

heat slightly, and stir around with the flat of a fork, always in the same direction, so that you are lifting the cooked part of the egg off the bottom of the pan. Another method is to lift the edges of the omelet with a narrow spatula to let the uncooked egg run under the cooked portion. This should take from 10 to 15 seconds.

Shake the pan back and forth over the flame while you're stirring or lifting. It's sort of like patting your head and rubbing your stomach. When the omelet is soft, creamy, and slightly set, lay your warm pre-cooked ingredient or herbs across the center of the omelet. Grab the pan handle from underneath with the left hand, and with the right hand flip one third of the omelet over the center, tilt the omelet pan up, and roll the omelet out onto a waiting warmed plate. This begins to sound like a scenario but actually the whole business takes only about 15 seconds or so, though probably a lot longer if you've never made an omelet before.

Things to Add to Omelets:

Creamed or plain chipped beef

Crumbled bacon

Strips of thinly sliced ham or bologna (fried)

Fried minced onions, scallions, green peppers, pimientos

Creamed or sautéed mushrooms

Minced leftover vegetables (especially spinach) or meat in a thick cream sauce

Freshly grated Gruyère, Swiss,

Parmesan, Romano, or cheddar cheese

Chopped fresh herbs: chives, parsley, chervil, tarragon, or thyme

Flaked cooked fish minus skin and bones (leftover or canned)

Minced lobster, crab, or shrimp

Chopped canned anchovies

Dairy sour cream to spoon over a finished herb omelet

Add anything you damn well please, so long as it is cut very fine and precooked—unless you use fresh herbs.

BAUERNFRÜHSTÜCK

This is a German dish and translates "farmer's breakfast." It *is* a little heavy unless you have to harvest an acre of cabbages right after the milking. Great for lunch and supper, though.

Serves 2

4 large eggs

4 strips bacon

1 onion, chopped

1 medium cold boiled potato, chopped

salt and pepper

Lay the bacon in a heavy, cold skillet and cook over medium heat, turning often until crisp. Remove and drain on paper toweling. If necessary, pour off all but 3 tablespoons of fat (into the juice can where you are thriftily conserving your bacon fat). Throw the chopped onion into the pan and cook over medium heat until soft; then add the potato and cook until both are lightly browned. Crumble the bacon into the pan.

Beat the eggs well with a little salt and pepper to taste.

Pour in the eggs and, as the omelet cooks, lift the edges with a narrow spatula or table knife so that the uncooked portion runs under the cooked part. When the top is about the consistency of very thick cream, the omelet is done. Regulate the heat and move the pan back and forth occasionally so that you do not burn the center bottom.

This is a great clumsy, delicious thing that can't be rolled out of the pan in the usual way. Instead, fold one half over the other, and lift it with two wide spatulas onto a hot platter. A sprinkle of parsley adds a lot of charm.

SOUFFLÉ OMELET

This is much easier to make than a real soufflé and, for some people, easier than a classic omelet. It is actually just a puffed omelet started on top of the stove and finished in the oven.

Serves 1–2

3 large eggs, separated
½ tsp. salt
   pinch of pepper
2 Tbsp. butter
¼ cup grated cheese or some other filling suitable for an ordinary omelet

Preheat the oven to 450°.
Beat the whites with the salt until stiff but not dry (a pinch of cream of tartar makes them mount higher) and in another large bowl beat the yolks until thick. Beat the pepper and filling into the yolks. Add one third of the egg whites to the yolks and mix gently. Turn the remaining egg whites onto the top of the yolk mixture and fold them in with a rubber spatula, scraping from the bottom of the bowl up over the top of the meringue until the yolks and whites are fairly well combined. Don't mix too much. It is better to have some clumps of white than an airless pancake.

Heat the butter in a heavy iron skillet until foaming hot. Turn the soufflé-omelet mixture into the skillet and cook undisturbed over medium-low heat for a minute or two. Then pop it into the oven to brown and cook on top. If the oven is too much trouble, you can brown it under the broiler, taking care that the omelet top is at least three inches from the heat source. It rises slightly. Have hot plates waiting and serve the omelet from the skillet, cut in half or in wedges.

CURRIED EGGS

About as Indian as Egg Foo Yong is Chinese, this will nevertheless be liked by almost any American. Don't serve it to anyone who has been in the Indian Service and is a stickler for authenticity.

Serves 2

2 Tbsp. butter	2 Tbsp. curry powder (or more
1 onion, minced	if you like)
2 Tbsp. flour (level, of course)	1 tsp. salt
1 cup milk, very hot	4 hard-cooked eggs
½ cup sliced mushrooms, cooked	2 slices toast

Sauté the onion in the butter until transparent. Stir in the flour over low heat, then beat in the milk with a wire whisk and continue cooking until the sauce is smooth and thickened. Add the mushrooms, curry powder, and salt, and taste. Quarter the eggs, lengthwise, add them to the sauce gently (so they remain relatively intact), heat through, and divide on each piece of toast. Serve instantly along with a green salad or some kind of raw vegetables—otherwise the flavor and texture can be a bit monotonous.

QUICHE LORRAINE

Traditionally, this egg, cheese, and bacon pie is baked in a flan ring, which is removed when the crust is half baked. The filling is then poured into the partially baked crust, and it's a disaster if the sides of the shell are not strong enough to hold the weight of the filling. But a quiche is a simple thing to master if you just proceed as for an ordinary one-crust pie. It is crucial to the success of this recipe that the pie shell be two-thirds baked (firm but still pale) before adding the custard. Use your favorite pastry recipe or pie-crust mix or a frozen shell.

Serves 6

1 9-inch pie shell, two-thirds baked	3 eggs
4–6 slices bacon, fried crisp	1½ cups Swiss cheese, grated
2 cups light cream (or half milk and half evaporated milk)	1 tsp. salt
	few drops Tabasco (or a little pepper)

Preheat oven to 375°.

Crumble the bacon into the prebaked pie shell. (If using a frozen pie shell, do not thaw. Bake completed quiche on lowest shelf of oven.) Beat the eggs, then stir in the cream, cheese, salt, and Tabasco and mix well. Pour this into the pie shell and bake in the lower third of the oven for about 35 minutes. Let the quiche rest at room temperature about 15 minutes before serving. Like pizza, a quiche has a way of searing the roof of your mouth if it is served right out of the oven. Resting it makes the pie easier to cut into neat wedges, too.

OMELET MEDITERRANEAN

An Italian dish with a catchy name, Uova in Purgatorio (Eggs in Purgatory), was the inspiration for this omelet. An earthy mixture of tomatoes, garlic, olive oil, and, of course, eggs, the dish is about as subtle as Anna Magnani. For this reason it can enliven the deadest taste buds and is a terrific hangover brunch entree.

Serves 2

4 Tbsp. olive oil	⅛ tsp. dried thyme
6 scallions, sliced thinly	4 eggs plus 1 Tbsp. water
1 clove garlic, minced	½ tsp. salt
2 Tbsp. parsley, chopped fine	¼ tsp. pepper
½ cup canned tomatoes, chopped small	

Heat 2 tablespoons of the oil in a small skillet. Add the scallions, garlic, and parsley and sauté over low heat a couple of minutes. Add the tomatoes and crush the thyme over the mixture. Stir everything together and let bubble gently while you beat up the eggs, water, salt, and pepper.

In a heavy skillet or omelet pan, heat the remaining 2 tablespoons of oil. When it is very hot, but not smoking, pour the egg mixture directly into the center of the pan. Stir with a table fork in a circular motion a couple of times until the omelet is sort of bunched up in the middle and still very wet. Stir in the tomato sauce and cook the omelet over medium-low heat, shaking the pan occasionally, until it is set but still moist. Fold one-third of the omelet over the center, grab the skillet by the handle, and roll the omelet out onto a waiting hot platter.

UOVA IN PURGATORIO

If you haven't passed Omelet I, never mind; the original Eggs in Purgatory is easy enough even for those still in Remedial Egg Frying. Just as with other regional or ethnic dishes, who knows what the "original" recipe for Uova in Purgatorio could have been. Anyway, my introduction to it came from the *New Yorker* magazine's gastronomical writer and gourmet-in-residence, M. F. K. Fisher. The recipe is from her book *How to Cook a Wolf*, published during World War II, when even affluent Americans had to grapple with the shorts. (The poor folks hardly noticed rationing, of course.) Mrs. Fisher's book is stylish, anecdotal, informative, and generally still valid, although some of her poverty was endured in Paris and eased by Moulin à Vent at 26¢ a liter.

Serves 4

"4 Tbsp. olive oil (substitute will do, dad blast it)
1 clove garlic
1 onion
2 cups tomato sauce (Italian kind is best, but even catchup will do if you cut down on spices)

1 tsp. minced mixed herbs (basil, thyme)
1 tsp. minced parsley
salt and pepper
8 eggs
slices of thin French bread, toasted

"Heat oil in a saucepan that has a tight cover. Split garlic lengthwise, run a toothpick through each half, and brown slowly in oil. Add the onion, minced, and cook until golden. Then add the tomato sauce and the seasonings and herbs. Cook about 15 minutes, stirring often, and then take out the garlic.

"Into this sauce break the eggs. Spoon the sauce over them, cover closely, and cook very slowly until eggs are done, or about 15 minutes. (If the skillet is a heavy one, you can turn off the heat immediately and cook in 15 minutes with what is stored in the metal.)

"When done, put the eggs carefully on the slices of dry toast, and cover with sauce. (Grated Parmesan cheese is good on this, if you can get any.)"

PIPERADE

Even the timidest tourist to the Basque Country of France has probably sampled this well-known *Basquaise* egg dish. It's sort of a cross between a Western omelet and scrambled eggs. However, the proportion of vegetables to eggs is far greater, and the dish is served as a separate course, sometimes with a slice of Bayonne ham. Prosciutto or Westphalian ham makes a good substitute.

Serves 4

3 Tbsp. olive oil
2 medium onions, sliced thinly
2 large red (or green) sweet peppers

2 good-sized fresh tomatoes, chopped
4 large eggs
salt and pepper to taste

Heat the oil in a heavy skillet (Teflon-lined is best) and slowly sauté the onions to a light brown. Cut the peppers into thin strips and add them to the pan. When the peppers are soft, add the tomatoes and cook, covered, about 10 minutes. Add more oil if the mixture seems too dry and watch that it doesn't scorch. Season with salt and freshly milled pepper, beat the eggs, and stir them into the vegetables. Cook, stirring gently, until the mass is semi-set but still soft—more like scrambled eggs than an omelet. Serve at once with or without a slice of ham.

STUFFED EGGS MORNAY

A delicious little supper dish that can be quickly rustled up from things usually found on the pantry shelf and a few eggs. Crisp green salad in a vinaigrette dressing offsets the soft voluptuousness of Stuffed Eggs Mornay. You can also make this with poached eggs replacing the stuffed eggs, but everybody knows about that.

Serves 2–3

4 large eggs
1 cup thick cream sauce (see recipe, page 32)
small can mushroom stems and pieces, drained and minced approximately ½ cup milk, heated

salt and pepper
4 Tbsp. grated Gruyère or Swiss cheese for sauce
2 Tbsp. grated Gruyère or Swiss cheese for topping

Preheat oven to 450°.
Start the eggs in cool water with a splash of vinegar in it. After it comes to the boil, lower heat and simmer the eggs gently about 10 min-

utes. Plunge them at once into cold running water. While the eggs are cooling, make the cream sauce. Shell the eggs, split them lengthwise, and remove the yolks and sieve them. To them add ⅓ cup of the cream sauce and the mushrooms. Mix well with a fork and season carefully with salt and pepper, preferably cayenne. Stuff the egg whites with this mixture. Warm the remaining sauce over low heat and thin to a medium consistency with hot milk; then stir in the 4 tablespoons grated cheese until the sauce is quite smooth. Spread a little of the sauce on the bottom of a small oval gratin dish just large enough to hold the eggs in one layer. Arrange the eggs over the sauce and pour the remaining sauce evenly over and around the stuffed eggs. Sprinkle with the remaining 2 tablespoons of grated cheese. Bake on the top shelf of the preheated oven for about 10 minutes, until the sauce is bubbly. Glaze the dish under a very hot broiler about three inches from the heat. This will only take a minute or so; you must watch it hawkishly and snatch it out when the top begins to brown ever so lightly. A sprinkle of fresh chopped chives is a pleasant touch if you happen to have any—a very light scattering of finely chopped fresh tarragon is nice too, but don't try to substitute dried herbs, for they must be either cooked or marinated to bring out their flavor.

VARIATION: 3–4 tablespoons finely shredded dried beef can be substituted for the mushrooms. If you use it, omit salt in making the cream sauce.

EGG CREAM

The most fascinating thing about an egg cream is that it contains no egg and no cream. It is a drink, also known as a Two Cents Plain (Harry Golden's book title), that seems to have originated in the Jewish candy stores of New York's Lower East Side. You couldn't fool a six-year-old into believing in the egg or the cream, so one has to conclude that irony and not chicanery prompted the name.

A successful writer once told me he knew he'd arrived when he could make his own egg creams at home. First you need a seltzer bottle (the kind people were always squirting into their whisky in movies of the thirties). Try a thrift shop for these. Put some kind of sweet syrup in the bottom of a rather tall glass, say chocolate, strawberry jam, or, for the Classic Two Cents Plain, simply sugar and water that has been boiled together. Pour in about an inch of milk, then foam it up to the top with seltzer. There it is—egg cream.

6

FISH

Any generality about fish is almost bound to be wrong somewhere. The endless wrangle between any two Frenchmen over what legitimately goes into a bouillabaisse is but one example. From one part of our country to another the fish vary as much as the trees and wildflowers, so the only useful categories are "fat" and "lean" fish. Recipes are more or less interchangeable within the two groupings.

Some of the "fat," or oily fleshed, fish are bluefish, mackerel, shad, eel, pompano, red snapper, herring, trout, rock bass, mullet, tuna, swordfish, and croakers. Some of the commoner "lean" fish are cod, porgie, sheepshead, grouper, fluke, striped bass, flounder, lemon sole, gray sole, whiting, catfish, and kingfish. Most of these have five or six other regional names, although they're all Atlantic fish. It's on this coast that I've picked up most of my fish lore—watching the haul-seiners cranking in their nets on the Amagansett beaches, poking around the Montauk docks, or ambling through the early morning din of the Fulton Street fish market. When I lived in the Village and shopped on (then) glorious Bleecker Street, a fishmonger with Italian panache used to separate a flounder from its bones and skin with two flicks of his knife while he was explaining to me how to starve snails for cooking.

I love all kinds of fish markets: wholesale port markets, street markets, big, noisy city markets, little ethnic markets, off-the-boat haggling in the Caribbean—in fact, any kind except those frosty little snob markets that traffic in precooked shrimp and lobster and an occasional pristine fillet of something. The best place to buy fresh fish in the city is in a market where the dealer knows his neighborhood demands and thus has a fast turnover, or in a big semi-wholesale city market.

Fresh fish have bright, bulgy eyes, red gills, firm flesh, and a pleasant sea odor. There is no reason for the fishmonger to hand you any billingsgate for making sure these standards are met. In the case of buying fillets already prepared, you'd better know and trust the management. Should some miraculous change occur in the price of shrimp and lobster so that we can all enjoy it again, some advice: never buy cooked shrimp or lobster. Dealers tend to cook the moribund lobsters they know won't last out the night, and they invariably overcook shrimp alarmingly. A live lobster is best bought from a pound filled with sea water; they can survive for some days solely on refrigeration but during this time the lobster becomes dehydrated and the flesh loses its juiciness. This is academic, even in the great seaport of New York, where the price of lobster is so high it has been removed from most restaurant menus. One understands about the effect of a stormy winter, poaching Russian ships, and all that, but there is no faintly plausible answer to the ridiculous price of shrimp. Soft- and hard-shell clams and mussels are still relatively cheap in the New York area, crabmeat is astronomical, small hard-shelled blue crabs with itsy-bitsy claws are declared a bargain at two dollars a dozen. About the only fish that could still be considered cheap in this area is whiting. Especially in fish marketing, it's quite pointless to decide what you want until you get to the shop and see what's fresh, plentiful, and reasonably priced.

Frozen fish is a flop—a fresh porgie is a thousand times better then a frozen Dover sole.

GRILLED FLOUNDER

Plain grilling, or broiling, probably retains the fullest flavor of a freshly caught fish more than any other method. Despite the popularity of grilling (and charcoal grilling), it is by no means the simple matter many people suppose it to be. How hot should the fire be, how far from the

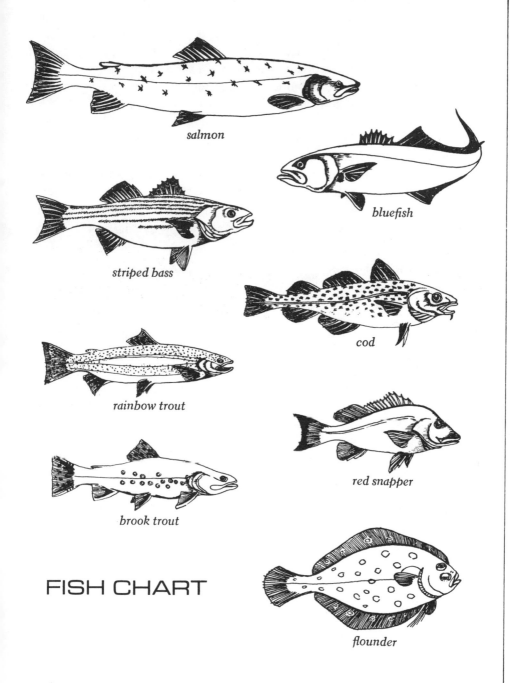

salmon

bluefish

striped bass

cod

rainbow trout

red snapper

brook trout

FISH CHART

flounder

flame or embers should the food be, when is the exact moment of perfection—neither overdone nor underdone? Grill cooks are born, not taught, and none of these questions can be answered precisely. On top of that, fish is delicate and tricky, disgusting if underdone, destroyed if overdone. Grilled fish must be watched *constantly*, the heat adjusted minutely, and the fish must be snatched from the fire and served immediately it reaches the perfect state. The fish should never be turned more than once because it breaks so easily. For this reason, you shouldn't choose fish any larger than a flounder unless you have a special fish-shaped French wire grill with legs to stand over a charcoal fire. For small fish, a long-handled hamburger grill that clamps together so that you can just turn the whole grill over simplifies matters.

Grilled fish in the average home stove is just too much bother for more than two people unless you are as swift and accurate as a tern.

Serves 2

2 whole flounder (about 1 lb. each)	lemon wedges
melted butter	hot plates or metal platters
chopped parsley	

Have the flounder gutted and scaled but left whole. Preheat the broiler for 10 minutes. Wash and dry the fish and season it inside with salt and pepper; then rub the entire outside well with melted butter. Lay it on the hot grill about three inches from the heat source, and when the skin starts to turn crisp and golden, reduce the heat slightly. The skin should never blacken and blister. Using two spatulas, roll the fish over and grill the other side until it too is a crisp, golden brown. This should take about 10 minutes in all; I usually cook the first side less than the second to lessen the danger of breakage. An alternate method, especially successful with rather large fish on an outdoor grill, is to lay the fish on a double thickness of buttered foil with widely spaced holes punched in it so that juices won't collect and steam the fish. When you think the fish is a little less than half done, pull the foil to one edge of the grill and roll the fish over directly onto the grill. This is not as attractive, but at least your fish is more likely to be in one piece.

Test the fish by inserting the blade of a small knife near the backbone. If it is opaque white right down to the bone, it is done. Lift it immediately onto hot plates, sprinkle with parsley, decorate with lemon wedges, and serve at once. One or two small, plainly boiled or steamed new potatoes are the only thing usually served with grilled fish.

FILLET OF LEMON SOLE À LA MEUNIÈRE

"Dusted with flour and fried" refers either to the usual condition of "the miller's wife" or to the way she cooked her husband's fish. As is the case with almost anything to be sautéed, "quickness" (in the sports-page sense) is essential to this dish. Also, be certain when buying your fillets that they will fit in your skillet. Perhaps American pot-makers will one day wake up to the need for a good, heavy, decently priced oval fish skillet, which is now available only in fancy imported cookware shops. A visit to a French culinary goods shop makes you realize why their food turns out more beautifully than anybody else's. A shallow oval Creuset baking dish is flameproof and can be used for sautéing fish.

Serves 2

2 fillets of lemon sole (or similar fish)
2 Tbsp. butter (not margarine)
lemon wedges
chopped parsley

flour, salt, and pepper
2–3 Tbsp. plain, flavorless salad oil (for economy; this ideally should be clarified butter)

Have ready before you start to cook the fish: the butter, slowly cooked to a light nut brown, the lemon wedges, the chopped parsley, and two very hot platters or plates. Anything else you plan to serve with the fish should also be ready.

Small whole fish may also be prepared in this manner. If you're buying flounder fillets, pick out the white sides (one side of a flounder is dark, the other light). Wipe off the sole, season it, and flour it lightly. When the salad oil is quite hot, but by no means smoking, lay in the fish fillets. When one side is light golden brown, turn the fillet over carefully and cook the other side; 3 or 4 minutes per side should do.

Do not overcook the fish—it will continue cooking just a bit on the hot plates and the bubbling brown butter will add to this. Lift the fillets onto the plates with two spatulas, pour over the brown butter, sprinkle with parsley, and decorate with lemon wedges. Thin, peeled slices of lemon with a caper at the center of each, laid along the length of the sole, look very pretty if you feel like getting fancy.

SAUTÉED FLOUNDER OR COD ROE

Everybody knows about shad roe—that it is delectable, available only in spring, and wildly expensive—but the roes of the humble flounder and cod are fine things, too, and cheap. Admittedly, they aren't to be found in run-of-the-mill fish markets, but ask for them a few times and maybe the dealer will catch on. (My fish man carries winkles, conchs, cod tongues, squid, and Irish seaweed, as well as these roes and all the usual things—one of the blessings of a mixed city neighborhood.) All roes are easier to deal with if parboiled. Otherwise you may hear a loud noise just before you find disembodied fish eggs clinging to your chest and chin.

Serves 2 (for very big roe fans, double the amounts below)

1 pair of cod roe (about 6 inches long) or flounder roe salted water to cover with 1 Tbsp. vinegar added 1 whole egg, beaten lightly dry bread crumbs	2 Tbsp. butter salt and pepper lemon wedges chopped parsley (optional) 2 strips thick-sliced bacon, cooked (optional)

Handle the roe very gently to avoid breaking the membrane. When the salted water is just below the simmer (small bubbles clinging to the bottom of the pan), slide in the roes, unseparated. Poach about 8 minutes, uncovered, and do not let the water boil. If the roes are larger or smaller, adjust the time. Drain and drop into very cold water for a minute. Very carefully, peel the membrance from the roes after separating the halves. If the membrane clings obstinately, just leave it on and let the diner worry about it—it's a little chewy but otherwise not unpleasant. If the roes are thick (more than an inch), split them in half lengthwise. Dip them in beaten egg, then in crumbs and sauté over low heat in butter, turning only once. Serve on hot plates with the grilled bacon and lemon wedges. Sprinkle with salt and pepper. Scatter with parsley.

COD-ROE PÂTÉ

This is what happened to my cod roe once when I let them get too cold before peeling them. The membrane stuck; I swore; I had a plate full of loose fish eggs. I remembered some kind of smoked cod-roe pâté (which comes in tins but doesn't exist in this country) in one of Elizabeth David's cookbooks. Hers, made with garlic and olive oil, sounds splendid, but this one I concocted from fresh roe has an altogether different character. To be served on thin, fresh toast squares with wine or drinks.

1 pair cod roe (approximately
  6 inches long)
4–5 Tbsp. slightly softened butter
1 Tbsp. minced shallot (or
  onion)

¼ tsp. dried tarragon or 1 Tbsp.
  fresh, chopped
¼ cup white wine
1 tsp. wine vinegar
salt and pepper to taste

Poach the cod roe as in the preceding recipe. Peel it and put the loose roe into a mortar or wooden bowl. Mash it thoroughly with the butter. Simmer the shallots and tarragon in the white wine and vinegar about 5 minutes, covered. It should have reduced to about one tablespoon; if not, reduce it. Cool to lukewarm; then strain into the cod roe and mix well with a fork until it is light. Season with salt and pepper (white preferably) to taste. Pile into a small terrine and cover with plastic wrap, smoothing the wrap down onto the surface of the pâté to eliminate all air. If you want to keep it a few days, melt some butter, and when it is cooled but still liquid pour a film an eighth-inch deep on top of the cod roe (omitting the milky residue of the butter) before covering it.

BAKED FISH FILLETS IN CREAM SAUCE

Filet of Sole à la Bonne Femme is one of the simplest and most enduringly pleasing ways to treat fillets of such fish as lemon or gray sole, flounder, or any of the sole family. The dish can be endlessly varied with different sauces and called something else, but the basic preparation remains the same. If you use large fillets of lemon sole, allow only one per serving, but fewer than 2 fillets of flounder per person would be unsatisfying.

Serves 4

8 flounder fillets, uniform size
  salt and white pepper
1 cup dry white wine
3 Tbsp. butter
2 Tbsp. shallots or onion, finely
  minced

½ lb. sliced mushrooms
2 Tbsp. flour
¼ cup heavy cream or ¼ cup
  milk beaten with one egg yolk
  chopped parsley

Butter a baking dish, salt and pepper the fillets, and lay them in the dish, folded in half. Pour the wine over them and bake covered with foil in a 350° oven for about 15 minutes, or until just cooked through. Remove to a buttered fireproof gratin dish and cover loosely with foil. Strain the fish stock into a small saucepan and reduce it to 1 cup. Slowly sauté the shallots and mushrooms in 2 tablespoons of the butter, without browning, for 5 minutes. Sprinkle them with flour and mix it into the butter well. Pour the boiling fish stock over this, stirring constantly with a wooden spoon until you have a thick, smooth velouté. Finish the sauce with the cream or the milk and egg yolk beaten together. If using egg yolk, be careful not to let the sauce boil. Season with salt and pepper. With a paper towel, mop up any juices the fish may have exuded. Pour the sauce over the fillets, covering them completely. Dot with bits of butter and run under the broiler to glaze the top and color it very, very lightly. Sprinkle with parsley and serve.

The entire dish can be made a few hours in advance except for the final broiler glazing. However, the fish will have cooled through to the bottom and must be gently reheated (not cooked) in a moderate oven and then run under the broiler.

COLD BAKED BASS

Once I bought a whole side of smoked salmon in Dublin, but that's as close as I've ever been to my dream of owning a whole, huge, gorgeous pink salmon to serve with three exquisite sauces. Salmon is almost worth its price, but I've never been able to discern the reason for the high price of swordfish, which I find coarse, dry, and insipid. To my taste, striped bass is the finest fish we have on the Northeast coast; and depending on the season, the weather, and a lot of imponderables, bass is sometimes fairly cheap. Substitute any other lean fish that's running in your part of the country.

Serves 6

1 whole striped bass, about 5 lbs.
salt, pepper, and lemon juice
1 cup dry white wine
3 Tbsp. softened butter
several sprigs fresh tarragon (or ½ tsp. dried)

2 Tbsp. minced shallot or onion
Cucumber Sauce
Aïoli (see recipe, page 40)
large bunch of parsley
slice of lemon and 1 caper

Be sure you have a pan large enough to accommodate a fish of this size; it can be laid cater-cornered. Have the fish gutted but left otherwise intact. Rub the interior with salt, pepper, and lemon juice; then insert the tarragon and a few bits of butter. Salt and pepper the outside of the fish and rub well with the softened butter. Lay the fish on a large double thickness of aluminum foil, cupping the edges to form a shell. Put this into the baking pan. Sprinkle with shallots and pour the wine into the foil shell. Seal the edges of the foil together into a loose envelope. Bake in a **preheated 350°** oven about 40 minutes. Make a tiny slit in the thickest part of the fish near the spine to see that the flesh is white all the way to the bone. Loosen the packet to let the steam escape and halt the cooking. Transfer the fish, foil and all, to a cool place. When it has cooled to room temperature, peel the skin from one side, then gently roll the fish over onto a long, clean platter and peel the other side. Cover with plastic wrap and chill. At serving time, cover the eye of the fish with the lemon slice and put the caper in its center. Surround the fish with a garland of freshly washed green parsley. Serve the Cucumber Sauce and Aïoli separately.

Cucumber Sauce

This sauce is better with shellfish and hot fish if mayonnaise is substituted for the sour cream. But this version has a light freshness that perfectly complements the tarragon-and-wine-flavored chilled bass. (If you double the cucumber and halve the sour cream it becomes a refreshing cool taste to serve with a hot curry.)

Makes 1½ cups approximately

1 6-inch firm green cucumber
1 cup sour cream
2 Tbsp. fresh dill weed, chopped (or, if you must, fresh parsley)
   salt and white pepper to taste

Peel, halve, seed, and soak the cucumber in cold salted water for 1 hour. Dry and chop it into fine cubes. Mix with the sour cream, dill, salt, and pepper.

FISH IN DILLED SOUR CREAM

Leftover baked fish can be used, perhaps simply mixed with some of the Cucumber Sauce (see preceding recipe) served with the fish. But poached fish from a firm variety is really more suitable. Cod, haddock, or kingfish (which is a big mackerel) are logical choices. There's quite a lot of dazzle in this hors d'oeuvre and it can be made with little bother or expense.

2 lbs. skinless fillets of cod, haddock, or a similar fish
1 cup dry white wine
1 cup water
1 tsp. salt
1 bouquet garni: 1 Tbsp. mixed
pickling spices, 1 sprig pars-

ley, 1 bay leaf, all tied in a
cheesecloth bag
2 cups sour cream
4 Tbsp. fresh dill, chopped
4 Tbsp. scallions, minced
salt and pepper to taste

Bring the wine, water, salt, and the bouquet to a boil and simmer 5 minutes. Cut the fish into large chunks (if they're too small, you'll wind up with mere flakes) and put them in a saucepan. Pour the wine mixture over the fish, cover, and poach very gently until done—probably not more than 5 minutes. Put an ice cube or two in the pan to stop the cooking and allow the fish to cool in the liquid. Drain. Mix together the sour cream, dill, and scallions and add salt and pepper to taste. Fold the fish and cream sauce together, breaking the fish as little as possible. Chill until serving time.

BAKED CLAMS CASINO

Originally, this was "Oysters Casino," and I don't know its history, but I like to think a Belle Epoque New Orleans chef concocted it for some big riverboat spender. Clams are a bit more cussed than oysters and can't be substituted in every case. But with care, cherrystone or littleneck clams will remain tender and juicy in this preparation. First, you have to go dig some clams and find someone who knows how to wield a clam knife. Fish dealers double the price of clams if they are required to open them for you. Anyway, once they have been opened, clams won't keep well on the half shell.

24 littleneck or cherrystone clams
4 Tbsp. minced onion
4 Tbsp. minced parsley
salt and Tabasco

24 thin squares of bacon large
enough to cover the clam
2 lbs. rock salt or large dried
beans

Open the clams over a bowl to avoid losing the juice. Loosen the clam but leave it lying on one shell half. Replace the juice if it has spilled. Push each shell down onto the rock salt or beans to keep it steady. Put a few grains of salt (see note) and a drop of Tabasco on each clam. Put a pinch of the onion and parsley, which you have mixed together, on top of each clam and cover with a square of bacon. Broil under moderate flame until the bacon is almost crisp and the clams plumped up. Hard-shelled clams suffer very little cooking or they toughen—they really need only to be heated through. Serve with lemon wedges.

NOTE: Buy a couple of extra clams if you don't dig your own. Taste a raw clam to see how salty they are before adding more salt.

CLAMS FLORENTINE

Once again adapted from an oyster recipe, these clams are normally served on the half shell. But there is an easier and cheaper way to make this rather rich hors d'oeuvre. Buy shucked clams by the pint or quart, allowing 6 or 8 littlenecks or small cherrystones per person. If you live near a beach, pick up some very large smooth clam shells. If not, those large white pearly clam shells from Japan sell at 6 for a dollar and can be used many times for almost anything you might want to serve in individual baking dishes.

Serves 4

24 shucked clams, littlenecks or small cherrystones
2 packages frozen chopped spinach
3 Tbsp. butter
1 Tbsp. minced onion
1 cup sauce Mornay (see recipe, page 34)

Cook the spinach according to package directions, breaking it up as soon as you can to prevent overcooking the outer part of the block. It is better, if you have time, to thaw the spinach first to avert this problem. Drain it well. Melt the butter and cook the onion in it until transparent but not browned. Add the spinach and stir until heated through and well mixed with the butter and onion. Season rather highly with salt and pepper. Make a bed of spinach in each clam shell—you may have a bit too much, but one package is not enough. Arrange 6 clams, drained, of course, on top of the spinach. Put a spoonful of sauce Mornay on top of each clam. Run under the broiler until the sauce bubbles and the clams are hot. You can't leave this unattended for one second—the sauce may burn and the clams vulcanize.

SALMON MOUSSE

Basic food products—flour, sugar, yeast, etc.—sometimes contain quite good recipes on or in them. Some are ill-advised brainstorms of an ad agency, but most are created by food professionals hired to promote one product. The Knox gelatine people try to tout their product for everything from strengthening fingernails to steadying a mousse. Upon request, the company will send out acres of recipes using gelatine, and I have found all of them reliable, if somewhat square. This salmon mousse is based on "Mrs. Knox's Tuna Mold," from which I have deleted a few colorful touches such as green of pea and red of pimiento. I like this as a light main course in summer, or a first course at any season.

Makes about 4 cups

1 envelope plain unflavored gelatine
1¾ cups milk
2 egg yolks (3 is better if eggs aren't very large)
1 tsp. salt
½ tsp. white pepper
2 Tbsp. scallions, minced

1 Tbsp. butter
1 16-oz. can salmon
1 tsp. Dijon-style mustard (Mr. Mustard, for instance)
2 Tbsp. lemon juice
2 Tbsp. fresh parsley, minced (optional)

Soften the gelantine in ½ cup of the cold milk. Whisk together the egg yolks, remaining milk, salt, and pepper. Stir the mixture into the softened gelantine and cook over low heat about 5 minutes, stirring constantly. Do not let the custard boil. Wilt the scallions in butter and add them to the custard. Chill until rather thick and syrupy. Drain the salmon and discard the skin and larger bones—don't worry about the wispy ones. Either pound the salmon, mustard, and lemon juice together in a mortar, or put it all into an electric blender with enough of the chilled custard mixture to keep the machine from clogging.

Stir in the minced parsley and pour the mixture into a wet 4-cup mold, previously chilled in cold water, or a lightly oiled mold. Cover with plastic wrap and chill until firm (at least four hours).

Ring molds set quickest; melon shape takes longest; the fish shape is O.K. but can be tricky to unmold with all those fins and bumps. A plain bowl can serve as a mold, too. I have an ancient enameled-iron ring mold that everything, hot or cold, slips out of effortlessly—but I don't think they're made any more. A Turk's head is undoubtedly one of the prettiest, and most cantankerous, molds you can choose.

The most important thing about any mold is that it must be of the proper capacity; it must be filled to within a quarter inch of the rim. If it is too full, hot water gets into the food when you're unmolding; if there is too much space between the roof and the rim, your mousse may get damaged in its long drop to the plate.

To Unmold

Always unmold things at least half an hour before serving time. The mousse may melt ever so slightly in the unmolding and will need to be put back in the icebox to firm up. If the mold is a simple shape, run a thin knife around the edge; if it's a fancy shape, just hope for the best. Dip the mold into very hot (not boiling) water for 1 or 2 minutes. Cover the mold with the serving plate and invert the mold onto it, giving it a couple of sharp downward jerks. If the food doesn't come out—back to the hot water. Some cooks lay a towel wrung out in very hot water on the bottom and sides of the mold. Like crepes and omelets, molded dishes require a certain deftness that only practice can bring, but it is well worth learning—you can always practice on Jello.

Serve the mousse with plain homemade mayonnaise (see recipe on page 37 or use your favorite blender recipe), the Cucumber Sauce on page 83, or a sauce rémoulade.

SPIKY CODFISH BALLS

I found this recipe handwritten on a flyleaf of my early edition of Fannie Farmer's *Boston Cooking-School Cook Book*. I believe the book's previous owner intended these codfish balls to be served at breakfast because her other handwritten recipes indicate a sophisticated table: *crème brûlée* and a punch made with brandy, rum, curaçao, orange, and lemons in prodigious quantities. These are truly wonderful for a big Sunday breakfast treat. I think my Boston lady might have served them with Tomatoes Gratin (see recipe, page 202) and hot biscuits.

Serves 4

2 cups peeled, diced potatoes
1 box (2 oz.) dried shredded codfish
½ tsp. baking powder
1 well-beaten egg

¼ tsp. pepper
2 Tbsp. minced scallions
oil for deep frying (at least a pint)

Simmer the potatoes in a small amount of salted water until tender (about 10 minutes). Drain, return to pot, and shake over low heat to evaporate any moisture. Put the potatoes through a food mill or a ricer. Put the shredded cod into a colander and rinse with cold water, but don't overdo it or the codfish balls will lack flavor. Squeeze out the water, then pull the codfish apart with your finger and mix it with the remaining ingredients except for the frying oil.

When the oil is very hot, but not smoking, scoop up a forkful of the codfish mixture and, using another fork, push it off into the hot oil. In about 2 minutes they should be golden brown and crisp outside and creamy hot inside. Drain on paper towels. "Always fork mixture," admonishes my Boston lady; this is what makes them spiky and light.

KEDGEREE

The English brought this back from India, where it originated as a catchall for little bits of leftovers, chiefly lentils and rice with spices. This kedgeree can be made from leftovers or you can buy a small piece of fresh cod or haddock—or really any kind of fish—and poach it in salted water. Every nutritional need is satisfied in this one-dish meal and it's easy to make in large quantities—communes take note. Vegetarians could substitute lentils for the fish.

Serves 4 generously

2 cups flaked, cooked fish
3 Tbsp. oil
1 cup thinly sliced onions
½ cup slivered green pepper
1–2 cloves garlic, minced
2 ripe tomatoes, peeled, seeded, and chopped (fresh or canned)

2 Tbsp. good curry powder (you must judge this spice)
2 cups cooked fluffy rice
salt and freshly milled pepper to taste
2 hard-cooked eggs, quartered

Slowly cook the onions, green pepper, and garlic in the oil until tender. Add the tomatoes and curry powder, and simmer 5 minutes. Add the rice and fish, season to taste, and heat through. Serve garnished with the egg quarters.

NOTE: Instead of fish, put in a half pound of cooked, chopped conch meat for a special (and very cheap) kedgeree.

STOCKFISCH (BACALAO)

Despite the fact that Nice is roiling with fresh fish, one of the favorite peasant dishes in this region is *Stockfisch*, "a savoury mess" made from dried salt cod the French import from Norway, according to Waverly Root. From his description in *The Food of France*, I have doped out this recipe, minus one ingredient I find loathesome: tripe. *Brandade de Morue* is another famous salt cod peasant dish of Provence, but it's quite a lot of work to make and although I think it's sublime, I've noted that few of my friends are bowled over by it. You will find the big, woody slabs of salt cod you need for *Stockfisch* in most Spanish food stores and fish markets. It's very dry and very salty and needs quite a lot of soaking.

Serves 6

1 2-lb. piece of dried salt cod
3–4 Tbsp. olive oil
1 large onion, thinly sliced
4 cloves garlic, minced
2 sweet peppers, red and green
2 cups tomatoes, peeled, seeded, and chopped
1 bay leaf

½ tsp. dried thyme
½ tsp. dried tarragon
¼ cup brandy or bourbon
  red or black pepper to taste
1 cup diced peeled potatoes
12 spicy Italian or Greek black olives

Soak the salt cod in a crock of cold water for 24 hours, changing the water three times. Then cut it in large chunks. Heat the olive oil in a large stew pot and add the onion, garlic, and peppers, cut in strips. Cover and simmer until soft. Add the tomatoes and their juices, the bay leaf, thyme, tarragon, brandy, and the cut-up fish. You may have to add a bit of water if the tomatoes weren't juicy. Add red or black pepper to taste but *add no salt*; the cod should take care of that. Some salt cod is saltier than other, and this is a problem no one can help you with. If the last soaking water is still very salty, it might be wise to parboil the fish a few minutes in fresh water to further rid it of salt.

Stir it all up well, cover, and simmer on low heat about 1½ hours. Add the potatoes and simmer until they are tender, about 10 or 15 minutes. Serve garnished with the black olives, which are also quite salty, and plenty of red jug wine. *Stockfisch* is too overwhelming for a white wine.

MUSSELS DUMAS

Once you could gather all the mussels you could eat on the rocky eastern tip of Long Island. But they're no longer so plentiful since I cunningly spread the word that they were edible and the local fish dealers realized that "summer people" (the weirdos) would pay cash for them. Mussels are hardly an endangered species, but if you find a good spawning spot where the blue-black mollusks are washed by sea tides, I advise you to keep it to yourself. Mussels remain one of the cheapest of all shellfish because of their mystifying lack of popularity. When you buy them, the shells should be firmly closed and undamaged. Don't buy small ones—there's nothing left when they're cooked—and be sure you aren't buying half a pound of rocks and seaweed clinging to the mussels.

The following recipe is adapted from one written by Alexander Dumas in his *Le Grand Dictionnaire de Cuisine*, published posthumously in 1873. My recipe was originally published in the East Hampton *Star*.

Serves 6–8

4 quarts mussels (in the shell)
12 small white onions
6 large red ripe tomatoes
2 cans undiluted beef bouillon
2 soup cans water
   big pinch saffron (probably
   one of the gifts presented to
   the Christ child by the three
   kings and you may have to
   do without it—there's no

feasible substitute in this
   dish)
¼ tsp. turmeric
¼ tsp. cumin powder
2 cloves garlic
1 Tbsp. olive oil
   salt and pepper to taste
1 bay leaf
2 cups dry white wine
   fried bread (optional)

Scrub the mussels well with a stiff brush (or one of those plastic things) under cold running water and de-beard them. Let them soak in a bucket of fresh cold water while you prepare the soup base. (Mussels and beef bouillon may sound incompatible, but have faith—M. Dumas was an accomplished amateur chef.)

Skin the onions by submerging them in boiling water for 30 seconds, then in cold for a minute so the skins will slip off. Treat the tomatoes the same way. Cut the tomatoes in half and simmer them together with the onions, saffron, turmeric, and cumin powder in the bouillon and water for about 1 hour. Add the peeled cloves of garlic to the soup and purée all in a blender. Return it to the pot, add the olive oil, and salt and pepper to taste. Simmer uncovered while you prepare the mussels and fry the bread.

Lift the mussels out of their soaking water and put them into a large pot with a lid. Bury the bay leaf in the middle of the shellfish and pour the wine over them. Cover and set over high heat until all the mussels are open, which should be in about 5 minutes. (Caution: if a few of the mussels won't open and feel unusually heavy, don't try to pry them open because they are most likely full of mud; just throw them away.) Stir top layer down to the bottom so that the mussels cook evenly.

Strain off most of the mussel liquor through a cheesecloth of four thicknesses laid in a sieve, and boil it down quickly to 2 cups. Keep the mussels covered in a warm place while this is going on. Add the reduced mussel broth to the soup base.

Put a piece of fried bread in the bottom of each large, flat soup plate, pile on the mussels, and ladle on the soup generously. This is to be eaten with spoons, forks, and fingers—and don't forget to provide some big bowls for the empty shells.

Fried Bread

Heat some olive oil flavored with a cut clove of garlic and a little salt in a heavy skillet. Cut some French bread in one-inch slices and brown it on both sides in the oil. Fried bread should be somewhat crisp and may be kept warm or reheated in the oven.

7

POULTRY

. . . poultry is for the cook what canvas is for the painter.
—BRILLAT-SAVARIN

Although in any country except our own chicken is treated as a delicacy, France's Henri IV's dream of "a chicken in every pot" has turned into a dreary reality. Almost no meat or fish is as cheap as chicken or, fortunately, as versatile. Even though our national craving for fried chicken is seemingly insatiable, it's worth pointing out that chicken can be braised, broiled, spitted, skewered, roasted, poached, stewed, and smoked. The blandness of chicken makes it an excellent host to a variety of seasonings and sauces. To add to this litany of virtues, chicken (except for old stewing hens, which have gotten just about as rare as their teeth) seldom takes long to cook, a fact many cooks fail to take advantage of. One of the drawbacks to cooking chicken properly is that for the brief time you're dealing with it, you have to pay attention—basting and turning and probing for just the right degree of doneness.

I can't begin to fathom what takes place in the kitchens that produce the birds for the aptly named "rubber-chicken circuit" of business and political luncheons. Perhaps they acquire that special springy muscle tone by being run to death.

There is nothing very difficult about choosing poultry. You need concern yourself with only one grade: U.S. Grade A, because if it's

Grade B or, God forbid, Grade C, the producer will not advertise such a thing and simply market it without a grade tag. The round "Inspected for wholesomeness by U.S.D.A." tag just means that the chicken is fit for human food, and is no guarantee of quality. Chickens, turkeys, and ducks should be broad-breasted and plump; the skin should be smooth, waxy, and pale with some golden-yellow fat showing beneath it. One of my old cookbooks advises the novice to "pinch the bird's windpipe; if it is supple the bird is young, if it seems hard and brittle, the fowl is best avoided." In countries where poultry is still bought live, the bird gets a chest massage and a couple of lusty pokes before the housewife makes up her mind. As for me, I'm content to let our highly trained corps of skilled Government chicken inspectors do this for me.

Besides quality and wholesomeness, which one is assured of if the poultry has been labeled with the inspection and grade marks, the only other thing to worry about is selecting the right bird for the right purpose. Even that is usually clearly marked as "fryer," "broiler," "roaster," and very occasionally "stewing fowl." It is a mistake to assume that substituting a younger chicken in such a recipe as "chicken fricassee" will improve it. The results will be quite the opposite because the mature fowl or stewing hen has a much more strongly developed flavor and the tougher fibers to withstand the long, slow simmering that produces a rich, aromatic stew.

Capon, the emasculated cockerel, is without doubt the finest textured, most juicy and flavorful poultry one can buy. Because it has a much higher ratio of meat to carcass, the capon with its much finer flesh and lack of waste may be a greater bargain than turkey even though capons cost from 25¢ to 45¢ more per pound.

Turkey, domesticated in France since it was the hit of the wedding breakfast of Charles IX and his queen, seems to have lost its cachet in its native land. Whether because it is cheap and plentiful, or simply because it is often ill-cooked, it's hard to account for this snobbery. Most turkeys are frozen these days (even some hastily thawed ones sold as "fresh-killed" at a much higher price). I think it is the thawing rather than the freezing that renders turkey flesh cottony and flat-tasting. A turkey should be thawed in the refrigerator, very slowly; it can take three to four days or even longer if you've bought a 20-pound Tom.

Another great improvement is the self-basting turkey, injected subcutaneously with corn oil to keep the bird moist and juicy. Though Mary McCarthy regards this as final proof of American degeneration, it doesn't really depart too much from the French tradition of stuffing the bird with butter, then barding it with unsmoked bacon to insure profuse lubrication from within and without. With any chicken to be roasted, it is my custom to lift the skin carefully from the flesh to stuff the interstices with softened butter. But this technique will be discussed in detail in specific recipes. A final word about the self-basting turkey: you still have to baste it occasionally if you want a juicy bird, although it does turn a fabulous brown left to its own devices.

Just about all the domestic duckling you will ever see will be frozen (unless you live near a duck farm, which is an olfactory experience to put you off duck forever). Because it has about a half inch of subcutaneous fat, duckling is said to withstand freezing better than other birds. Again, slow thawing is important if you're to avoid winding up with a dry, stringy critter and a quart of expensive duck fat. Duckling seems cheaper than it really is. It costs a bit more than chicken and a little less than capon, *but*: one 4½-pound (average weight) duckling will serve only two or at most three people once most of its fat is roasted out. French and other foreign recipes are colossal catastrophes when applied to the doughty Long Island duck; all (7,500,000 raised each year) are descended from nine White Pekin ducks who sailed around the Horn from China with a Sag Harbor master in 1873. Even if Americans *liked* rare duck, the hour-and-a-half roasting time recommended in French books for the Rouen or Nantes duckling would leave our Pekin ducks as tender as a Spanish wineskin. Possibly this is because our ducklings are really full-grown when they're killed at seven or eight weeks and, though young, are technically not "ducklings" at all.

Goose is not very economical because there is relatively little meat on its large, bony carcass. But it is lovely for a holiday dinner if there aren't too many guests. A 9½-pound goose, the usual weight of the young goslings sold in the United States, will serve only about eight people. Nearly all come to market frozen and are seldom larger than 10 pounds because they are killed at about five months old. Goose exudes even more fat than duckling (valuable cooking fat that should be saved), but the flesh can be strangely dry if the goose is not basted often during roasting.

The same U.S.D.A. standards apply to all poultry as well as chicken. Fresh-killed poultry is invariably superior in flavor and texture to frozen birds, but it is also more expensive. Since chicken is so cheap to begin with, the qualities one relinquishes in buying frozen poultry hardly seem worth the small saving.

Chicken sautés are simple family dishes, easily made and endlessly variable with sensible use of whatever is at hand. Basically, a sauté consists of a disjointed young fryer, faintly browned in oil or butter, then flavored with herbs or garlic, red or white wine, and such vegetables as mushrooms, tomatoes, shallots, onions, etc. Since the chicken can be bought for around a dollar, it seems permissible to me to indulge moderately in a few luxuries such as heavy cream, artichoke hearts, fresh mushrooms, and wines. The variations distract the family a bit from noticing the chicken quota in the menu.

COQ AU VIN

This is probably the best-known chicken sauté in the Western world. It is not a chicken stew, as one might be led to believe by those Coqs au Vin so relentlessly dished up in little French restaurants. Several nasty restaurant experiences of this dish led me to believe (given my culinary Francophilia) that Coq au Vin *couldn't* have come out of the French cuisine—perhaps was made up by the same American who gave us that ersatz "French dressing." There are many good ways to make it, I discovered in various books—even with white wine—but this is the method that best solves the problem of how to get the sauce right before the chicken falls to rags.

Serves 4

3 oz. smoked slab bacon
1 2½- to 3-lb. fryer, disjointed
  flour
  more oil or bacon fat if necessary
1 lb. small white pearl onions
¼ cup cognac (or bourbon)
3 cups dry red wine
  bouquet garni: 2 cloves garlic, mashed, 1 small bay leaf,

1 sprig of parsley, and ¼ tsp. dried thyme, tied in cheesecloth bag
  salt and freshly milled pepper
1 Tbsp. flour
1½ Tbsp. butter
½ lb. small whole button mushrooms or larger ones quartered

Cut the bacon into short fat matchsticks and lay them in a cold, heavy, cast-iron casserole large enough to hold all the above ingredients. Slowly try out the bacon and, when it has rendered most of its fat, remove it with a slotted spoon and reserve. Dust the chicken pieces with flour (reserve the back, neck, and giblets for another use) and brown them carefully in the fat remaining in the casserole, adding more fat if necessary. Drop the little onions into boiling water for 30 seconds, drain, and plunge them into cold water; the skins will slip off easily. Pierce an "x" in the root end to prevent the centers from oozing out. Brown the onions with the chicken, then remove them. Heat the cognac in a ladle, pour it over the chicken, and set it alight. Keep your face and hair well clear of this operation, as the flames can shoot up quite fiercely. Add the wine, the bouquet garni, and salt and pepper to taste. Remember, it is best to underseason at first and correct in the final moments any sauce or soup that will reduce in cooking.

Simmer the chicken 30 minutes, stirring occasionally. Add the onions and mushrooms and simmer 10 minutes longer (if the onions are larger than one inch in diameter, put them in early enough to be done when the chicken is tender, about 40 minutes in all). Strain the sauce into a smaller saucepan, keep the chicken and vegetables warm, and boil the sauce rapidly until you have about 2 cups. Thicken this with a *beurre manié* made by mixing the flour and butter to a paste, then dividing it into pea-sized balls. Whisk these into the boiling sauce piece by piece until the sauce becomes thick and shiny. Discard the bouquet garni, pour the sauce over the chicken (reheat if necessary), and serve either in the casserole or on a hot deep platter. Sprinkle with chopped parsley and bacon, and serve with boiled potatoes.

COUNTRY CAPTAIN

An oddly East Indian dish wedged smack dab in the middle of land-locked, up-country cookery, this is an old Southern specialty dating from colonial times. Georgians hold that the concoction is their very own because a sea captain gave his Savannah hosts the recipe in exchange for their hospitality—not the most tactful gesture. Another theory about the peculiar name is that the dish is really an East Indian one transported by English colonial officers to the West Indies, where "curry capon" gradually blurred to "country captain." Pretty farfetched, I guess, but so is

Kentucky's "burgoo" and an early settlers' cocktail called Whistle Belly Vengeance.

Whatever it started out as, the dish is by now truly Southern, despite some of its regionally uncharacteristic ingredients.

Serves 4

1 fat fryer (2½ to 3 lbs.)
2 Tbsp. bacon fat
2 Tbsp. butter
1 large onion, sliced thinly
1 green bell pepper, seeded and cut in julienne strips
2 cloves garlic, minced
1½ tsp. curry powder (or more)

1 1-lb. can tomatoes, chopped
1½ tsp. salt
1 tsp. white pepper
1½ tsp. dried leaf thyme
2 Tbsp. black currants, rinsed
¼ cup toasted, sliced almonds
1½ Tbsp. parsley, chopped
chutney

Preheat oven to 350°.

Disjoint, wash, and dry the chicken. Split the breast. Save the back, neck, wing tips, and giblets to make soup or stock. Brown the chicken pieces in the bacon fat, using a heavy iron skillet. Set it aside. If the fat has burned, rinse out the pan. If not, simply add the butter and, when it melts, sauté the onion, bell pepper, garlic, and curry powder. Add the tomatoes and their juice, salt, pepper, and thyme. Simmer, uncovered, for 10 minutes.

Put the chicken back into this sauce, baste it well, cover it, and braise it in the oven for about 30 minutes. During the last 10 minutes of cooking, add the currants. Don't overcook—a tender young fryer will simply disintegrate to tatters and bones if cooked too long. Sprinkle the Country Captain with toasted almonds and parsley and serve it with a big bowl of rice and chutney.

SAUTÉED SUPRÊMES

Suprêmes are skinned and boned chicken breasts; in other words, fillets. Butchers tend to double the price of the chicken for carrying out this simple operation. I love going into my Famed Surgeon routine: separating muscle from bone with my beautiful, bitter-sharp carbon steel knives. If you are repelled by the idea, then you'll just have to go on paying and paying (and frequently not getting what you want because the butcher knows less than you do). If slight cowardice is the only problem, get yourself some good knives and have a go at it. So you get a few raggedy results—the chicken is reparable because breast meat adheres nicely. I admit at once that everything I know about boning I learned from Julia Child's books, and about butchering from studying the carcasses in the *Larousse Gastronomique*.

Serves 4

2 whole fryer breasts (four halves)
4 thin slices *unsmoked* bacon (see note)
1 Tbsp. sherry (optional)
1 lb. marble-sized pearl onions (or no larger than 1½-inch diameter)
1 cup raw rice

3 Tbsp. clarified butter or margarine
½ lb. sliced fresh mushrooms (or use canned if fresh ones are too pricy)
salt and pepper
½ cup dry white wine or vermouth
chopped fresh parsley

Split the breasts and pull off the skin with your fingers. Beginning at the bottom point of the breastbone, lift the flesh away from the bones with a small, pointed, stiff knife. Work upward, blade against bone, until you reach the wing (or you may cut it off first). Detach it at the joint, reserve it, and continue pulling and cutting the flesh away until it is free of the bone. Doing it is the way to learn how; describing the structure of the breastbone minutely is just a waste of time.

Put the chicken bones, skin, an onion, a bit of celery, and whatever else you fancy—thyme or bay leaf—into a pot with cold water to cover and a little salt. Simmer to a rich broth you can use for cooking the rice that is so good with this dish. Or you can save it to make soup.

There is a thick white tendon on the underside of the *suprême* which should be removed. Sever the thinnest end of it; then, using the point of your knife, pull out the thick end. Grasp this with a towel and pull out the tendon, using your fingers to keep the flesh from tearing raggedly. If this final nicety stretches your patience, just forget it. Most people have been eating their chicken complete with bones, tendons, and, up to the present century, feet.

Rub the boned breasts with sherry (or brandy). Rinse the unsmoked bacon in cold water, dry it, and wrap it in a figure eight around the *suprêmes*. Fasten ends together with a wooden toothpick on the ugly side.

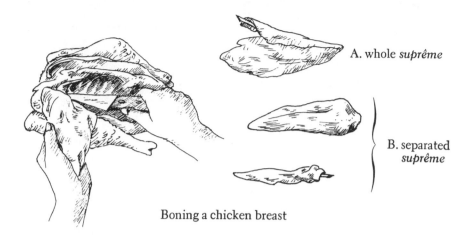

A. whole *suprême*

B. separated *suprême*

Boning a chicken breast

The *suprêmes* should be prepared in advance up to this point, wrapped in wax paper, and refrigerated until about half an hour before dinner. They will need 20 minutes to come to room temperature and about 8 minutes to cook. The onions should be peeled in advance also. All the work is in this preparation—the final dish is cooked in just 15 to 20 minutes, depending on the size of the onions.

Half an hour before serving time, put the rice to cook in the broth made with the bones. Slice the mushrooms and chop the parsley. Melt the butter or margarine in a heavy skillet. Roll the onions around in butter to coat evenly. Brown them lightly, shaking the pan from time to time. When they are half tender, put in the chicken breasts and sauté, turning often, until they are golden brown and springy to the touch, about 8 minutes in all. Season the dish with salt and pepper. Remove to a warm platter and cover with foil. Add the sliced mushrooms to the skillet and sauté 5 minutes; then stir in the wine or vermouth, scraping up any brown juices in the bottom of the pan. Pour the juices over the chicken and arrange the onions and mushrooms around it. Sprinkle with chopped parsley. Serve with the pilaf cooked in broth and some small garden peas or a salad, or both. If you're feeling especially generous you may wish to serve two *suprêmes* to a customer, but I think one of those richly flavored fillets is enough to satisfy most appetites.

VARIATION: If you have some, add a few tablespoons of heavy cream to the wine sauce at the very end and heat to bubbling.

NOTE: If you can't find unsmoked bacon (lean salt pork which has been brine-cured but not smoked), use regular thick-sliced bacon, but put it in 1 quart of cold water, bring it to the boil, and simmer 5 minutes to remove some of the smoke flavor, which will utterly dominate the chicken if this step is omitted.

SUPRÊMES WITH CHINESE MUSHROOMS

This recipe is little more than a variation on the preceding one for Sautéed Suprêmes, but the flavor is markedly different and quite unusual. The only substitution permissible in this dish is Japanese dried mushrooms (*shiitake*) for the Chinese (*doong gwoo*); otherwise the dish loses its character. (You will find the mushrooms and a lot of other good things at Oriental food stores; for instance, rice flour for thickening sauces to a velvety smoothness, an instant tempura mix to fry chicken and vegetables in, marvelous dehydrated soup-and-noodle all-in-one lunches that come in a small packet.) This is not to be construed as any kind of authentic Chinese dish; I just always keep some Oriental food stores on hand and this is what happened.

Serves 3–4

½ cup dry white vermouth plus ½ cup water, boiling hot
1 package (1½ oz.) dried Chinese mushrooms
salt and pepper
flour
6 *suprêmes* (see preceding recipe)

3 Tbsp. butter
½ cup chopped scallions
2 Tbsp. fresh tarragon, chopped (or 1 tsp. dried)
1 Tbsp. flour
¼ cup milk

Pour the boiling vermouth and water over the dried mushrooms and let them stand 30 minutes. Cut them in 4 or 5 pieces each and put them back into their soaking liquid. Rub salt, pepper, and a little flour into the *suprêmes*. Melt the butter in a heavy skillet, put in the *suprêmes* and scallions, and cook, turning often, until they color nicely and are springy to the touch, about 8 minutes—perhaps a bit longer if the *suprêmes* are large. *They must not overcook* or they will be tough and dry. Remove sauce, add the tarragon, the mushrooms, and their liquid to deglaze the pan. Stir over a brisk flame; then mix the flour and milk together smoothly and beat into the pan juices. When the sauce is thickened, pour it over the waiting chicken breasts. Try to work quickly so that it will not be necessary to reheat the *suprêmes* in the sauce—this tends to toughen them. You may like to serve the *suprêmes* on slices of bread fried in butter, with plain white rice, or just with a green vegetable such as zucchini, garden peas, spinach, or broccoli.

CHICKEN, BRAISED OR ROASTED?

Factory-farmed chickens, about the only kind available any more, get very large very quickly. Thus, while they are admirably tender and cook at average weight (3½ pounds) in three-quarters of an hour, their flavor is incredibly bland. They need help in the form of carrots, onions, garlic, wine, and herbs if anything interesting is to be made of them. Therefore, I think for this kind of young "roaster," braising is more satisfactory than open baking in the oven, a method more suitable to large turkeys or juicy capons. Braised chicken doesn't require the constant attention to basting that oven roasting does, and it also provides a nice little effortless sauce in the bargain. Roasting chickens are generally the cheapest of all poultry except for stewing hens. One reason roasted or braised whole chicken looms as such a chore is the conviction held in America that there must always be a stuffing. This adds to the preparation and cooking time and is rather boring, too. The basic unstuffed chicken can be varied immensely with different herbs—tarragon, thyme, basil—and such spices as cardamom, cumin, curry, and ginger.

Serves 4

1 fat roasting chicken (3½ lbs. approximately)
salt and pepper
1 Tbsp. butter plus 1 Tbsp. oil
1 onion, minced (½ cup)
1 carrot, finely chopped

small clove garlic, split
sprig of tarragon or parsley (or a pinch of dried tarragon or thyme)
¼ cup white vermouth or dry white wine or water

Wash and dry the chicken inside and out. Just inside the vent on each side are thick clumps of smooth, yellow fat. Remove the fat, chop it roughly, and mix with salt, pepper, and whatever herb you have chosen. Put this back in the cavity and truss up the bird with string, pushing the legs up against the breast, then tying them together at the vent; snap the wings to the back of the chicken, bring the string around to hold the

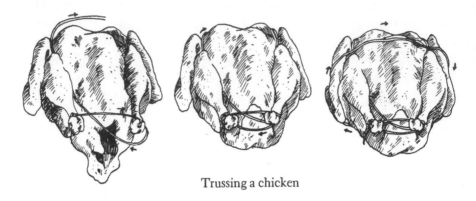

Trussing a chicken

wings close to the body, and skewer the neck skin to the back. If the bird is not trussed it flops all over the place when it is being turned and the finished beast has a rather unattractive sprawl.

In a heavy casserole (with a cover) in which the chicken just fits, heat the butter and oil. Put the chicken in on its side and when the skin is puffed and golden brown, turn it carefully until you have the same effect on all sides. (The only way I've discovered to turn the chicken without damaging the skin is with my hands protected by clean kitchen mitts. You must above all *not* use kitchen forks, which just provide perfect drainage holes for all the fat, herbs, and juices you're trying to keep trapped in the chicken.) Take out the browned chicken and add the minced onion, carrot, garlic, and tarragon or parsley to the casserole. Stir them around and cook briefly; then pour in the vermouth or wine and stir up any browned bits in the bottom of the casserole. Replace the chicken, laid on its side, on top of the vegetables. Cover and braise on a very low fire or in **a 325° oven** for 20 minutes. Turn the chicken on its other side and braise another 20 to 25 minutes or until the juices run yellow when the thigh is pierced.

Set the chicken on a warm platter, skim off excess fat from the pan juices, spoon some over the chicken, and put the remainder in a small bowl to be served at the table.

CORNBREAD STUFFING

There are truly an amazing number of delicious stuffings in my French cookbooks, and they are usually made with highly seasoned forcemeats.

But these are practically pâtés and add enormously to the cost of a roasted or braised chicken. The customary stale bread, celery, onion, and sage stuffing recalls depressing attempts at festive meals on the day before we left school for our Christmas or Thanksgiving holidays. For this stuffing you may bake your own cornbread, using a mix that does not contain sugar, or, easiest of all, buy a bag of Pepperidge Farm cornbread stuffing mix to use as a base. If you make your own cornbread, make it very thin and leave it out to harden in the air for 24 hours before using it. Also, you will have to supply the seasonings that are already in the prepared dry stuffing mix.

For a 3½-lb. bird

½ lb. loose sausage meat
1 large clove garlic, minced
½ cup chopped onion
   the liver from the chicken

½ cup parsley, chopped
½ bag of cornbread stuffing mix
   prepared according to package directions

Put the sausage in a cold skillet, then fry it slowly to brown the meat and render the excessive fat found in most commercially made sausage. Pour the fat off, leaving about 1½ tablespoons in the skillet. Stir in the garlic, onion, and liver from the chicken. When the onion is limp, turn off the flame, remove the liver, chop it, and return it to the skillet along with the prepared cornbread stuffing and the parsley. Mix it all well together and stuff the chicken.

VARIATIONS: Instead of sausage, buy a ½ pound of chicken livers and sauté them in butter until they are pink inside, remove from the pan, chop them roughly, and add them to the recipe at the end. Mushrooms, hard-cooked eggs, and water chestnuts, thinly sliced, are some other good things to add to this stuffing. (My mother used to put whole oysters in her cornbread stuffing—but those were the days when we used shrimp for bait.)

POACHED CHICKEN À LA CRÈME

Simmered in a rich broth, poached chicken is a moist and delicious foundation for many dishes. Although it's easy enough to do, not many people bother since few of us have to worry about what to do with an elderly hen whose laying days are over. Nevertheless, when you happen to find one, "there's a dance in the old dame yet": the deeper flavor of a mature hen provides a fragrant stock for soups or sauces; the flesh a foundation for white or brown fricassees, chicken fritters, croquettes, or an old-fashioned chicken pudding. A French farm wife might make a *galantine* of hers, boned and stuffed with pâté, then poached in white wine. Roasting chickens can be successfully poached, but don't substitute one in this particular recipe because their tender young flesh needs much more flavoring and much less cooking.

Serves 4–6

1 mature stewing fowl, 4½ to 5 lbs.
2 Tbsp. butter
2 or 3 large carrots, sliced
2 medium onions, sliced
2 cloves garlic, mashed
1 bay leaf
couple of sprigs of parsley

3 or 4 quarts chicken broth if possible; if not, water
pinch of dried thyme
pinch of dried tarragon (or 1 branch, fresh)
the washed giblets
salt and pepper

ᶠ **Preheat oven to 325°.**

Wash the fowl and remove the giblets from the cavity. Look it over for quill stumps, which may have to be removed with tweezers. Tie the wings to the body and tie the legs *down* (normally one pushes them up toward the breast) as far as possible because they must be submerged in broth, while the breast is exposed only to steam. Rub the breast well with a little softened butter. (Old recipes recommend a great deal of butter, but a plump old fowl yields a good quantity of fat of itself, which should be saved for other cooking purposes; if you have got a dried-out stringy old bird, it is really good for nothing except its stock.)

The type of pot is really important here: it should be rather narrow, oval, and deep enough to allow the chicken's legs to be covered with stock. Melt the butter and put in the carrots, onions, garlic, bay leaf, and parsley. Stir them around to coat with butter, then put the chicken on top of the vegetables. Pour the heated broth (it can be canned or made from bouillon cubes) or water around the chicken until it covers the legs. Put in the thyme, tarragon, pepper, and giblets. Bring it to the simmer and salt it lightly (how much will depend greatly on whether you have used broth or water). Seal the pot with aluminum foil, put on a heavy cover, and set it in the oven for about 2 hours. After a half hour, see that the pot is merely bubbling gently, not boiling rapidly. Otherwise the broth will waste away and the flesh will be dry and worthless. No one can determine the life that late she led, and it may take another hour to become tender. When it is, take the chicken from the pot, strain the broth into a bowl (discarding all the vegetables and giblets; they've given their all), and put it in the icebox. When the fat congeals, lift it off, put it into a jar, cover, and refrigerate. Pull the skin off the chicken and the meat from the bones, keeping it in fairly large pieces. This is most efficiently done with your fingers. Pack the meat into a bowl and cover it tightly to keep it moist. If you propose to keep all or some of the meat for another meal, slosh some of the broth on it.

Now, you may either make Chicken à la Crème for two and chicken salad for two, a couple of quarts of chicken soup with rice or noodles, or soup plus four generous servings of Chicken à la Crème, curried chicken, chicken pot pie, or whatever.

Sauce for Chicken à la Crème

4 Tbsp. chicken fat	squeeze of lemon juice (about
5 Tbsp. flour	a quarter of a lemon)
2 cups hot chicken broth	salt and pepper to taste
½ cup heavy cream	½ cup sliced cooked mushrooms
	2 Tbsp. sherry (optional)

Melt the chicken fat in a heavy saucepan. Stir in the flour and cook, stirring constantly, for 1 or 2 minutes. Off heat dump in the boiling chicken broth, whisking rapidly with a wire whip. Return the sauce to the heat and whisk and taste as you add the lemon juice, salt and pepper, and sherry, if used. When the texture and flavor please you (if you like a thinner sauce, add a little more broth) stir in the mushrooms and chicken. Serve on a bed of rice cooked in some of the chicken broth. Sprinkle with chopped parsley. Peas are good with this and so is a spinach salad.

VARIATION: You can make a sort of chicken *pot-au-feu* out of this by straining the broth, cooking some fresh vegetables in it such as carrots, potatoes, onions, peas, whole kernel corn, a couple of chopped tomatoes, etc. (even okra), and when they are all done, putting the meat, stripped from the bones as directed, back into the soup.

GALANTINE

Classically, a *galantine* was poached, boned, stuffed chicken, but nowadays it can mean a breast of veal, a duck, or a turkey prepared in this way. Pâtés and *galantines* are both fairly cheap to make but a lot of work. Gourmet shops get so much money for a simple *pâté de campagne*, which is really nothing more than gussied-up meatloaf, they rarely bother with anything so time-consuming as a *galantine*. You may not wish to go to all this bother very often (even though its mastery will award you instant celebrity), but a *galantine* makes a beautiful and uncommon centerpiece for a party buffet. It can be made two or three days in advance, the ingredients are cheap (we'll forget about the truffles French farm wives seem to have lying about by the basketful), and its construction is enjoyable if you have the leisure. (If you regard cooking as a chore rather than a pastime, this dish is not for you.) The *galantine* puts to excellent use the leftover broth from the Poached Chicken à la Crème, where it eventually winds up as a rich, shimmering, golden aspic covering the *galantine*.

Serves about 10

1 6- to 7-lb. roasting chicken (fresh, not frozen)	1 carrot, sliced
few drops cognac	1 medium onion, sliced
2 quarts rich chicken broth	2 sprigs of parsley
½ calf's foot, split vertically	1 cup dry white wine

Forcemeat Stuffing

½ lb. salt pork, cut in ¼-inch dice	1 tsp. salt
½ lb. lean fresh pork, ground	¼ tsp. pepper
½ lb. stewing veal, ground	½ cup minced onion
¼ cup cognac (or Madeira)	2 Tbsp. butter
½ tsp. ground allspice	¼ lb. cubed cooled ham or tongue
1 tsp. dried thyme	

Have the butcher bone the chicken for you, or if he won't or can't, tackle it yourself. Split the bird up the back and begin pushing against the carcass with a sharp, rather short, stiff-bladed knife. When the back is free, remove the thighbones and the first joint of the wing bones; the pinions are then clipped off. By now the bird probably resembles an old shirt, but it really will look all right in the end. *Don't pierce the skin.* This is tricky, but keep moving your knife carefully up toward the ridge of the breastbone and try not to pierce the thin skin stretched over it. If you do, don't panic—it can be patched with a transplant from some less conspicuous place. When you have freed one side of the breast, start again on the other underwing and cut out toward the breast ridge. We will hope the butcher has done all this for you because there's more trouble ahead. You must detach the flesh of the chicken from its skin without puncturing it. When you have the meat out, cut the dark meat in cubes but cut the breast in long fillets about half an inch wide. Sprinkle the meat, light and dark, with a little cognac and put it back in the shapeless skin. Cover and refrigerate while you make the forcemeat stuffing.

Cover the diced salt pork with two inches of boiling water and let it stand 15 minutes. Drain, rinse with cold water, and dry. Mix together thoroughly the ground pork, veal, diced salt pork, ham or tongue, cognac, and spices, including salt and pepper. Sauté the onions in the butter until transparent but not browned. Stir them into the meat mixture. Fry a little ball of the mixture so that you can taste it for seasoning. You may want to add more salt, pepper, or a bit of crushed garlic. Add the cubed dark meat of the chicken to this pâté mixture. Lay the chicken, breast side down, on a large white dish towel which you have rubbed with softened butter. Pat a layer of the forcemeat into the breast cavity to flavor and lubricate the breast fillets, which are arranged on top of this layer. Press the remaining forcemeat into an oblong and put it in the chicken. Press some of the meat out into the thighs and wings so that the thing begins to look like a chicken again. Lap the skin over the back incision and sew it up. Roll the chicken up tightly in the buttered towel and tie it like a sausage at each end. Tie it around the middle, too, but not too tightly.

Put the *galantine* into a similarly shaped deep pan (a fish-poacher is ideal) and pour the heated chicken broth over it. Add the chicken bones, calf's foot, carrot, onion, parsley, and wine. Cover and poach just under the simmer for 2 hours, maintaining the liquid level to cover the *galantine.* Turn the *galantine* over occasionally if it doesn't do so of its own accord. When it is done, leave it to cool in the broth for an hour. Take it out of the broth, which must now be boiled hard until it is reduced to about half its volume. Reroll the *galantine* in a fresh, clean cloth and tie it as before. Put a board on it and weight it with cans for 2 hours, then refrigerate. Strain the reduced broth through damp cheesecloth laid in a sieve. Chill in a wide, flared bowl until it sets to a jelly and the fat is hard. Carefully lift off this cake of fat and discard. Remove any tiny bits that cling to the jelly. If your aspic looks murky, bring it to the boil and stir into it 2 slightly beaten egg whites. Simmer and stir for 5 minutes, by which time the particles causing the murk should have adhered to the egg white. Simmer undisturbed for 10 minutes, lift off the caked egg white, and strain the aspic again. When it cools to a lukewarm, syrupy state it is ready to spoon over the chilled (disrobed) *galantine*. You can decorate this with little flowers made of bits of egg white (hard-cooked, of course), black olives (for the truffles you haven't got), perhaps a few slivers of tinned pimiento—but don't overdo it or it will look like one of those monster delicatessen turkeys. In fact, if you have no hand for decorating, leave it alone and just arrange a pretty necklace of fresh watercress leaves around the *galantine*. Slice thinly and serve with no other accompaniment as a first course or as part of a buffet.

SOUTH CAROLINA FRIED CHICKEN

Fried chicken in the South comes in about as many different styles as its politicians—crusty or soggy, plain or baroque. I prefer my chicken and my politicians the same way—crusty and plain. Fried chicken is so simple to make this is hardly a recipe at all; I include it only because more people have asked me how I make it than any other thing. (Nobody ever asks about a real culinary triumph such as a perfect, jewel-bright natural aspic.) One fryer will serve one, two, three, or four people.

1 fresh-killed frying chicken, disjointed
1 cup flour (approximately)
  salt and pepper
1 quart peanut oil

Fryers are left in rather large clumsy pieces as they are sold in supermarkets. When you get one home, you will have to finish the job of disjointing it properly. Cut the wings from the breast halves and tuck them into a triangle. Detach the thighs from the drumsticks. Take a heavy cleaver and cut the breast halves in two, making 4 pieces of white meat to haggle over. (But the chief reason for doing this is so that it cooks more quickly and hasn't time to dry out.) Chop off the Pope's Nose and give it to the cat, then whack the back section in half. My cats get the neck and innards, but you can fry the neck too, although I see no point in it.

Heat the oil to shimmering hot, but not smoking, in a deep heavy kettle, the type that are called Dutch ovens or chicken fryers, depending on where you're from. I use a heavy iron wok because you need less oil to get more frying space—the curved bottom achieves this. However, the cheap, thin woks are not satisfactory for frying chicken because they overheat if you do more than quick stir-frying in them. You can also use a spider (black iron skillet), but then the chicken must be carefully turned with tongs because a spider is too shallow for deep frying.

Wash the chicken and drop it, a few pieces at a time, into a bag which contains about a cup of flour seasoned with salt and pepper (I sometimes add some dried thyme or paprika to this, but it's heresy). Do the legs and thighs first, as they take longer to cook. Shake the pieces around in the bag to coat them well and, as you remove each piece, press the flour into the chicken with your hands. Put it into the hot oil and prepare another piece. This is important because if you flour all the chicken and add it all at once, the temperature of the oil will decrease and the crust will be greasy and soggy. After the legs and thighs have been frying for about 10 minutes, add the breasts and bony parts, again one by one, regulating the heat to keep the oil temperature steady. Continue frying over medium heat 15 minutes, when the chicken should be a deep gold, crusty without and juicy within. Drain it on lots of paper towels and keep it warm in a low oven. Refrigeration ruins fried chicken, but if it's absolutely unavoidable, at least let the chicken cool completely at room temperature, then spread it out in a pan, and cover it with foil before refrigerating.

There! Everything you probably didn't even want to know about frying chicken—especially since Colonel Claghorn seems to be doing the job for everybody in the country.

CHINESE FRIED CHICKEN

An otherwise intelligent and perceptive writer I know remains curiously indifferent to the mysteries and subtleties of Chinese food. Or perhaps not curiously at all, since this is the only thing he ever orders except for the damn roast duck. This fried chicken is pleasant for a change, and you needn't fear serving it to people who really don't like Chinese food. The pieces, cut small enough to be maneuvered by chopsticks, make the chicken suitable finger food at parties and picnics, too. Madame Buwei Yang Chao is a doctor who wrote perhaps the most charming and competent Chinese cookbook available in English, *How to Cook and Eat in Chinese*. This recipe is hers except that I have omitted the sugar she recommends.

Serves 4–6

2 spring chickens, total 4 lbs.
2 Tbsp. sherry
3 Tbsp. soy sauce
1 tsp. salt

1 cup flour
1 small onion or 2 scallions
    enough lard or vegetable oil
    for deep frying

"Chop chicken into pieces about the size of eggs. Cut onion into small sections. Put it in a bowl with the chicken and add the sherry, soy sauce, salt. . . . Then let it stand for 1 hour in the icebox. Then dip each piece into the cup of flour so that it is all wrapped with flour. Heat enough oil for deep oil frying and put the chicken in. Fry for two minutes."

NOTE: In Chinese restaurants the pieces are smaller—maybe she meant pullet eggs. Also, if Mme. Chao's directions are a bit terse for you, review my interminable recipe for South Carolina Fried Chicken (page 108).

CHICKEN TEMPURA

Tempura is normally made with vegetables or sea food, but the method works splendidly if you use only the white meat of chicken and cut it in slices. Naturally, it must be boned and skinned. Any tempura must be eaten as soon as it is cooked, as the delicate cornstarch-batter crust soon wilts.

Serves 3–4

2 whole chicken breasts, skinned and boned (from fryers)
¼ tsp. freshly grated ginger (or the same amount powder)
2 Tbsp. Hawaiian Teriyaki Sauce (Kikkoman) or plain soy sauce
1 scallion, minced very fine
1 quart peanut oil, approximately

Batter
2 egg whites
½ cup cold water
¾ cup cornstarch

Sauce

2 Tbsp. dry sherry
3 Tbsp. teriyaki or soy sauce
   finely minced scallion, optional
1 tsp. hot vinegar (see note), optional

Flatten the breast fillets with the side of a cleaver or a rolling pin or whatever you have around. Cut them into pieces about three inches long and three quarters of an inch wide. Put them into a small bowl and sprinkle with the ginger, teriyaki or soy sauce, and the minced scallion. Cover and let stand for half an hour if possible.

Beat the egg whites slightly, then beat in the water. Stir in the cornstarch. If you can't handle chopsticks for putting things into hot fat, use tongs, and for getting the pieces out, a slotted spoon—but chopsticks are a lot less trouble once you get the hang of it (pester an Oriental friend or waiter for instruction).

Heat up the peanut oil until it will brown golden a cube of bread in 30 seconds. Dip each piece of chicken in the batter, then drop it quickly into the hot oil. The pieces will be golden, crisp, and cooked through in about 3 minutes; never crowd them or they will stick together. You will have to work quickly and serve quickly as any tempura tastes best just when it finishes cooking. Drain the pieces on paper toweling and keep warm in a low oven until all are fried. Obviously, you can't make this for many people unless you have two woks, are very skilled with chopsticks, have an Oriental wire skimmer for deftly scooping up the pieces as they are done, and have "quick hands." A little dish of sauce is served to each person, made from the sherry, teriyaki or soy sauce, minced scallion, and hot vinegar. I think the Japanese would use plain rice vinegar; my hot vinegar is strictly from Dixie.

NOTE: Wash and dry a jar of about 1-cup capacity. Wash and dry 3 *chipotle* chiles (these are small red dried peppers you can buy in Spanish or Mexican food stores). If these are not available, substitute the dried red chiles called *pequin*, which Spice Islands sells all over the country. Pound them in a mortar or put them in a blender and pour about a cup of boiling white or cider vinegar over them. Add 1 teaspoon mustard seeds and store, tightly covered in the icebox, a week before using. Hot, very hot flavoring (a few drops does a lot for a clam on the half shell, too).

ROAST TURKEY

The complaint most often made about turkey is that it's "too dry." Generally, the reason Mum's Thanksgiving bird bombs out is that she's had it in the oven since daybreak. In the days when you had to go out in the woods and wing your own, maybe turkeys *were* tough and really needed all that long, slow cooking. But modern domestic turkeys are bred so fast they haven't time to get tough. Besides that, they have such enormous heavy breasts they can hardly move. The best way to roast them is as fast as you can. It is now possible to buy just the breast, which is very good broiled, and so is a small turkey split in half. A 10- or 11-pound hen turkey is a smart buy even for a small family because there are so many delicious leftover dishes to be made from it. Ham and Turkey Gratin, turkey salad, creamed turkey, Turkey Florentine (on a bed of spinach), Turkey Divan (on a bed of broccoli, masked with hollandaise sauce), are a few possibilities.

Serves 8–10

1 10-lb. hen turkey	1 rib celery
1 cup brandy or bourbon	4 sprigs parsley
butter, softened	thyme, tarragon, or whatever
salt and pepper	herb or spice you like
1 onion stuck with 2 cloves	

Wash the turkey and dry it. Rub the brandy or bourbon into it, inside and out, especially between the flesh and skin of the breast. Put a good amount of softened butter here too, mixed with salt and pepper. Wrap the bird rather loosely in foil and put it in the icebox overnight. An hour before you wish to cook it, remove it from the icebox so that it can come to room temperature.

Preheat oven to 450°. (That's right, 450°.) Sprinkle the turkey inside with salt and pepper and put in the onion, celery, and parsley, with whatever herb or spice you have chosen. (If you've always used sage, try to think of something else this time.) Rub the turkey all over with butter, salt and pepper it, and truss it up (see recipe for Braised Chicken, page 101, for trussing instructions). Lay it on its side on a rack placed in a shallow baking pan and put it in the oven. After 20 minutes turn it on its other side—use heavy mitts or dish towels so that you won't break the skin. After another 20 minutes turn the turkey breast side down and baste it well. This bird is supposed to be a dark, rich brown, about the color of a pecan. If it begins to get too dark, reduce the heat about 15°. To avoid burning fat, put a little water in the pan. Stuffed or unstuffed, the turkey should roast about 18 to 20 minutes per pound. This will depend on how high you are able to keep the oven temperature. Roast the bird breast side up, basting every 5 minutes, for the last 20 minutes of cooking time. It is done when the thick underside of the thigh runs yellow juice when pierced. A turkey needs a good long rest in a warm place to recollect its juices—at least 20 minutes. Room-temperature turkey is much easier to carve thinly, thus serving more people, and the meat will be much juicier. Turkey is always nearly cold by the time you get it carved anyway and has to be hotted up with gravy. A 10-pound turkey roasted in this way will require about 3 hours and 20 minutes.

NOTE: Any stuffing used should be fully cooked—no raw meat, etc. It is safest to cook the stuffing separately in a tightly sealed casserole.

ROAST DUCKLING

If you happen to live on Long Island or in New York City, it's possible to buy fresh-killed ducklings, but in most localities only frozen ones are available. Perhaps because of their heavy layer of subcutaneous fat, ducks seem to weather the freezing process better than other poultry. You don't have to worry about getting an old, tough bird because duck farmers have figured out a way to fatten the ducks to between 4 and 5 pounds by the time they are eight weeks old. You *do* have to worry about how to get rid of all that fat while retaining a juicy bird with a crisp skin. Through many an experiment, I would arrive at one or the other of these objectives, but never simultaneously. The following unorthodox method is mine alone, agrees with no other cookbook, and demands a good deal of blind faith, but it does produce the perfect roast duckling. One bird serves only two or three people, thereby somewhat nullifying its low price per pound. But a duck is still cheaper than most roasts and supplies at least the illusion of luxury.

Serves 2–3

1 duckling, 4–5 lbs.
   salt and pepper
1 pint chicken stock
   the giblets and neck
1 cup dry white wine

1 onion, chopped
2 cloves garlic, finely chopped
   parsley
1 carrot, finely chopped
1 tsp. thyme (dried)

Thaw the duck slowly (2 days in the refrigerator) if possible. However you do it, don't remove the bird from its plastic bag until it is thawed. Remove the neck and giblets from the cavity, wash the duck, and dry it. Pull out as much fat as you can from the vent and the crop. Put the giblets and neck into the stock and wine along with the onion, garlic, parsley, carrot, thyme, some pepper, and a very little salt. Cover and simmer for an hour so that you will have a well-flavored braising liquid.

Preheat the oven to 450°. Salt the duck inside and out (pepper too); skewer the cavity closed and the neck skin to the back. Prick it all over with a sharp fork, especially the legs and thighs. Put it on a rack in a shallow open pan, breast side up. Pour about a pint of hot water into the pan and set it in the middle of this very hot oven for 45 minutes. The duck won't burn but the fat will when all the water evaporates; you must check often and add a little water if this happens. Not only because duck fat is valuable for cooking, but also because the smoke and smell of burning fat might win you a visit from the Fire Department.

It is important to have a heavy covered casserole exactly the same size as your duck, otherwise the braising liquid will dry up, too much dry heat will circulate around the duck, and its flesh will be dry and stringy.

Reduce the oven temperature to 350°. Transfer the duck to the casserole, strain the giblet broth over it, cover, and braise half an hour in the oven. Uncover and roast 20 minutes longer so that the skin will retain its crispness. Total open roasting and braising time is 1 hour and 35 minutes. Admittedly, this combination of cooking methods is more trouble, but it produces the ideal result. Skim the fat from the pan juices. Reheat and season, adding a splash of Madeira or port if you have it, and serve as a sauce for the duck.

8

BEEF

Because we prefer it above all other flesh, fish, or fowl, beef is priced out of almost every penny-pinching household. Yet we will have it, even if it means bologna sandwiches after the wad is shot on steak. But the steaks, the most expensive cuts, account for only a small part of a beef carcass, and the rest of the animal affords some fine eating if one but knows what to do with less familiar cuts. The fanciful names butchers bestow on some of the cheaper parts—"California roast" for a blade of chuck, "pinwheel" for soupmeat from the shin, "Cross-cut Rib Roast," which is chuck from the shoulder and has nothing to do with a rib roast—are, to put the kindest light on it, confusing. A semiprofessional course in meat cutting would probably benefit the novice cook more than all the moussaka and chicken mole classes in the suburbs.

Meat packers have their beef graded (voluntarily—it is not a Federal law) by the United States Department of Agriculture. These grades, Prime, Choice, Good, Standard, and Commercial, are your most reliable and important guides to quality. If the packer has declined to have his meat graded, I think it is fair for the consumer to decline to buy it. The following information is from the U.S.D.A.:

Prime-grade beef is the ultimate in tenderness, juiciness, and flavor. It has abundant marbling—veins of fat within the lean, which enhances both flavor and juiciness. You will seldom see Prime beef except in the most expensive restaurants and luxury butcher shops. Fairly confident of the consumer's ignorance, many butchers fling about the term "prime" when it is merely their opinion and not the U.S.D.A. grade. You may be certain that any meat packer with Prime beef to sell will not be shy about having it so labeled with the government's purple grade shield.

Choice beef is the highest grade we are likely to find in a supermarket, and it is the most commonly sold everywhere. Although it has slightly less marbling than Prime, it is almost as tender, juicy, and flavorful. Choice beef has slightly less waste than prime. Rump, eye-round, and sirloin tip of this high quality may, like standing rib roast, be dry-roasted in the oven, but only to the medium-rare stage or they will be too tough. If medium or well-done beef is required, these cuts should be braised. I don't have one, but I imagine that roasting on an electric spit would require the tenderest (rib or rib-eye—not eye-round) cuts of Prime or Choice beef.

Good is a grade often marketed under "house" brands by chain markets and is considerably cheaper than Choice. It is too lean to be very juicy or particularly tender, but it has very little waste and is a thrifty buy for braising and stewing. The standing rib roast, except for filet mignon, which is the tenderest cut in the animal, could probably be successfully roasted to rare even in this grade.

Standard is quite lean, but, because it comes from young animals, it is relatively tender. Because it is lean and young, it is also relatively tasteless and somewhat on the dry side. It needs help with seasoning and saucing.

Commercial beef comes from the portly, middle-aged steer, and although it is heavy, well-marbled beef with richly developed flavor it needs long, slow, moist cooking to tenderize it. A good buy, if you can find it.

There are three lower grades, Utility, Cutter, and Canner, not sold at retail. The U.S.D.A. says, "They go mostly into ground beef or into processed meat items such as hot dogs"—but maybe you'd rather not think about the quality of our star-spangled favorites.

No matter *what* grade of beef you buy, some cuts of meat will not be tender enough for open roasting and quick cooking. Only the expensive steaks and rib roast cut from the top of the animal's rib

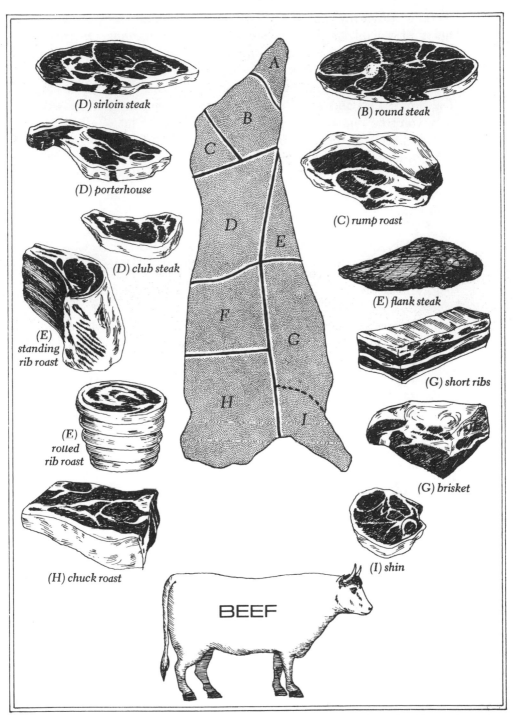

(D) sirloin steak

(B) round steak

(D) porterhouse

(C) rump roast

(D) club steak

(E) standing rib roast

(E) flank steak

(E) rolled rib roast

(G) short ribs

(H) chuck roast

(G) brisket

(I) shin

BEEF

Beef Chart: A. soupbone; B. round; C. rump; D. loin; E. flank and suet; F. rib; G. plate; H. chuck; I. shin section are really suitable. Marinades can sometimes soften the fibers of a flank or shoulder steak enough for grilling, but on the whole, cuts from the fore and hindquarters—all the chuck and round steaks and roasts—must be slowly and gently braised or simmered to achieve tenderness. Study the accompanying chart and get to know the various cuts and what part of the animal they come from—then you won't be unpleasantly surprised when those "luau tidbits" turn out to be chewy little chunks of round steak. In New York City meat cutters are compelled by law to label meat generically as "chuck," "round," "sirloin," etc., underneath such poetic flights as "butterfly" steaks. If the meat in your market is not plainly and informatively labeled, ring the bell and ask the butcher to identify it.

EMPANADAS (BEEF TURNOVERS)

Empanadas are the sandwiches of South America: they may be eaten hot or cold, they may be sweet or savoury and served either as hors d'oeuvre, a main course, a snack, or a dessert. Any food that versatile is certainly worth learning about. These *empanadas* are filled with *picadillo* (a sort of Mexican hash made with ground beef) and are best eaten hot. Leftover meats, fish, refried beans, *ratatouille*, cheese and onions, or any moist but not too sloppy filling makes delicious *empanadas*. (I was introduced to them as a sweet snack called "fried pies" by my Aunt Helen, who filled them with apricots and packed them off to me—starving on boarding-school food—in battered round tin boxes.) They're really *supposed* to be fried, but I find baking them simpler and the turnovers less rich and heavy. It doesn't matter whether you bake or fry, but it is essential that the filling, whatever it is, be chilled before it is put in its pastry pocket.

Makes approximately 1 dozen 6-inch turnovers

Picadillo

2 Tbsp. olive or salad oil	½ tsp. ground cumin
1 lb. ground chuck	¼ tsp. ground allspice
1–2 cloves garlic, minced	3 Tbsp. tomato paste
⅔ cup finely chopped onion	½ cup water
salt and pepper	1 Tbsp. capers, chopped
1½–2 Tbsp. chili powder (or more if you have a hot tooth)	

Beef Empanada

Heat the oil and sauté the ground beef, breaking up the chunks with a fork. Add the garlic, onions, and salt and pepper to taste. Cook, stirring, until the onions are transparent. Stir in the chili powder, cumin, and allspice and cook briefly over low heat to rid the spices of their "raw" taste. Finally, stir in the tomato paste, water, and capers and simmer about 5 minutes, covered. If the *picadillo* is too dry, add enough water so that the mixture is quite juicy but not runny. Spread out on a platter and chill in the refrigerator while you make the pastry.

Pastry
   2 cups flour, sifted
   1 tsp. baking powder
   ½ tsp. salt
   ⅔ cup vegetable shortening (Crisco, Spry, etc.)
   6 or 7 Tbsp. ice-cold club soda (or plain water)

Sift the flour, baking powder, and salt together; then, with a pastry blender or two table knives, cut in the shortening until it is in bits the size of small peas. Sprinkle on the cold club soda (I don't know why this makes better, crisper pastry for me than plain water, but it does) spoonful by spoonful, pressing the dough together with a fork. Use just enough club soda to hold the flour and shortening together. Form the dough into 2 balls, handling as little as possible. Roll 1 ball out on a floured pastry cloth or board to about one-sixteenth-inch thickness. Using the lid of a coffee can or something sharp-edged and about six inches in diameter, cut out circles of pastry and lay them aside on waxed paper. Repeat with the second ball of dough.

Spoon about 1 heaped tablespoon of the chilled *picadillo* onto the center of each pastry circle, moisten halfway round the edge with ice water, fold the pastry over to form a half moon; then crimp the edges tightly together with a fork, unless you have deft pastry crimpers around the house to help with this operation, which is, admittedly, rather time-consuming. Complete the remaining turnovers. Either fry the Empanadas a few at a time in about one inch of very hot oil for about 5 minutes (they must be well-drained on lots of paper toweling), or bake as follows: **Preheat oven to 425°.** Arrange the turnovers about an inch apart on a greased cookie sheet, prick each with a sharp fork, brush with melted shortening or salad oil, and bake about 15 minutes until they color a pale golden brown.

NOTE: These freeze well, unbaked. Thaw before baking as above. Hors d'oeuvre Empanadas should be only about three inches in diameter. The large ones are fine for a buffet bash—they're easy to eat, can be made in advance, are quickly cooked; and I don't know many other ways to feed six hungry people on one pound of ground chuck.

MEATLOAF

I have at least six recipes for this in my notebooks, and I like them all but I never follow any of them. A select circle of meatloaf fanciers has pronounced this version Best of Breed. It is a kissing cousin of the French *pâté de campagne* and, indeed, is very good cold.

Serves 4–6

2 Tbsp. bacon fat
1 medium onion, minced
1 large or 2 small cloves garlic, minced
2 slices day-old bread, trimmed
¼ cup parsley, finely chopped
1 lb. ground chuck beef
½ lb. ground veal (stew meat)
½ lb. ground pork shoulder

¼ cup cognac or good bourbon
1 egg, beaten
1½ tsp. salt
½ tsp. freshly ground pepper
¼ tsp. ground allspice
½ tsp. dried thyme (leaf)
1 bay leaf
2 or 3 strips bacon

Preheat oven to 350°.

Assemble all ingredients on your worktable and put the meats into a large mixing bowl. The ground meat is easier to work at room temperature. Heat the bacon fat and sauté the onion and garlic until soft and transparent. Crumble the bread to fine soft crumbs (easy in a blender) and sprinkle over the meats. Scrape the onions into the meats, add the parsley, cognac, egg, salt, pepper, allspice, and thyme. Mix thoroughly with your hands; a spoon is tedious and an electric mixer overdoes the job, producing a rubbery texture.

Pack the meatloaf mixture into a 1-quart loaf pan (cheap aluminum-foil loafpans are available in most supermarkets), lay the bay leaf on top, and cover the meatloaf with bacon strips. Set in the preheated oven on the middle rack and bake for 1½ hours. Leave the loaf in the pan and put it in a warm place for 20 or 30 minutes before slicing; otherwise it will crumble terribly.

For a very firm texture to serve as a cold pâté, put another loaf pan on top of the meatloaf and weight it for 4 or 5 hours with about 1 pound of canned goods evenly distributed. Seal tightly with aluminum foil and chill before serving, but the meatloaf should not be too cold or the flavor will be bland.

MEATBALLS STROGANOFF

Beef Stroganoff litters the menus of nearly every pretentious restaurant in the country and is almost never any good. I think the reason for this is that the dish should be made with filet (tenderloin), but because the steak is cut in strips and covered in sauce, restaurateurs believe the client won't notice if he substitutes a cheaper cut of beef. If you can't afford filet, it's better to go all the way with economy and use ground round steak, which is just as certain to be tender.

Serves 3

1 clove garlic (large)
1 small onion
1 Tbsp. butter
1 lb. ground round steak
1 egg, beaten
¼ cup soft bread crumbs, fine
1 tsp. salt

freshly milled black pepper
2 Tbsp. salad oil
¼ lb. fresh mushrooms, sliced (optional)
½ cup beef bouillon
1½ cups sour cream
chopped parsley

Mince the garlic and onion and sauté in the tablespoon of butter until soft. Mix with the ground steak, egg, bread crumbs, salt, and pepper and shape into balls about the size of a walnut. This recipe makes about 18 meatballs. Don't make larger balls because they get misshapen in the browning process and tend to fall apart.

Heat the salad oil to smoking hot in a large heavy skillet. Put in 6 or 8 meatballs—they must have room to move around—and brown on all sides, shaking the pan constantly 4 or 5 minutes. Remove the meatballs, cover, and keep warm while you repeat the operation until all the meatballs are cooked, nicely browned on the outside and medium-pink inside. If at any time you notice the fat getting burned or meat particles sticking to the pan, pour out the oil, wash the pan, and start over with fresh oil.

If using the mushrooms, sauté them in a small skillet while doing the last batch of meatballs. When these are all done, pour off the remaining fat and deglaze the pan with ½ cup of beef bouillon, lower the heat, and stir in the sour cream, spoonful by spoonful, and *do not let the sauce boil or it will curdle*. When the sauce is hot through, pour it over the combined mushrooms and meatballs, sprinkle with chopped parsley, and serve at once with rice or buttered noodles.

PARIS BROIL

Flank steak is the long flat, lean muscle normally used for what we call London Broil. Any one of a number of minute miscalculations can render it inedibly tough. Tartar horsemen strapped meat under their saddles to tenderize it; the Japanese keep their beer-fattened cattle boozily immobile and massage them constantly to, I am told, a melting pliability. Here is a somewhat less dramatic, but effective, method of softening the long, fibrous tissues of this cut, which has no bone and no fat. A marinade of plain red or white dry wine will do the trick, but the herbs and garlic add interesting flavor. However, nothing will help unless these two rules are strictly observed: the steak must be broiled quickly with intense heat only to the rare stage. It must then be sliced thinly on a bias almost parallel to the carving board. This sounds hard, but it isn't if you have a proper carving knife, fairly long and very sharp.

Serves 4

1 flank steak (average is about 2 lbs.)

1 cup dry (white) vermouth or other dry red or white wine

lots of coarsely cracked black pepper (twist the peppercorns into a tea towel and crush them with a hammer)

1 large clove garlic, mashed (or, if preferred, 1 Tbsp. minced onion)

½ tsp. dried thyme leaves
salt and softened butter

Wipe the meat dry with paper towels; *never* wash meat unless it has fallen into something disgusting. Pick out a nonmetallic casserole just big enough to cram the steak into. In it mix together the vermouth or wine (red gives a rather gamy taste, nice for a change), pepper, garlic, and thyme. *Do not add salt.* Salt draws the juices from the meat, leaving it dry and tasteless. Roll the steak in the marinade to coat all sides; then fold it in three (like an omelet) and press it down into the casserole. Cover and leave at room temperature (unless the weather is hot) for 3 or 4 hours. Turn the meat every hour; then refrigerate 1 hour before broiling. Otherwise you may not be able to keep the steak rare.

Preheat the broiler to red-hot and then some with the rack as close to the flame as possible. Dry off the steak, rub it with salt and butter, and lay it on the hot grids. Broil, taking care it doesn't flame up, a maximum of 5 minutes on either side. Remove to a warm carving board (a carving board is not a luxury since you can use the smooth reverse side for a chopping board) and carve thin diagonal slices at the table, serving some of the natural juices on each helping.

NOTE: A platter of cold, thinly sliced steak is a fine buffet dish. It is immensely easier to slice when it is cold. Serve it with coarse salt and a sharp Dijon-style mustard.

BRAISED STUFFED SHOULDER STEAK

Shoulder steak is sometimes sold as London Broil, and if it is from well-aged Choice-grade beef is often tender enough to broil. But this recipe is an unusual and pleasant change from plain broiled steak, and is a safer method when one is uncertain of the quality of the beef.

Serves 6

1 shoulder steak, 2 inches thick

2 Tbsp. bacon fat

Stuffing
2 Tbsp. butter
⅓ lb. mushrooms, chopped
2 medium onions, chopped (1 cup)

1 slice day-old bread, trimmed
salt and pepper
¼ cup parsley, chopped

(*Continued*)

Braising Liquid

½ cup dry red wine (preferably a Burgundy)
2 sprigs parsley
2 Tbsp. meat jelly (see note)

Have the butcher butterfly the steak (split but not completely in half) or do it yourself if he looks puzzled by the request. Dry the meat thoroughly, salt and pepper it, and make the stuffing.

Melt the butter in a heavy braising pan with a lid and sauté the onions 5 minutes. Add the mushrooms and sauté another 5 minutes. Off heat, stir in the bread crumbled to fine soft crumbs, the parsley, and a little salt and pepper. Lay this stuffing on one half of the meat and fold the other half over it like an omelet. Sew or fasten with skewers around the outside edges. Wipe out the braising pan, put in the bacon fat, and brown the steak well on both sides. Pour off any excess fat; then put the wine, parsley, and meat jelly into the casserole with the meat. If you haven't got any meat jelly, substitute a half cup of canned beef bouillon and thicken the sauce with a little arrowroot or cornstarch after the steak is done and has been removed.

Cover and braise the stuffed steak slowly over a low heat (or in the **oven at 325°**) until it is quite tender, which may take 2 hours or more. Turn the meat occasionally, baste with the juices, and add more butter if the meat seems dry. Dish onto a hot platter, remove the skewers, pour the pan juices over the steak, and carve it in fairly thick slices across the grain of the meat. Braised carrots (they could be done in the casserole with the steak) and cauliflower with brown butter are good with this.

NOTE: Meat jelly is most useful to give flavor and body to stews, soups, and sauces. It makes use of food that otherwise would be discarded.

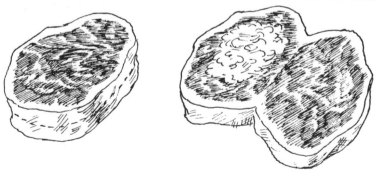

Butterflying beef

Save all the carcasses of roast chicken, duck, etc. and all the roast meat bones and lean trimming from beef, pork, and veal. Store in the freezer until about 3 or 4 pounds accumulate. Buy a veal knucklebone and have it cracked. Put everything into a big stock pot with four quarts of water, a little salt and pepper, a few sprigs of parsley, 2 carrots, 2 onions stuck with cloves, and a large stalk of celery and bring to a boil. Skim, half cover, and simmer 4 or 5 hours. Strain and store in ½-pint Mason jars. The fat that floats to the top will seal the jelly and keep it from spoiling, but the jars should be kept in the icebox. Lift off the fat and discard as you use each jar.

BEEF AND LEEKS À LA FLAMANDE

Because things made with leeks and beer seem vaguely Flemish to me, I tacked the *à la Flamande* onto my own invention according to the established French custom. It is a robust country stew with rich flavors bringing to mind a black iron stove and strings of things dripping from kitchen rafters. However, the dish could be made on an electric hotplate. Unfortunately, leeks are hard to come by in some parts of the United States, but if you shop the ethnic food markets, you should find them most of the time. If they're too dear, substitute plain old domestic onions.

Serves 4–6

2 lbs. lean chuck, in 2½-inch cubes
1 lb. beef flanken (short ribs), same size
flour, salt, and pepper
2 Tbsp. oil plus 1 Tbsp. butter
2 cups beer
1 quart beef bouillon
2 cloves mashed garlic
1 medium onion, chopped

1 tsp. dried thyme, crushed
½ bay leaf
6–8 carrots, scraped and cut in 4-inch lengths
8–10 small leeks, about 1-inch diameter at root (or 3 cups sliced sautéed onions)
2 Tbsp. cornstarch
¼ cup Madeira

Preheat oven to 325°.

As I said, this *can* be done on a top burner, but I think oven stews more savoury and the danger of scorching is almost nil.

Dry the beef and dust it with flour, salt, and pepper. Heat the oil and butter to almost smoking and brown the beef over medium heat, turning

often. Remove the meat and brown the chopped onion (and the sliced onions if you have no leeks). Add beer, bouillon, garlic, and herbs, stir up the browned bits, and return the meat to the casserole. Cover and simmer while scraping and cutting the carrots.

Cut off the roots and most of the tops of the leeks, leaving them about six inches long. Peel off tough outer layer and split leeks lengthwise from the top halfway down the length. Wash them carefully under cold running water to remove the sand that lurks in the green tops. Set them aside until about *1 hour before the stew is done*. Add the carrots to the stew, correct the seasoning, cover it, and bake in **a 325° oven** about 2½ hours. (Don't forget to add those leeks.) Pour off the liquid into another saucepan. Skim off the fat (if you have time, put the saucepan in the freezer until the fat congeals, which makes child's play of an otherwise rather tedious job), bring the liquid to a boil, and stir in 2 tablespoons cornstarch mixed with ¼ cup of Madeira. Cook, stirring constantly, until the sauce is smooth and thickened. Pour it over the meat and vegetables, reheat, and serve in the casserole, sprinkled with fresh parsley. Boiled noodles and beer go with this dinner.

BRESLAW OF BEEF

Eliza Acton published her marvelous book, *Modern Cookery*, in London in 1845, some sixteen years before Mrs. Beeton's better-known *Book of Household Management*, which has stayed in print for over 100 years. Miss Acton's immensely superior book (to which Mrs. Beeton is clearly quite indebted) was out of print for a century. Happily, a London publisher has brought out a facsimile of Eliza Acton's 1865 revision of her masterwork. Except for changing the English weights to American volume measurements, the recipe is exactly as she wrote it. What is a "breslaw"? I don't know, but I agree with Miss Acton's note under the title: "(Good)."

"Trim the brown edges from half a pound of undressed [without sauce] roast beef, shred it small, and mix it with four ounces of fine bread-crumbs, a teaspoonful of minced parsley, and two-thirds as much of thyme, two ounces of butter broken small, half a cupful of gravy or cream, a high seasoning of pepper and cayenne and mace or nutmeg, a small teaspoonful of salt, and three large eggs well whisked. Melt a little butter in a deep dish, pour in the beef, and bake it half an hour; turn it out, and send it to table with brown gravy in a tureen. When cream or gravy is not at hand, an additional egg or two and rather more butter must be used. We think that grated lemon-rind improves the breslaw. A portion of fat from the joint [roast] can be added where it is liked. The mixture is sometimes baked in buttered cups.

"Beef, ½ lb.; bread-crumbs, 1 cup; butter, ¼ cup; gravy or cream, ½ cupful; parsley, 1 teaspoonful; thyme, ⅔ of teaspoonful; eggs, 3 or 4, if small; salt, 1 teaspoonful; pepper and nutmeg, ½ teaspoonful each: bake ½ hour."

The amount of thyme is a bit too much for my taste and I add some chopped scallions to this spicy baked hash. Mace is better than nutmeg for this dish.

STEAK AND KIDNEY PIE (OR RAGOUT)

Meat pasties existed in English cookery long before anyone ever thought of putting sweetened fruit between crusts. They were a mainstay of medieval cooking but are now almost extinct, except for Shepherd's Pie and this old favorite. However much I thank the English for the *idea* of these dishes, I don't care for the way they actually make them today. This is not authentic, but I was born a Lancaster and I have a right to my own version.

Serves 4

1½ lbs. bottom round steak (½ inch thick)
1 or 2 veal kidneys
flour
salad oil
1 large onion, thinly sliced
1 small carrot, minced
1 cup dry red wine

1–1½ cups beef bouillon
pinch of dried thyme
salt and pepper
½ lb. fresh mushrooms, sliced thickly
½ recipe of pastry (see Empanadas recipe, page 118) or use a packaged pastry mix

Cut steak into generous bite-sized pieces. Wash and dry the kidneys and cut them into half-inch pieces, discarding all fat. Dredge lightly in flour, shaking off excess. Film a heavy iron skillet with oil and when it is almost smoking hot, brown the steak pieces and remove. Add a bit more oil, then brown the kidneys and onions together, but do it gently— burned onions are awful. Return the steak to the skillet, add the carrot, wine, bouillon, thyme, and salt and pepper to taste. Undersalt to begin with, as the liquid reduces by about one third. Cover and simmer slowly (on an asbestos pad) for about 2 hours. Stir occasionally to make certain the ragout doesn't stick or scorch. About 10 minutes before it is done, quickly sauté the mushrooms in butter; then stir them into the ragout at the last minute.

Cool the steak-and-kidney mixture to room temperature and pour it into a two-inch-deep casserole. Cover it with chilled pastry rolled an eighth inch thick; seal it well and prick the top. Bake in a preheated 400° oven 15 to 20 minutes or until the crust is golden, the pie bubbling. Or if pastry-making bothers you, serve the ragout with mounds of parslied mashed potatoes, or some little hot biscuits made from those prefab icebox cylinders.

LIVER AND ONION PIE

Calves' liver costs, at the moment, a few cents less per pound than live lobster. But beef liver can be wonderful and many people prefer its more distinct flavor. The only way to be sure you're getting liver from at least

"Choice" grade beef is to buy from a reliable butcher. Liver, for obvious reasons, cannot bear a grade mark, and I shudder to think what might be lurking in those plastic supermarket packages. Also, liver, as any organ meat, should be absolutely fresh and never frozen.

Serves 4

1 lb. beef liver, sliced ¼ inch thick
4 thick slices bacon
flour
2 large onions, sliced thinly
¼ lb. mushrooms, sliced (optional)

1 clove garlic, minced
pepper
bay leaf (½ if large)
½ tsp. dried oregano
½ cup beef bouillon, heated
pastry (make half quantity Empanadas, page 118)

Preheat oven to 375°.

Wipe the liver with paper towels and cut it into pieces roughly three inches square. Slowly fry the bacon until it is three-quarters done, then remove, cut each slice in half (or do this first) and lay them on the bottom of a nine-inch Pyrex pie plate. Pepper the liver and dredge it very lightly in flour. Pour off all but 3 tablespoons of bacon fat and, in the same skillet, sauté the liver very quickly over brisk flame. This is only to brown the liver, not to cook it. Lay half the liver on the bacon and put the rest aside. Fry the onions in the same skillet, adding more bacon fat if necessary. When they are half cooked (they should be soft and lightly browned when done), add the mushrooms and garlic. Stir about 5 minutes over low flame; then spread half the vegetables over the liver and cover with the remaining pieces of liver and another layer of onions. Lay the bay leaf on top, sprinkle oregano over all, and pour on the beef broth. Cover with pastry, slash top, and bake for about 30 minutes or until the crust is nicely browned.

VARIATION: Duchess potatoes are an excellent covering for the pie and are easy to make with instant mashed potatoes. Use a "7-serving" package prepared as follows:

Use ¼ cup less water than specified in the package directions. Beat the potatoes well, then beat in two egg yolks and a pinch of nutmeg. Either put the mixture into a pastry bag and pipe it over the top, or delicately mound it on with a spoon, completely covering the liver and onions, and bake as directed.

CREAMED CHIPPED BEEF

Creamed chipped beef got a bad name—and I mean a really bad name —around World War II, when it was prepared for mess halls by conscripted ironmongers and mechanics. There was also a tinned meat called "Spam" that was much abused; its manufacturer complained recently about this lasting damnation and said the G.I.'s were really eating *fake* Spam. I've tasted the real thing and I can't see why anyone would counterfeit it. But creamed chipped beef, properly made, spooned over a smoking hot, freshly baked Idaho potato, just *couldn't* have been what our soldiers were making somewhat coarse remarks about.

Serves 2

2 large perfect Idaho baking potatoes	1 cup hot milk
2 Tbsp. butter	1 2½-oz. jar dried beef
½ cup scallions, minced	pepper to taste
1½ Tbsp. flour	chopped fresh parsley

Preheat the oven to 350°.

Scrub the potatoes under cold running water, dry them, and rub them with salad oil. Place the potatoes on the middle oven rack for about 1 hour. Do not wrap them in aluminum foil; this villainous practice is what accounts for all those sodden, sticky "baked" potatoes served by bad restaurants. The foil steams, rather than bakes, the potatoes.

About 10 minutes before the potatoes are fork tender, make the chipped beef. Melt the butter in a small heavy saucepan and gently simmer the scallions a couple of minutes. Stir in the flour and cook over low heat a minute longer. Dump in the hot milk all at once and beat madly with a wire whisk until the sauce is smooth and thickened. Shred the dried beef with a sharp knife and stir it into the cream sauce. Add pepper to taste.

Slit an "x" in the top of each potato, then gently press the sides until some of the mealy white inside pops through the "x." Divide the creamed chipped beef over the two potatoes and sprinkle with parsley. This must be eaten at once and if you wanted salad you should have thought of that before.

BAKED MARROWBONES

Marrowbones, as noted elsewhere, cost next to nothing and are richly flavored, very nutritious, and highly prized by those who know that looks aren't everything. (In French cooking, it is a great delicacy.) Marrow tastes like essence of beef, but it looks, undeniably, like fat. Despite this, its devotees are many and passionate. This recipe adapted from an old cookbook makes marrowbones an attractive dish by covering them with Yorkshire Pudding. This amount is intended as a light supper dish or late-night snack.

Serves 3–4

Preheat oven to 450°.

1½ lbs. small marrowbones, sawed into 1½-inch lengths. Arrange the marrowbones in a square cake tin, standing on their ends if possible. Put them in the hot oven for about 5 minutes, or until you see about an eighth of an inch of fat swimming in the bottom of the pan. Have ready the following batter to pour over the hot marrowbones.

Yorkshire Pudding

> 2 eggs
> 1 cup milk
> 1 cup sifted flour
> ¾ tsp. salt

Beat the eggs until very light, then beat in the milk with a rotary or an electric mixer. Gradually beat in the flour and salt, adding a third of the flour at a time, until the batter is very smooth. The texture will be thinner than you might expect if you have never made Yorkshire Pudding before. Pour it around and over the marrowbones; then return the hot pan to the oven and **bake at 450°** for 10 minutes. **Reduce the heat to 350°** and continue cooking another 15 or 20 minutes, until puffed and brown. Serve at once. Each person will need a small, narrow knife to push the marrow out of the bones and spread on the pudding.

SPANISH BEEF STEW

Olives in the stew may sound bizarre, rather like the famous French roast chicken that is stuffed with a whole pound of garlic. Like the garlic in the chicken, the olives in the stew change magically in the long cooking to impart an elusive flavor. I confess that I am at a loss to describe this taste because I can think of nothing comparable. You'll just have to take it on faith that the combination results in a delicious and unusual dish.

Serves 4

2 lbs. boneless chuck, trimmed and cut into chunks about 2 inches square
flour
3 Tbsp. olive oil
salt and freshly milled pepper
2 large onions, chopped (about 2 cups)
1 cup beef bouillon
½ cup dry red wine

2 large cloves garlic, crushed
2 ripe tomatoes, seeded and chopped, or 2 Tbsp. tomato paste
2 Tbsp. fresh thyme (or ½ tsp. dried)
1 cup small green olives, stoned
1 1-lb. can garbanzos (chickpeas) (optional)

Dust the meat with flour and heat the oil very hot in a heavy pot such as an iron Dutch oven. Brown the beef on all sides, sprinkling it with salt and pepper as you do so. Lower the heat, add the onions and cook, covered, until they are limp. Add the bouillon, wine, garlic, tomatoes or tomato paste, thyme, and olives, bring everything to the simmer, and taste for seasoning. The stew should be but lightly salted because the olives will take care of that. It is always best to adjust seasoning in a soup or a stew when it is finished and has reduced to its proper consistentcy. Cover and either simmer the stew on a top burner or put it in the middle of a 350° oven for 1 hour. After this time add the drained garbanzos, if you are using them, and continue cooking gently for about 1 hour longer. Because there isn't a great deal of added liquid, the meat will need occasional stirring and basting with the sauce. If there is excess oil, skim the stew before serving.

NOTE: If you don't care for garbanzos, leave them out and serve the stew over mounds of steamed rice.

SMOKED TONGUE

For the bunch of people who spend more time foraging than drinking at parties, nothing beats a big platter of cold, thinly sliced tongue with horse-radish sauce, some tingly mustards, and several good, heavy breads. Most old cookbooks advise soaking a smoked tongue in cold water overnight, but I never soak it at all and it works out.

1 smoked beef tongue, usually 3½–4 lbs.	1 carrot, sliced (1 cup)
cold water to cover	couple of celery tops (or 1 tsp. celery seed)
2 cloves garlic, peeled and split	about 1 Tbsp. freshly ground
1 onion stuck with four cloves	coarse black pepper
1 bay leaf	

Wash the tongue and put it in a kettle with enough water to cover. Add remaining ingredients and bring to a boil. Reduce heat and simmer slowly about 3 hours. It should be very tender when pierced with a sharp fork. Cool the tongue in the broth. (As you have deduced by now, all this takes a long time but no skill or attention.) Remove the tongue and slit the skin (use a small sharp knife) from the tip to the root end. Peel carefully and pull the small bones out of the root end; trim off any ragged or fatty stuff at this end. Wrap it in aluminum foil, lay it on its side in the icebox, and weight it with a book. (Weighting makes slicing easier.) Leave it overnight. Now, if you haven't got a very heavy sharp knife, get one—or throw yourself on the mercy of your butcher and his slicing machine. Lay the tongue on its side on a cutting board and, beginning at the tip, make wafer-thin, slightly diagonal slices. Arrange the slices in an overlapping circular pattern, decorate with watercress or parsley, and cover with plastic wrap if it isn't to be eaten right away.

NOTE: Save the stock the tongue cooked in. It makes superior bean soup (see recipe, page 11). Skim the fat from the stock, strain it, and either freeze it or store it in the icebox and use within two days.

9

VEAL

Possibly because we have always treated veal so unimaginatively, this delicately flavored meat has never been very popular with Americans. According to a Department of Agriculture survey, we eat only about 4 pounds a year per capita in contrast to the Frenchman, who eats about 15 pounds of veal a year. It is a certainty that those 15 pounds aren't all escalopes cut from the hind leg, the choicest and most expensive part of the young animal. Heavily breaded, fried in oil, then doused with tomato sauce, this cut is served up in American restaurants as "breaded veal cutlets." Odds on it will be the *only* veal dish on the menu, too. This strange preference of course drives the price of veal escalopes (or scallopini) to ridiculous heights, but it does have the pleasant effect of leaving the butcher with a lot of less popular parts of the carcass he must get rid of at enticingly low prices.

Breast of veal, boned and stuffed with an aromatic herb, pork sausage, and onion mixture is a dish that doesn't shriek its parsimony. Cut in long strips across the breast, pieces of veal called *tendrons* by the French are braised slowly with wine and vegetables to make a stout country stew. Shoulder is an excellent cut for Blanquette de Veau and the less familiar brown veal ragout known as Veal Marengo.

Chops and roasts from the ribs and loin are too costly to be considered in this book. But whatever veal you choose, the flesh should be a very pale pink, almost white, if it is a true milk-fed calf slaughtered before its fourteenth week. Some of the dark reddish meat sold as veal might more properly be labled "baby beef." Plume de Veau is the finest, and hideously expensive, quality, and only a small quantity is produced. Italian butchers generally have the best genuine milk-fed veal, and they know best how to slice perfect escalopes and separate the muscles into neat, compact seamless roasts.

Veal, like beef, is graded Prime, Choice, Good, etc., but if you see no grade mark, the color of the flesh still tells you a good deal about it. It can be lightened and tenderized by marinating it in milk. Veal is never aged and should be cooked within a day or so of purchase. Because it is all lean (thus good for dieters, cholesterol worriers, and people in delicate condition), veal is too dry to broil. Except for chops and escalopes, which are quickly turned in butter, veal needs long, gentle, moist cooking, and it also benefits from the subtle influences of wine, herbs, and vegetables.

BLANQUETTE DE VEAU

A mainstay of French home cooking, or *cuisine bourgeoise*, this veal stew can be simpler than the recipe I will give. But, because I have a special fondness for this dish, and for all its seeming lavishness it isn't expensive, I can't bring myself to adapt this for economy. What follows is the best way I know to achieve the subtle, rich creamy blend of veal, button onions, and mushrooms bound in a golden sauce of cream and egg yolks.

Serves 4–6

2 lbs. stewing veal, boneless shoulder, cut in 1½-inch cubes
1 carrot, scraped
1 peeled whole onion, stuck with 2 cloves
2½ cups chicken broth
½ cup dry white wine
1 bouquet garni: 1 split clove garlic, 2 sprigs parsley, ½ tsp. dried thyme, and 4 peppercorns, all tied in a cheese-cloth bag

12 pearl onions (about 1–1½ inches diameter)
½ lb. small whole fresh mushrooms or, if absolutely necessary, the equivalent, canned (3½ oz.)
1 Tbsp. butter
2 Tbsp. flour
½ cup heavy cream
2 egg yolks
2 or 3 Tbsp. chopped fresh parsley

Cover the veal with cold water and bring it to a boil just long enough for the scum to rise. Remove this; then rinse the veal briefly in cold fresh water. Wash the pot, too; then return the veal to it and put in the carrot, onion stuck with cloves, the chicken broth, and wine. Tuck the herb bouquet in the middle of it all and bring the veal to a simmer. Cover and cook gently about 1 hour and 15 minutes or until just tender, not falling apart.

Meanwhile peel the pearl onions by dropping them into boiling water for about 1 minute, then plunging them into cold water. Cut off the root end so the skins will slip off easily. Cut a tiny cross in the root end of each, which helps to prevent the hearts from bulging out of the onions as they cook. Drop them into the simmering veal about 25 minutes before you think it will be tender. If you miscalculate or the veal is old or cantankerous, remove the onions when they are done and set aside until the meat is tender.

Clean the mushrooms and save the stems for another dish (soup, sauce, or stew). Add these to the stew about 5 minutes before the veal is done. Or simmer them separately in a bit of lemon juice and water, then add them at the last.

When the veal is nicely tender, drain it in a colander set over a saucepan and discard the clove-stuck onion, the carrot, and the herb bouquet. Put the veal, onions, and mushrooms in a warm covered dish and make the sauce. Boil down the stock rapidly until it reduces to about 2 cups. In another heavy saucepan, melt the butter and stir in the flour to make white *roux*. Pour in the boiling stock and whisk smooth. Beat the cream and egg yolks together; then beat into the veal velouté. Return the meat, onions, and mushrooms to the sauce to reheat gently. *Do not boil*: the egg yolks will curdle. (There is one other bad thing that can befall a blanquette de veau—and a noncooking friend of mine found it right away: she had commissioned the dish from some catering service, then put it over the pilot light on her stove and left it for about three hours— until it turned sour and separated.) Correctly thickened with cream and yolks of egg, the dish does not hold well, which may explain its absence on restaurant menus. It can be made in advance—even a day in advance— up to the final thickening with cream and egg.

Serve the blanquette sprinkled with parsley in a very hot dish along with some butter noodles or rice. Have the plates hot, too, as this tends to cool rather quickly, which is a compelling reason for serving the dish at a sit-down dinner even though it seems like a good idea for a buffet.

VEAL SAUTÉ MARENGO

Although this stew is made with the same cut of veal as the preceding Blanquette de Veau, it has an utterly different character. Olive oil, garlic, tomatoes, and orange peel lend it the earthy, peasant quality of Pagnol country, a dish Fanny might have made for Marius. The French really prefer the crunchiness of the *tendron* (breast of veal) for this as well as for the Blanquette de Veau, but most Americans will prefer a stew made with the neater, leaner meat of the shoulder.

This dish is pure essence of Provence, and only fresh herbs will truly capture it. I realize that fresh tarragon and thyme are not to hand in the average kitchen. But if I can grow them on a window sill in the fug of Manhattan's Upper West Side, so can anybody except an Eskimo. If dried herbs are all you can get, at least be sure to use only the best and freshest you can find.

Serves 6

½ cup flour for dredging the meat, seasoned with salt and pepper

3 lbs. boneless veal shoulder, cut in 2-inch cubes

¼ cup olive oil

1½ cups onions, finely chopped salt and pepper

1 cup dry white wine

1 cup light chicken broth

1½ cups *drained* canned tomatoes, chopped (or puréed in a blender)

2 cloves garlic, crushed

1 Tbsp. fresh tarragon, minced (or ½ tsp. dried)

1 Tbsp. fresh thyme, minced (or ½ tsp. dried)

2-inch strip of orange peel

½ lb. fresh mushrooms, whole if small enough, otherwise quartered

2 Tbsp. minced fresh parsley

Preheat oven to 325°.

Dry the veal cubes with paper towels and shake them in a bag with flour seasoned with salt and pepper. Choose a heavy casserole with a lid, and heat the olive oil to nearly smoking. Quickly brown the veal in two batches. It just won't brown if you crowd it all in at once. Lower the heat, put in the onions, and sauté until limp. Put all the meat back into the casserole, season lightly with salt and pepper, and add all the remaining ingredients *except* the mushrooms and minced parsley. Bring the stew to a simmer on a top burner; then cover it and set it on the lower rack of the preheated oven for about 1¼ hours. Test after 1 hour, and, if the veal seems almost done, add the mushrooms, which have been washed, dried, and stemmed. They should simmer in the stew 10 or 15 minutes. The sauce should be a rich, reddish brown about the consistency of heavy cream. If it seems too thin, thicken it with a little cornstarch mixed with cold water, but add only a little at a time—the sauce should not be too thick. Strew the top with the minced parsley and serve it up in its own baking casserole. Rice is essential with Veal Sauté Marengo (noodles can be served, but they seem to me out of harmony with things Provençal) and a green salad rounds out the meal. A great dish for a dinner party, it can be made a day or so in advance and will wait patiently for guests who can't be pried away from their drinks.

STUFFED BREAST OF VEAL

About the only place you're likely to encounter this lowly but absolutely delicious illusion of a roast is in a small French *pension*, where the bread *à discrétion* is carefully observed, the wine measured exactly. It is often eaten in French households, although no one would serve it to guests, and of course it is much too humble for restaurants to bother with. Not out of frugality, but simply because one can't get stuffed breast of veal anywhere, I have ventured to serve this to guests. No one has ever seemed insulted.

1 breast of veal, weighing about 3½ lbs.
   salt and pepper
   lemon juice

Stuffing

  1 package Pepperidge Farm
    herb stuffing mix
  ½ lb. pork sausage (loose)
  1 cup minced onion

2–3 Tbsp. minced celery
3 Tbsp. minced fresh parsley
1 egg, lightly beaten

Vegetables

  6 carrots, peeled and quartered
  6 medium-small onions, peeled but whole

Braising Liquid

  1 cup beef bouillon
  1 Tbsp. tomato paste
  ¼ cup Madeira (optional)

Preheat oven to 325°.

Have the breast of veal boned and the pocket slit for stuffing. Rub it inside and out with salt, pepper, and lemon juice. You may substitute your own favorite stuffing, of course, but this sausage and herb mixture does give strength and flavor to an otherwise insipid piece of meat. Veal is rather like a good fashion model; bland itself but so very, very adaptable.

Mix up the stuffing according to the directions on the package. Lightly grease a skillet; then slowly fry the sausage meat, breaking it up with a fork into small particles. If it exudes a great deal of fat, pour off all but 2 tablespoons. Add the onion and celery and cook gently until limp. Turn this mixture into the prepared bread stuffing, add the parsley, and bind it together with the beaten egg. Fill the pocket with this stuffing (but don't pack it tightly—remember, stuffing expands) and sew up the opening securely. Put the stuffed breast into a heavy casserole of about the same dimensions as the meat and add the carrots and the bouillon mixed with the tomato paste. Cover and bake for 1 hour. Add the onions and bake for 1 hour longer. When it is done, thicken the sauce slightly with a little cornstarch mixed with the Madeira, or water if there's no Madeira or port around. Serve with the braised vegetables and spoon a little sauce over each slice of veal and stuffing. Stuffed breast of veal is delicious cold, and it is much easier to slice, too.

OSSI BUCHI

Ossi Buchi is a dish that often gets unnecessarily complicated with herbs belonging more properly to Neapolitan cookery than to Milanese. This is a northern Italian specialty, however, and should not be spiced up with a sensational array of discordant flavors. Veal shanks won't often be found in supermarket bins, but sometimes the butcher has them if you ask. Italian butchers will nearly always have them, and probably better ones from a younger calf.

Serves 4

2 veal shanks, sawed into 2-inch lengths
2 Tbsp. butter plus 1 Tbsp. olive oil
1 medium onion, chopped small
1 medium carrot, minced
1 cup fresh tomatoes, skinned and chopped, or the same amount of canned Italian plum tomatoes

¾ cup dry white wine
1 cup chicken stock
1 clove garlic, crushed
1 small bay leaf
  salt and pepper to taste
1 Tbsp. grated lemon peel
2 Tbsp. fresh parsley, minced

Brown the veal shanks in the butter and oil heated together in a heavy casserole or Dutch oven. When they are golden, remove them; then cook the onion and carrot about 5 minutes in the same pan. Add the tomatoes and stir briefly. Stand the veal shanks on their ends in the casserole so that the marrow won't fall out. Add the wine, stock, garlic, and bay leaf; when it bubbles, season the sauce with salt and pepper, cover, and simmer for about 1½ hours, or longer if the shanks are not from the youngest animal. When the meat is tender, serve it in its casserole sprinkled with the grated lemon peel and minced parsley. The classic accompaniment is a good *risotto* cooked in chicken broth and enriched with butter and Parmesan cheese.

ROAST VEAL À LA BONNE FEMME

One of my favorite cookbooks was written by Joseph Donon, *chef de cuisine* to Henry Clay Frick, whose splendid mansion is now the Frick Museum housing his magnificent painting collection. The old millionaire's tastes and that of the family of New York aristocrats later served by M. Donon ran to simple excellence made with the best of everything. I learned to adapt some of his recipes to a humbler purse. The master's recipe for roast veal starts out, "Have the butcher bone the loin, lard it, and roll it for roasting." I advise you to buy a well-shaped piece of rump of veal and if you want it larded, buy a larding needle and learn to do this yourself—it isn't difficult. Volume II of *Mastering the Art of French Cooking* by Simone Beck and Julia Child explains this process perfectly. Although the book is expensive, it can be found in any good library.

Serves 8

1 4-lb. piece of veal rump, boneless
¼ cup softened butter
salt and pepper
3 carrots, thinly sliced
2 medium onions, thinly sliced
½ tsp. dried thyme
½ bay leaf
1 cup thin beef bouillon
2 cloves garlic, crushed

2 sprigs parsley
garnish: 16 glazed pearl onions, 16 boiled new potatoes, 16 small whole carrots (or larger ones cut in three-inch-long quarters), steamed in butter. This is what makes it *à la bonne femme* (in the style of the good wife).

Preheat oven to 450°.

Tie the rump into a neat, firm shape, as cylindrical as possible, with white butcher's cord. Rub the softened butter into it and sprinkle the roast with salt and pepper. Put it into a pan just large enough to hold it and roast it uncovered at 450° until it is golden (about 20 minutes). **Reduce the temperature to 350°**, put the sliced vegetables, garlic, and herbs under the veal, and pour the bouillon around it. Cover and braise for a further 1½ to 2 hours, basting occasionally with the pan juices. When it is fork tender, remove it to a warm place to rest (reabsorb its juices) while you make a little sauce. Skim off as much fat as you can and pour the juices, with or without the cooking vegetables as you choose, into a small saucepan. Bring it to a simmer. Off heat stir in a small amount of cornstarch mixed to a paste with cold water, adding it little by little to the juices until you reach a medium-thin consistency. Return it to the heat and cook, stirring constantly for 2 or 3 minutes. Remove the strings and put the roast on a hot platter (or carve it in thinnish slices and reassemble it on the platter in the kitchen). Surround the roast with the glazed onions, new potatoes, and carrots and sprinkle them with fresh minced parsley. Dribble a bit of sauce over the roast and serve the rest in a hot gravy boat.

JAMAICAN "CURRY GOAT"

A Kingston friend who now lives in Brooklyn regularly makes up great batches of her native specialty to serve at parties. There being a fearful shortage of goats in Brooklyn these days, she substitutes veal or lamb but still calls it "curry goat." Dorothy's would singe the fuzz on your upper lip, so this version is considerably less incendiary.

Serves 4

2 lbs. boneless veal stew meat (shoulder or breast) flour
2 Tbsp. salad oil (coconut oil is the real thing)
1 large onion, minced
2 cloves garlic, crushed or minced fine
1 Tbsp. good, fresh hot curry powder (or more to taste)

½ tsp. ground cumin
¼ tsp. crushed red pepper
    pinch of powdered broth
2 cups chicken broth
2 Tbsp. lime juice (or substitute lemon)
    salt to taste
½ cup minced scallions

Dust the veal with flour. In a heavy cast-iron skillet with a cover, heat the oil to almost smoking. Put in some of the veal and brown it over medium heat, turning the pieces often. This should be done in two batches, otherwise the pan will be too crowded to do this job correctly. As soon as the meat is golden, remove it and toss in the onion and garlic. (You may have to add a bit more oil at this point.) When the onion is transparent, stir in the curry powder, cumin, red pepper, and ginger. Cook, stirring over low heat, to toast out the raw flavor in the spices. (Indian cooks always do this and it makes a great deal of difference in the finished flavor—it also makes a difference in the way the house smells for the next two days if you forget to close the kitchen door.) Pour in the chicken broth and bring it to the simmer, stirring up all the browned bits with a wooden spoon. Return the meat to the skillet, baste with the broth, cover tightly, and simmer over very low heat for about 1½ hours, or until very tender. Stir occasionally to prevent scorching and add a bit of stock or water if the sauce seems to be thickening too much. It's supposed to be rather on the thin side with all the heaviness in the seasoning—not like your Aunt Em's Sunday night "chicken curry," glutinous with flour and exotic with a half teaspoon of curry powder. Stir in the lime juice and season to taste with salt just before serving.

Serve the "curry goat" in a heated dish and sprinkle the top with the minced scallions. There should be plenty of fluffy white rice to go with it. Some chutney is good with the curry and you can also serve little dishes of chopped yolk and white of hard-boiled egg, ground peanuts, and shredded coconut. These are East Indian touches I tacked on and the chopped scallions are really the only thing you *must* add. Beer is better with curry than wine, but if you must, serve a dry chilled white wine, such as a Riesling.

VEAL, HAM, AND MUSHROOM BOUCHÉES

Bouchées ("little mouthfuls") are airy, crisp shells made of French puff pastry and they are usually served, filled with some rich, velvety mixture, as a first course. However, two of them make an excellent main course, and since they are so rich nothing more than a green salad need be served. If you don't know how to make French puff pastry, never mind: Pepperidge Farm does. The patty shells are sold frozen in most supermarkets and they are of a superior quality. This veal and ham mixture is but one of many fillings; you might also try a mixture of chicken and ham or mushrooms or a mélange of sea food. Sweetbreads are traditional in *bouchées*, but they're usually very expensive now.

Serves 3, or 6 as hors d'oeuvres

1 package of 6 frozen (or home-made) patty shells, or pastry for a double-crust pie	2 cups chicken broth
	3 Tbsp. butter
	3 Tbsp. flour
1 lb. boneless veal (any cheap cut will do)	3 or 4 scallions, minced
¼ lb. mild boiled ham, sliced thin	½ cup light cream (or half-and-half)
½ lb. fresh mushrooms, sliced	1 egg yolk
	1 egg white

Cut the veal into strips about half the size of your little finger. Simmer it in the chicken broth for about an hour or until it is quite tender; then add the mushrooms and simmer 5 minutes longer. Drain and reserve the broth, which should be reduced by fast boiling to 1½ cups. Prepare the patty shells according to the package directions or make the pie crust and prebake the bottom one in a moderate oven of about 350° for 5 minutes. Then brush it with slightly beaten egg white, which will prevent it from getting soggy.

Dice the boiled ham and add it to the veal and mushrooms. Melt the butter and simmer the scallions in it, taking care that nothing browns or colors. Stir in the flour, bring the reduced stock to boiling, and off heat pour it all at once into the *roux*, beating madly with a wire whip so that the sauce will be smooth as cream. Next beat the cream and egg yolk together and beat this into the sauce, which should now be quite thick. Stir it over low heat for a few minutes; then add the veal, ham, and mushrooms. When everything is hot through, fill the baked, cooled patty shells and serve at once.

If you are making the pie, fill the waiting partly baked shell with the creamed veal and ham and fit a top crust over it, fastening the edges well. Slash it in a couple of places and bake the pie in a hot oven, about 400°, until the top crust is a pale golden brown—this crust is all you really have to worry about since the filling is completely cooked and the bottom crust is half cooked before the final baking. This should take no longer than 15 or 20 minutes if you have rolled the top crust quite thin.

VARIATION: Leftover chicken, boned, skinned, and cut in small pieces, may replace the veal in this recipe. In this case, you will have to substitute canned chicken broth, unless there is some left from the original dish. Or poach a fryer for this and there will be plenty of broth.

ROGNONS DE VEAU

Tripe, brains, heart, kidneys, etc., are delicately alluded to in this country as "variety meats." But I think most Americans would tend to agree that the English term, "offal," is more accurate. Although most of them are good values, I'm convinced that the national aversion to "innards" will most likely resist them down to the last food stamp. (I must own that I've never been able to stomach tripe—not *à la mode de Caen* or anybody else's mode.) However, I do think that anyone who at least likes liver can become a kidney convert. Stick to the French word—it may help to obliterate unwelcome associations, if you have any.

Raw veal kidneys should look firm, shiny, dry, and pale brownish rose in color. They must be absolutely fresh and should be used at once, or at least on the same day bought. Try to avoid frozen ones because you don't know how long they were lying around *unfrozen*, and upon thawing, they release a lot of blood and are the devil to brown. Kidneys should not be soaked in water (this used to be standard practice—possibly to freshen them in prerefrigeration days) because they absorb it quickly and then release it just as quickly in a hot pan. The result is a watery mess that stews and toughens the kidney.

This is a simple preparation and a good starting point for more elaborate dishes made with mushrooms, cream, truffles, and brandy—the night you open on Broadway.

Serves 2

2 veal kidneys
2 Tbsp. clarified butter (see note)
2 Tbsp. good bourbon or brandy
1 small onion, minced and sautéed in a little butter

salt and pepper
juice of ½ lemon
1 Tbsp. chopped parsley

Preheat oven to 200°.

Rinse the kidneys quickly in cold water, dry them, and split them. Remove as much as you can of the white knot of fat on the underside. Have all your ingredients ready, plates hot, and anything else you plan to serve already prepared—fried bread, rice, or mashed or scalloped potatoes are good with kidneys.

Use a heavy skillet and get the clarified butter to sizzling. Toss in the kidneys and keep the pan moving back and forth over high heat to coat them well in butter and brown on all sides. Lower the heat slightly and shake constantly until the kidneys are just slightly pink in the center, about 6 or 8 minutes all told. Turn off the heat. Have ready the 2 tablespoons of bourbon or brandy heated in a ladle, pour it over the kidneys, set it alight and, when the flames die, salt and pepper the kidneys and remove them to hot plates. Keep them warm in the low oven. Add the sautéed onions to the skillet, squeeze in the lemon juice, and add a few drops of water to make a little sauce in the pan. When it bubbles, pour it over the kidneys and sprinkle with parsley. Send everyone to the table at once.

NOTE: Clarified butter is made by melting butter over low heat, letting it settle, then pouring off the clear butter, leaving the milk solids in the bottom of the pan. The milk solids are what causes smoking and burning when butter is heated to a high temperature.

10

LAMB

A lamb is an animal under a year old; after that, the sheep becomes mutton. However, very few American sheep are allowed to reach this stage, when the meat becomes heavier, fatter, and more strongly flavored. At one time I imagine we ate as much mutton as the English and French: but as our beer got paler, our whisky blended, our bread softer and whiter, the national taste blander and blander, mutton disappeared and with it a cheap and delicious meat. Lamb is so expensive that except for the innards, bony neck, and breast, the animal contains practically no bargain cuts. Shanks *seem* cheap, but weighing the meat stripped from the bone, it comes to over $1.45 per pound.

Lambs must be slaughtered before they are overage; they can't be labeled pricy "Genuine Spring Lamb" if they're over three months old. "Milk-fed baby lamb" is astronomically expensive, the most tender and the least flavorful. "Yearling lamb" is the most flavorful and cheapest, but not quite so tender. All the lamb sold by retail butchers is U.S.D.A.-graded Prime or Choice. The best lamb in America is raised (and most of it eaten) in the Eastern states. But even among this small band, many grow up in the belief that a lamb is composed entirely of chops.

Loin chops are, of course, the choicest and most expensive cut. Rib chops are a little cheaper and quite attractive, but they have almost no meat on them. Shoulder chops can be reasonable, an especially good value if you get the pinbone chops rather than the blade cut, which are bony and tedious to eat. Shoulder, boned and rolled, makes an excellent roast. The leg makes the best roast of all that is within the scope of this book. The paper-frilled rib chops curved into a crown roast, its center stuffed with a pungent dressing; the magnificent saddle of lamb, which is the entire loin section with two filets on the underside; the royal baron, which is both hind-quarters joined by part of the saddle, are all luxurious banquet cuts that have vanished from all but the most opulent tables. Thank God there are a few lithographs and dim early sepia tints to remind us of how they looked. In fact, should you come into an inheritance and want to order one of these roasts, you might have to take along a drawing to refresh the butcher's memory—and he'd have to be an old man at that.

One important point about all lamb, whatever the cut: it should be well aged. The French specify that it be *bien rassis* ("well settled") because freshly slaughtered lamb will always be juiceless and tough no matter what the grade. If possible, ask the butcher for a well-aged cut (do this with beef, too). Most of them take notorious advantage of the buyer's ignorance (which they presume, usually correctly), so if you're unsure of the butcher, or your own judgment, it's best to wrap the lamb loosely in wax paper (*not* plastic or foil) and age it a few days in the refrigerator.

GIGOT À LA BRETONNE

Gigot is simply leg of lamb and *à la Bretonne* means that it will be served with white beans (dried marrow or pea beans). Even in France, it does not necessarily mean that you're getting the delicate young lamb fed in the salt marshes of Brittany (*l'agneau pré salé*). It is an unpretentious, yet nonetheless classy dish, which makes it appropriate for a dinner party as well as a family meal.

Half a leg of lamb is adequate for four people. Buy the shank half because American butchers cut the whole leg so inanely it is next to impossible to carve. If you want a whole leg, insist on having the two hip chops cut off (for another meal) and the pelvic bone removed. If the long thigh-bone is removed as well, it is then a "Frenched," or "short," leg of lamb, which is extremely easy to carve. But few butchers know how to do this

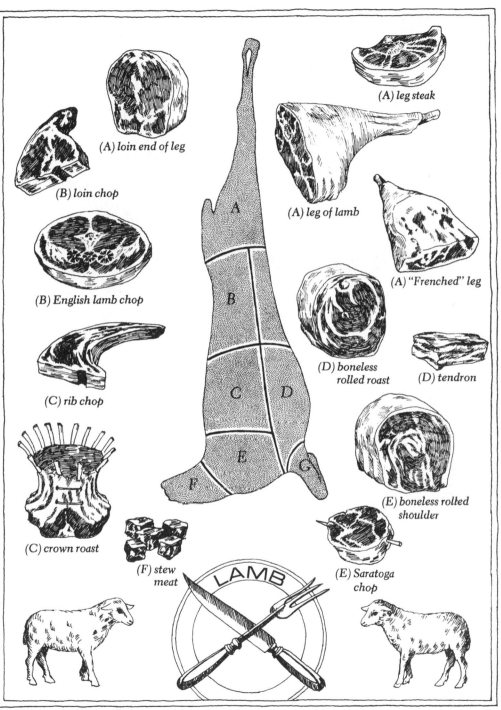

(A) leg steak

(A) loin end of leg

(A) leg of lamb

(B) loin chop

(A) "Frenched" leg

(B) English lamb chop

(D) boneless rolled roast

(D) tendron

(C) rib chop

(C) crown roast

(E) boneless rolled shoulder

(F) stew meat

(E) Saratoga chop

LAMB

Lamb Chart: A. leg; B. loin; C. rib or rack; D. breast; E. shoulder; F. neck; G. shank

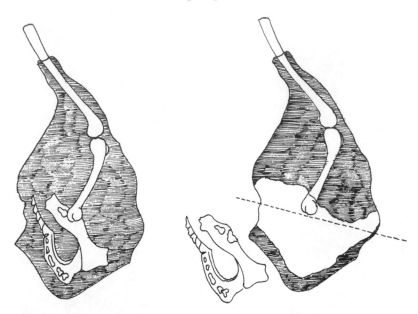

without slashing open the entire leg. If you want to try it yourself (after the hip chops and pelvic bone are removed), use a sharp, stout blade to scrape along the bone, loosening the flesh all around. Turning the top flesh of the leg inside out as you go, continue until you reach the ball joint, where, by twisting the bone and poking with the knife tip, you can detach the long bone. The shankbone should extend about two inches beyond the flesh so that you have a "handle" for carving. The fell (parchmentlike skin) should not be removed; it keeps the leg in shape. The boned end of the leg may be stuffed or not, but either way must be tied back in shape. A whole leg of lamb averages about 6½ pounds trimmed, and will serve eight people quite generously, ten adequately.

Serves 8–10

The Beans

1 lb. dried white beans (Great Northern, marrow, navy, or pea beans)

1½ quarts light chicken stock

1 onion stuck with 2 cloves

1 bouquet garni: 1 bay leaf, 1 sprig parsley, 1 fat clove garlic, six peppercorns, ½ tsp. dried thyme, tied together in a cheesecloth bag

1 carrot	1 cup skinned, chopped ripe
1 cup onions, chopped	tomatoes (fresh or canned)
1 Tbsp. butter	pan drippings from the lamb
3 Tbsp. parsley, finely chopped	salt and pepper

Wash and soak the beans as directed on page 46. Simmer them in the chicken stock with the onion stuck with cloves, bouquet garni, and carrot. Add no salt. The beans should be cooked well in advance because they are so unpredictable: they may take anywhere from 1½ to 3 hours to cook. Test a bean now and then to see how they're coming along, but don't stir them unnecessarily because they break easily. Don't let them boil dry, but most of the broth should be absorbed by the time the beans are tender. When they are, drain them, reserving the liquid, but discard the onion, carrot, and bouquet.

Sauté the chopped onion in butter until transparent, add the parsley and tomatoes, then simmer for 10 minutes or so. Put the beans in a casserole and pour the tomato mixture over them and about ½ cup of the bean liquid. Season to taste with salt and pepper and mix very gently. If the beans are at room temperature, they will require about 20 minutes to reheat in **a moderately hot 375° oven.** Time this to coincide with the Gigot, because the final flavoring is the pan juices from the lamb. When the lamb is finished and resting 15 minutes in a warm place, pour off the fat from the roasting pan. Deglaze it with a cup of boiling water, reduce this to ½ cup, and pour it over the beans.

The Gigot

1 leg of lamb, about 6½ lbs.
2 cloves garlic, slivered
   fresh or dried thyme (optional)
   olive oil
   coarse salt and freshly milled pepper

Preheat the oven to 450°.
Tie the boned part of the leg into shape. Roll the garlic slivers in thyme mixed with salt and pepper. Make tiny incisions spaced over the leg and shove the garlic and herb into them with a small stick (a swizzle stick or a chopstick). Rub the lamb with olive oil, sprinkle it with salt and pepper, and lay it on a rack in an open roasting pan. Brown the lamb for 20 minutes, then **lower the oven heat to 375°** and continue roasting for approxi-

mately 1 hour and 10 minutes, or until a meat thermometer registers 160°. (Rare lamb, 150°.) This will give you pink, juicy roast lamb—disregard the lamb setting on most thermometers; it presumes a desire for incinerated lamb. This is the standard way to roast lamb, however you are serving it. A dry red wine is nice with Gigot à la Bretonne, and some kind of salad should follow it.

VARIATION: Gigot d'Agneau Boulangère

Leg of lamb "baker's style" (or any other roast *boulangère*) means that potatoes and onions are roasted under or around the meat. Roast the lamb as in Gigot à la Bretonne. About 45 minutes before it is done, peel 1 large potato and 2 onions per person. Parboil the potatoes 5 minutes, drain, and dry them over low heat; then put them along with the onions into the roasting pan with the lamb. Baste them with the pan juices, salt, and pepper and turn once after 20 minutes.

STUFFED SHOULDER OF LAMB

Shoulder isn't all the bargain it's cracked up to be unless you happen to stumble on it at a special price. The reason is the unseen waste, especially if you are buying from a butcher who weighs and *then* trims remorselessly. If you see it in a supermarket case already trimmed, ask the butcher to bone it for you but leave it untied. (In an old book of James Beard's, written in calmer times, the old master suggests taking your herb stuffing along to the butchershop and having him put it in before he ties up the roast!) A leg may also be cooked in this way.

Serves 4

1 3-lb. trimmed piece of lamb shoulder	1 clove garlic, minced
olive oil	2 Tbsp. parsley, minced
3 Tbsp. butter	1 cup soft bread crumbs
½ cup chopped onion	salt and pepper
	rosemary or thyme (optional)

Preheat the oven to 375°.

Wipe the meat with a damp paper towel; then rub the interior with olive oil. Melt the butter and fry the onions and garlic in it. Stir in the parsley and bread crumbs and season with salt and pepper and a bit of rosemary or thyme, if you like. Spread this over the inside surface of the shoulder and roll it up. Tie it securely at one-inch intervals. Rub the rolled roast with olive oil, salt and pepper it, and lay it on a rack in an open pan for about 1½ hours for medium-rare, pink lamb. I put little faith in meat thermometers—mine lies a lot—but the reading is supposed to be 150° for rare, 160° for medium rare.

LAMB CURRY

There is, in the veal chapter, a dish called Jamaican "Curry Goat." (I'm not going to explain it twice.) Lamb may be substituted for the veal in that recipe (page 142), and beef bouillon for the chicken bouillon. Although a curry made from raw lamb is infinitely better than one made from leftover cooked meat, this curry isn't bad at all because the meat is steeped, rather than cooked, in the hot curry sauce. When you're down to the end of a leg of lamb, this makes a creditable supper for two or three people.

2 Tbsp. butter or salad oil	½ cup sliced mushrooms (optional)
1 large Bermuda onion, very thinly sliced	2 cups cold, cooked lamb, cut in small, ragged pieces (cubed meat always looks canned to me)
1 clove garlic, minced	
1–2 Tbsp. fresh, hot curry powder (to taste)	
2 cups chicken or beef bouillon	1 hard-cooked egg, chopped (optional)
salt to taste	2–3 scallions, minced (optional)

Heat the butter or oil and gently sauté the onion and garlic in it (you may add more garlic if the roast had very little). When the onions are transparent, stir in the curry powder, the amount depending on what kind of curry powder it is, how old it is, and how hot you think is hot. Stir it around and cook a minute or two. Pour in the bouillon, stir in the tomato paste, and add salt to taste. If the mushrooms are raw, simmer them in this sauce 5 minutes. Stir in the cold lamb, mix well, turn off the heat, and let it sit for at least half an hour—the longer the better—to absorb the flavors. Reheat briefly, but do not cook, and serve over mounds of cooked white rice. The chopped egg and scallions should be strewn over the top of the curry. A fresh green salad or cucumbers in yoghurt and a cooling beer will temper the after-burn a really good curry should have.

Of leftovers, Prosper Montagné advises, "Where there are abundant leftovers the administration of the kitchen is very bad. . . . Sometimes, however, foodstuffs are served in large quantity on purpose—when, for example, they will be served at a subsequent meal. . . ." In accordance with the great chef's pronouncement, there are only recipes for *planned* leftovers, such as this one, in this book.

LAMB RAGOÛT PROVENÇALE

Although this stew never came closer than Central Park West to the thyme- and lavender-scented fields of Provence, I did borrow many of the robust and distinctive flavors of that region. We ate very little lamb when I was a child. And when we did it was apt to be a wizened chop or a brown-to-the-bone leg soused with green mint sauce. So I banished these memories with olives, garlic, thyme, onions, zucchini, and wine with my lamb.

Serves 4

3 Tbsp. salad or olive oil
2 lbs. boneless shoulder of lamb
1 cup onions, thinly sliced
2 cloves garlic, minced
1 Tbsp. flour
1 1-lb. can stewed tomatoes (2 cups)
½ cup dry vermouth or white wine
1 small bay leaf
1 tsp. dried thyme (if you have

fresh thyme, use 2 Tbsp. added during last 15 minutes of cooking)
10–15 small, pitted olives, black or green or a mixture of the two
2 small, slender zucchini, sliced but unpeeled (see note)
salt and freshly milled pepper to taste

If you can buy the lamb, boned, trimmed, and cubed for stewing, you're fortunate. Most likely you'll have to buy the meat in one piece and trim and cut it in one-and-a-half-inch cubes yourself. Lamb neck is, of course, much cheaper and may be used, but there's no practical way of boning it and the meat is scanty. You will have to add more vegetables to compensate for this.

Dry the lamb and brown it in the oil, which ideally should be of the olive. Add the onions, stir and sauté about 5 minutes, and toss in the garlic and cook, stirring, another 2 or 3 minutes. Sprinkle the tablespoon of flour over the whole business and cook, stirring to distribute it evenly. Pour in the tomatoes, with their juices, add the wine, dried thyme (fresh thyme is added last, it doesn't withstand long cooking), bay leaf, and olives. You might add a bit of crushed red pepper now if you like it, but no salt—the olives are taking care of that. Cover and simmer about 1 hour and 15 minutes. Add the sliced zucchini when the meat is quite tender. The vegetable will be crisp-tender in about 10 to 15 minutes. Taste for seasoning (salt and pepper) and serve with rice or hot French bread.

NOTE: If zucchini is too expensive or unavailable, substitute 2 Italian sweet peppers, seeded and cut in strips, to be sautéed with the onions.

BREAST OF LAMB SAINTE MÉNÉHOULD

Pigs' trotters are usually prepared in this manner, and they may be substituted for the breast of lamb in the recipe. Most modern Americans shudder at the thought of a pig's foot, but at one time they were considered quite a delicacy. God knows what else will be banished from our tables with the ascendancy of a generation that thinks fried chicken comes from little men in white coats. This meal is rather a lot of trouble, but not in the least difficult to make. If you have more time than money, this is for you (lamb breast costs 29¢ a pound at this writing).

Serves 4

3 lbs. lean breast of lamb
2 carrots, sliced
2 onions, sliced (about 2 cups)
    bouquet garni: 1 mashed clove
    garlic, ½ bay leaf, pinch thyme,

2 sprigs parsley, 6 bruised peppercorns tied in a cheesecloth bag
2 quarts thin beef stock
    salt and pepper

Preheat oven to 325°.
First of all, there is no such thing as *lean* breast of lamb—the term is

relative. If there is a large bone on the underside, get the butcher to remove it. Very lightly salt and pepper the breast of lamb. Spread the sliced vegetables in the bottom of a heavy braising kettle (with cover) and lay the lamb on top. Tuck the bouquet garni under the lamb. Pour the cold stock over the meat and bring it to the simmer on a top burner. Add no salt unless your stock is salted insufficiently. Seal it with foil and a lid and braise slowly on the lower rack of the oven for about 2 hours. The breast is done when the bones can be easily pulled out. When the meat is cool enough for handling, remove the bones. Press the meat between two plates with a weight on top (I use an old flatiron), and chill it. It is best to do all this the day before it will be grilled and served. Chill the broth and degrease it—this is very important because there will be a lot of fat, which will ruin your soup if left in the broth. Lamb fat isn't much good for anything unless you're thinking of homemade lanolin, so throw it out.

Grilled lamb breast isn't very filling (albeit rich); therefore you will need the soup to follow.

The Soup

> the degreased lamb broth with vegetables
> 2 parsnips, peeled and cut in fat sticks
> ½ head of green cabbage, shredded
> 2 potatoes, peeled and diced
> ½ cup frozen Fordhook lima beans (optional)

Bring the broth to a simmer and taste it. If too weak (unlikely but possible) reduce it until you have a good rich flavor. If too strong, thin the broth with a bit of water. Add all the vegetables and cook about 15 minutes until the vegetables are just tender.

Breading and Grilling Lamb Breast

> prepared mustard
> 1 large egg, beaten with 1 tsp. water
> 1½ cups dry bread crumbs
> ½ cup salad oil or melted butter

Cut the breast into strips two inches wide. Smear them with mustard. Dip each piece in the beaten egg; then coat with bread crumbs, pressing them in with your hands. Lay them on a rack to dry for half an hour. Sprinkle the breaded meat with the oil or butter and grill until browned and hot through, about 8 minutes in all, turning once. Serve on hot plates with lemon wedges and parsley or a sauce vinaigrette. I think it's rather heavy, but some people like a sauce rémoulade with this dish.

DIZI (IRANIAN MUTTON AND CHICK-PEA STEW)

This dish shattered my lifelong prejudice against Middle Eastern food. Probably because it departs from their custom of studding gorgeous meat dishes with such unpleasant surprises as cherries or quinces or simply unidentifiable sweet fruits. My loathing of sweet with meat harks back to my Carolina childhood, when the ham was sometimes garlanded with pineapple or swam in a positively perverted raisin sauce. Dizi is exotic but not weird.

Serves 6

1 cup chick-peas (garbanzos)
1 cup pinto beans or California pink beans (authentically these should be fava beans, but they are hard to find)
3 lbs. lean, boneless lamb shoulder, cubed, or lamb neck with bone
  salad oil
1 cup onions, chopped
½ cup canned tomatoes, drained and chopped

1 quart water or thin beef bouillon
1 Tbsp. salt (a little less if using bouillon)
  black pepper to taste
  juice of half a lemon
2 cloves garlic, crushed
1 tsp. ground cumin
½ tsp. turmeric
¼ tsp. dried thyme (optional)
½ cup chopped scallions
  lemon wedges (optional)

Wash and soak the chick-peas in cold water overnight (they are the most intractable of dried legumes and will brook no short cuts). Separately, wash and soak the pinto beans overnight or use the quick method described in the chapter on Beans, Rice, and Pasta. Next day, drain both dried legumes, cover with fresh water by a depth of two inches above the beans, and simmer them in separate pots for about an hour. They will be only partly cooked. If you are using canned garbanzos, add them in the last hour of cooking.

Choose a heavy earthenware or iron casserole of about 3-quart capacity and be sure it has a close-fitting lid. Film it with oil, and when it is quite hot brown the lamb, which you have carefully dried with paper towels; otherwise it will just hiss at you instead of browning. When the meat is browned, pour off any excess fat; then stir in the onions and cook gently until they take color. Add the tomatoes, water or bouillon, salt, pepper, lemon juice, cumin, and turmeric. (Turmeric is a violent ochre but it has very little flavor; its main function is to color. Cumin is one of the spices in curry powder but it isn't hot. Mexicans are fond of cumin, and they also share the Middle Eastern taste for fruits in the stew—indeed, they surpass the Oriental cuisine in a concoction of lentils, pork, bananas, onions, apples, pineapple, and other things that make it resemble an explosion in the cookhouse.)

Now add the beans, stir the whole business up, and cover. Heat to bubbling on a top burner; then set in **a preheated 325° oven** for about 2½ hours, or until the beans and meat are quite tender, but not mushy. Take out a cupful of beans and liquid and purée it. Stir this back into the stew, sprinkle it with the chopped scallions, and send it to the table along with plenty of French bread, some lemon wedges, and perhaps a dish of cucumbers in yoghurt or sour cream.

SAUTÈED LAMB KIDNEYS MADEIRA

Most people in this country don't know how to cook kidneys for the very good reason that they have no desire to eat them. In countries where they are liked very much indeed, France and England, everybody knows so much about cooking kidneys that no one can agree about how it is done. I have a persuasive kidney nut in the house and am a convert. Consequently, I've tried everyone's suggestions because in my background kidneys were not mentioned in mixed company. The disagreements have to do with soaking or not soaking, slicing or leaving whole. Beef kidneys *must* be soaked to remove some of the intense flavor and scent (my kidney conversion has not extended to beef kidney as yet, however), but the matter is optional when dealing with the much more delicate and milder lamb and veal kidneys. If these kidneys are cut in small pieces, they tend to lose all their juices, in which they then stew and toughen. Lamb and veal kidneys should be cooked briefly and at high heat and just to the pink stage. An exception to this rule is Steak and Kidney Pie (see recipe, page 127). This method may be used for either lamb or veal kidneys, but the latter will require about 10 minutes cooking, whereas the tiny lamb kidneys will be done in about 4 or 5 minutes. At any respectable middling French restaurant the *rognons de veau* (veal kidney) runs about $6 à la carte. You can make this dish at home (either lamb or veal) for $1.50 or less for two people.

Serves 2

6 or 8 lamb kidneys (depending on your passion)	4 Tbsp. clarified butter
milk	¼ cup Madeira
flour	½ cup chopped mushrooms, cooked in butter
salt and pepper	2 Tbsp. chopped parsley

Wash the kidneys and cut them in half or leave them whole if you prefer rather rare kidneys. (Veal kidneys should have the fat cut out of the center.) Soak them in cold milk to cover for about 1 hour in the refrigerator. Dry them, season with salt and pepper, and dredge them lightly in flour. Heat the clarified butter to bubbling in a heavy skillet, then put in the kidneys very quickly. Sauté, shaking the pan and turning the little morsels, for about 4–5 minutes. The trick is to have the pan very hot and keep it moving (rather like making an omelet) so the kidneys never begin to stew. The flour helps prevent this and also thickens the little sauce. If they're not brown, they're not brown—but don't overcook them. Pour in the Madeira and cook and stir 1 minute. Add the mushrooms, give it a good quick stir, and serve up at once on hot plates. Scatter the chopped parsley over the top. Warmed French bread, plain bread fried in butter, or a white-hot baked potato are especially pleasant with kidneys. So is a spinach and bacon salad (see recipe, page 23).

CURRIED KIDNEYS

I am fond of Indian food and will curry anything that will stand still for it. With all their dietary laws, I have no idea whether Moslems and Hindus eat kidneys any way at all, but if they did, it might be this way. Again, one may use veal kidneys as well as lamb kidneys, keeping in mind that a calf's kidney is about four times the size of a lamb's. Always buy them fresh and use them quickly.

Serves 2

6 lamb kidneys (or 1 large veal kidney)

½ cup yoghurt

3 Tbsp. butter or oil

2 cloves garlic, minced

1 cup onion, finely chopped

½ small, dried red pepper, crushed

1 tsp. cumin

½ tsp. turmeric

¼ tsp. ginger (freshly grated is best)

½ cup fresh tomato, skinned and chopped

salt

2 Tbsp. lemon juice (to replace expensive cardamom seeds—see note)

2 more Tbsp. butter

2–3 Tbsp. minced scallions

Wash the kidneys, cut them in half or a veal kidney in sixths, and put them to soak in the yoghurt. Heat the butter or oil, or a combination of the two, in a small heavy casserole. Put in the garlic, onion, red pepper (you may wish to modify this), cumin, turmeric, and ginger and stir well. Cook gently until the onions are limp. Add the tomato and salt to taste. Cook over low heat, stirring occasionally. This is really a quick dinner— the rice and curry sauce cook in about the same length of time. In a skillet melt the remaining 2 tablespoons of butter. Dry the kidneys and pour their yoghurt marinade into the bubbling sauce. Quickly sauté the kidneys, sprinkling them with a little salt—about 2 minutes should be enough—and stir them into the waiting sauce. Add the lemon juice and more salt if necessary. Serve at once over rice and strew the chopped scallions over the top. If for some reason you want to make the sauce in advance, it won't be harmed. But you must sauté the kidneys at the last minute, and, once they are in the sauce, the dish must be served or the kidneys will toughen.

NOTE: Lemon juice cannot actually replace cardamom, but that rare and precious spice does have a predominantly lemony influence on food.

11

PORK AND HAM

The pig, that encyclopedic creature.

—GRIMOD DE LA REYNIÈRE

Charcuterie is not one of the great American arts, but even so, we do manage to use every scrap of our porkers. And we have such magnificent pigs. Although increasingly leaner, more succulent breeds have been developed here, the domestic pig isn't a native American. The ancestors of those fierce "razorbacks" that roam the Southern forests were all Chinese. Pigs vary more than people from country to country, depending on how they're bred and what they're fed. (Last summer I tangled with a roast from an Irish hog who must have been fattened on ground tires.)

The United States Department of Agriculture inspects all pork for wholesomeness, but does not grade for quality because our porkers are slaughtered so young—at about six months old—the meat is almost uniformly lean and tender. There are "yield grades" for the guidance of wholesale buyers which determine the ratio of lean meat to fat, but that is quite detectable to the naked eye of the dumbest consumer by the time the retail cuts are displayed in the store. Good pork should be firm to the touch, pale grayish-pink meat and white smooth fat.

Pork used to be more popular in America than any other meat except beef—especially with farmers, because they knew what to do with it, how to make sausages and head cheeses, how to cure and smoke hams. Maybe because of the population shift to the cities, weight consciousness (God, do we go on about our weight!) or some other reason, pork consumption has dropped although its quality has risen. The price of pork has risen too—it used to be one of the cheapest meats—because around 1965 the pig farmers, to prevent economic destruction, staged a revolt, cut back production, and refused to market their hogs until the price rose.

Even so, the quickly cooked loin chops and the delectable center-cut loin or crown roasts, the luxury cuts, are cheaper than any comparable cut of beef. Whole fresh leg of pork, which doubles in price after it becomes cured ham, can still be found for as little as 47¢ per pound. The trouble with it is, the whole leg weighs about 14 pounds, enough to feed the starting line-up of the Dallas Cowboys. Most butchers will halve them, though, and there are picnic shoulders that run about 6 or 7 pounds before boning. Rolled Boston butt makes a neat, compact roast for a small family. Spareribs used to be dirt cheap but have gone up because of their popularity, and aren't any great bargain. We buy them anyway, compensating for quantity with irresistible flavor and the primitive joys of bone-gnawing. Slab bacon is a bit more expensive than some presliced bacon, but is usually a better buy because it doesn't dissolve into lard. Smoked jowl bacon is even cheaper and quite good—indispensable for cooking.

Ham hocks provide great flavor and a bit of meat in vegetable dishes. My grandfather made peppery sausages out of heaven only knows what parts of the pig, the head was turned into a gelatinous, pressed cold meat called "head cheese" (which I hated), and even the blood was used to make "blood pudding," which are black sausages (*boudin*, in France) to be eaten hot with mashed potatoes. Shredded pig's ear in vinegar is something I once ate, somewhat unenthusiastically, at a Chinese dinner. Pigs' feet are pretty good *à la Sainte Ménéhould*, and although I haven't tried it yet, there is a recipe for Pig Tails 'n Beans in my copy of *Princess Pamela's Soul Food Cookbook*. So there he is, good from stem to stern, and you can see why poor regions keep pigs (and goats, which provide milk and fend for themselves).

Ham has been so debased by large meat-packing companies it's difficult to give any guidelines for buying it. Like American beer, ham

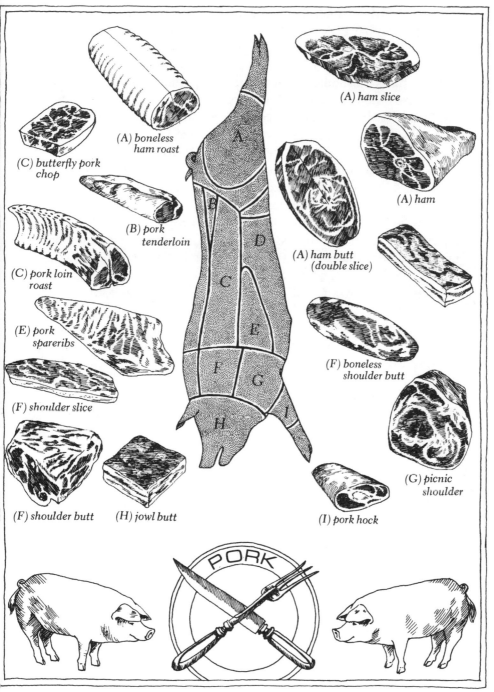

(A) boneless
ham roast

(C) butterfly pork
chop

(B) pork
tenderloin

(C) pork loin
roast

(E) pork
spareribs

(F) shoulder slice

(F) shoulder butt

(H) jowl butt

(A) ham slice

(A) ham

(A) ham butt
(double slice)

(F) boneless
shoulder butt

(G) picnic
shoulder

(I) pork hock

PORK

Pork Chart: A. ham; B. tenderloin; C. loin; D. flank; E. spareribs; F. shoulder
butt; G. picnic shoulder; H. snout and jowl; I. hock

has been ballyhooed, bleached out, flavor-flattened, and watered down (literally). A U.S.D.A. ruling now in litigation states that if ham contains up to 10 per cent added weight, it must be labeled HAM— WATER ADDED; if more than 10 per cent, it must be labeled IMITATION HAM. I think it should all be labeled "imitation ham." The only true ham is the rich, dark red, salty meat arrived at by careful curing and hanging in the cool sweetness of smoke-houses in Virginia, Kentucky, Tennessee, and maybe a few other states. The best country ham I've ever eaten comes from Trigg County, Kentucky, from an old family firm that numbers their hams and smokes them over sassafras. They cost about $2.00 a pound, but sliced paper thin, an 11- or 12-pound ham goes a long, long way.

Smithfield County ham, the name most people know, is costly for the true ham, but they also sell in supermarkets a country-cured picnic shoulder that is a buy at 99¢ a pound. The little boned, rolled picnic shoulders packed in a string bag are flavorful but sometimes are very fat and wasty. All you can go by is feel—squashy ones are usually fatty and firm ones leaner.

Ordinary mass-produced hams of the "tenderized" type (partly cooked) are reasonably priced and can be made more interesting by braising them in a little wine and herbs. Completely cooked, ready-to-eat hams appear to be gradually replacing all other kinds. And what a shame—ham will become as standard and dull as a loaf of Wonder Bread. Blandness keeps spreading over American food like an oil slick—maybe we should be worrying more about what's being taken out than what's being put in.

You probably noticed that commercial hams are nearly always sold in halves. This is so the butcher can remove the choice center slices and sell them at a much higher price. If possible, get a friend to split a whole ham with you to outwit this cheating. These hams don't keep particularly well because they are smoked very lightly, if at all.

Another form of ham, not so familiar to Americans, is the German *Kassler Ripchen*. This is the loin of pork, cured in brine, then smoked. It is sold ready to eat by German butchers in the Yorkville section of New York, and sometimes it can be found at a much lower price in supermarkets in German neighborhoods. These thick pink chops may be served hot or cold and are particularly good with a wine-soaked Alsatian *choucroute garni*. Canadian bacon is made from the cured loin of pork too, but it's pale, watery stuff by comparison with *Kassler Ripchen*. The best Irish bacon, which looks more like a slice of ham, contains a good deal of the loin and is perhaps the crown prince of all bacon, anywhere. It's too expensive in the United States to eat for breakfast, but a good slice laid alongside an omelet would make a delicious little supper.

Even the most costly cuts of pork and hams are, on the whole, cheaper than beef. A serving of lean roast beef contains almost the same number of calories as one of lean roast pork.

Trichinosis does still occur in this country and it shouldn't. The trichinae are destroyed if all pork (especially sausages and hams and various cool-smoked meats) is heated throughout to a temperature of 131°.

FRESH HAM, BONED AND STUFFED

The ham, or leg of pork, is an enormous piece of meat, but it can almost always be bought in shank or butt halves. The shank half is the more attractive for this roast. Shoulder is a bit cheaper than the leg and more difficult to bone, but the flavor and texture of the meat is essentially the same. Shoulder is not, strictly speaking, "ham," whether fresh or smoked, but it is labeled that way in many markets. Others label it *calas* or *callie* and in some regions it is a *hand* of pork. Both shoulder and leg have much juicier, darker, richer meat than the loin, which is more finely textured and leaner, and therefore more easily dried out through overcooking. I think the leg is better roasted and the shoulder braised.

Serves 8

1 6- or 7-lb. shank half of fresh pork leg	2 Tbsp. chopped parsley
3 Tbsp. butter	1 cup soft bread crumbs made from day-old bread
3 cloves garlic, finely minced	3 Tbsp. minced scallions
3 Tbsp. fresh chopped thyme or 1 Tbsp. dried	1½ cups thin beef broth
½ tsp. salt and ½ tsp. pepper	2 tsp. cornstarch
	2 Tbsp. Madeira (optional)

Have the bone removed up to the knuckle without splitting open the leg. If the butcher doesn't know how to do this, do it yourself—you will save yourself a lot of money and frustration by learning how to bone and cut meat at home. Start at the thick end of the leg, cutting always against the bone. When you get to the ball joint, insert the point of the knife to cut the tendons and twist the bone until it comes loose. If you like rich brown crackling, leave the skin on the top side of the leg. If not, reserve the pork skin (freeze it) to thicken stews. Melt the butter and sauté the garlic about 3 minutes. Stir in thyme, salt, pepper, parsley, bread crumbs, and scallions, let the mixture cool, then stuff the leg. Warm stuffing can cause meat to spoil unless it is to be cooked immediately and I presume anybody would want to get all this boning and stuffing done in the morning or even the night before serving it.

Preheat oven to 450°. Sew up the opening and tie the roast at one-inch intervals. Rub the exterior with salt and pepper or make some gashes in the skin. Rub some additional garlic, thyme, salt, and pepper into these slits.

Put the ham on a rack in a shallow pan and roast it 20 minutes to a golden light brown. Put a cup of water in the pan and cover the roast loosely with foil. **Lower the heat to 325°** and continue baking for 2½ hours, or until very tender. Uncover during last half hour to crisp the rind, which is now "crackling." Let the meat rest for 15 minutes or so in a warm place while you make a little sauce for it. Pour off most of the fat, leaving about 2 tablespoons. Add 1½ cups thin beef broth or water and deglaze the pan over high heat, scraping up all the meat drippings. Pour this into a small saucepan. Mix 2 teaspoons cornstarch with 2 tablespoons Madeira (or water) and stir it into the broth with a wire whisk. Cook, whisking over low heat, until smooth and thickened. Season to taste.

You cannot slice through crackling very easily, so remove it in one piece before carving the leg. Cut it in squares with kitchen shears and serve a little with each helping of roast pork.

BRAISED SHOULDER OF PORK

Like many pork roasts, this is absolutely delicious cold and it makes a handsome buffet dish surrounded by its own amber jelly, black olives, and watercress. It is also much easier to carve cold because boned cuts of meat tend to fall apart when they are hot.

Serves 6–8

1 fresh pork shoulder, about 5 lbs. after boning	salad oil and butter
all the skin from the shoulder and the bones	1 medium onion, chopped
	1 carrot, chopped
	2 Tbsp. parsley, chopped

2 Tbsp. fresh thyme, chopped (or 1 tsp. dried leaves)

2 cloves garlic, minced

salt and pepper

1 cup dry white wine or vermouth

Have the shoulder boned completely or have just the knucklebone left in, but be sure to get all the rind and bones from the butcher because that's what makes your jelly. (A small piece of calf's foot will *insure* the set.) Have the bones sawed into three-inch lengths and cut the skin into three or four pieces. **Preheat oven to 325°.** Wipe the meat with paper towels; then salt and pepper it inside. Scatter the parsley, thyme, and garlic on the inner surface, roll the roast up, and tie it at close intervals.

Heat some butter mixed with oil in a heavy skillet and brown the roast. Remove it to a Dutch oven or something similar. In the skillet sauté the onion and carrot, stirring over low heat, for about 5 minutes. If there is excess fat, drain it off. Pour in the wine or vermouth and scrape up the pan drippings. Pour this, and the vegetables, into the braising pan with the pork roast. Add boiling water to half the depth of the roast— for this reason you should have a braising pan almost exactly the same size as the meat, otherwise you will have to add too much water, and the pork will tend to boil rather than braise. Cover and set on the lower rack of the oven. After 1 hour, turn the roast. After 2 hours, remove it to a small shallow pan, add a splash of the broth, **turn up the oven to 350°,** and roast until the fat is crisp and browned, about half an hour. The total cooking time is about 2½ hours. This last open roasting isn't really essential if you don't care to bother with it . . . it's only for looks. Let the roast cool to room temperature, wrap it, and chill it before removing the strings. Boil down the broth to about 2½ cups; strain it and chill it. When the fat congeals, remove it entirely. You may want to add some fresh chopped and blanched parsley to the aspic after this, in which case you will have to remelt it. Clarifying is simple enough, but while improving the looks, it removes a lot of flavor.

To Clarify Meat Stock

Strain the stock, chill it, and remove every trace of fat. Wipe the surface of the jelly with a damp paper towel. When the jelly melts to cold stock, beat in one egg white and its crushed shell for each pint of stock. Set it on the fire and slowly bring it to the simmer, gently agitating the broth with a wire whisk. After the egg turns white and rises to the surface, turn the heat very low and leave it alone for 15 minutes. Carefully strain the clarified broth through several thicknesses of damp cheesecloth laid in a strainer. You may add some minced herbs or a spoonful of port, Madeira, or brandy at this point. After chilling, break up with a fork and serve around the chilled sliced pork.

ROAST PIG EN SANGLIER

Whether or not this actually tastes like wild boar (the *sanglier*) I couldn't vouch for, but it *does* have an interesting and decidedly "gamy" flavor after being steeped in wine and flavorings. The French do a similar thing with leg of lamb which they call *en Chevreuil* because it tastes quite a lot like venison. The fresh ham, or leg, is the best cut for this treatment.

Serves 8–10

1 6- or 7-lb. shank half leg of fresh pork
2 cups Burgundy (California is fine for this—see note)
½ cup wine vinegar or cider
½ cup chopped onions
2 carrots, thinly sliced
3 cloves garlic, mashed
4 sprigs of fresh thyme (or 2 tsp. dried)

8 juniper berries, mashed (or ¼ cup gin)
2 bay leaves
2 whole cloves
1 tsp. cracked black pepper
1 can beef bouillon and 1 can water
2 Tbsp. oil or bacon fat
2 Tbsp. flour
salt to taste

Have the leg half boned or not, as you prefer, but the marinade penetrates better if it is boned. Ask for the bones, sawed up. Remove the rind but keep it; trim the fat smoothly to about ¼-inch thickness. Make several gashes in the fat all the way down to the flesh. Bring wine and vinegar to a boil with the vegetables, herbs, and spices and simmer 5 minutes; then let it cool. Put the leg into a china or earthenware vessel that just leaves room for the marinade (I use an old stoneware crock). Pour the cooled marinade over the leg, cover it, and put it in the refrigerator for 4 days, turning at least once a day.

Take the leg out of the icebox 2 hours before you wish to cook it. Put the marinade with all the vegetables into a saucepan. Add the bones, pork rind (save half the rind for another stew or something), and the beef bouillon and water. Simmer this for 1 hour; then strain the stock and discard all the vegetables, herbs, and spices.

Preheat oven to 350°. Brown the leg (after drying it well) in oil or bacon fat. Remove it and sprinkle 2 tablespoons flour in the casserole. Stir and cook slightly. Pour in the hot, strained broth and beat it smooth with a whisk. Put the leg back into this sauce, baste it, cover the casserole, and bake it slowly in the preheated oven for about 2½ hours or longer until the meat is very tender. Remove the roast pork to a warm platter and keep it in a warm place, loosely covered with foil. Skim off as much fat as possible from the sauce, check it for flavoring and consistency, and, if necessary, correct the seasoning or reduce the sauce to a medium thickness. It should not be too heavy in texture, as the flavor is quite strong and rich. This wonderful sauce just begs for the subtle bland counterpoint of creamy mashed potatoes. Obviously, not a dish for dieters or hot weather. Cranberry sauce might be served with this and the freshness of a green salad would make a pleasant *digestif* to end the meal. Or maybe a Brioschi.

NOTE: Shop around for the driest and least "grapy" Burgundy—some of the Californias taste more like Kool-Aid than wine.

PORK LOIN WITH RIPE OLIVES

Perfect served cold at a large buffet, this is an adapted version of a luxurious dish I discovered in Elizabeth David's *French Provincial Cooking*. The classic Enchaud de Porc à la Périgourdine is a specialty of the truffle region, where the cooks throw around the famous "black diamonds" as if they were turnips. Black olives can somewhat duplicate the appearance of truffles, but unfortunately not the flavor, which is exquisite and unlike anything else. Whenever I get any unexpected money, I present myself with a tiny tin of truffles and make this dish the real way.

Serves 10 for dinner or 20 as part of a buffet

1 center-cut boned loin of pork of about 6 lbs. (it can be as small as 3½ lbs. but no less)	salt and pepper
	1½ cups thin beef stock (dilute if canned)
6 medium-size California ripe olives, water-packed	1 cup dry white wine
1 or 2 cloves garlic, slivered	¼ calf's foot (or ¼ lb. fresh pork rind cut in strips)
½ tsp. rosemary, crushed (see note)	1 Tbsp. Madeira (optional)

Any butcher will bone a loin of pork for you (or he should be drummed out of the corps). Ask him to saw the rack and chinebone into two-inch lengths. **Preheat oven to 400°.** Pare the fat to a smooth covering about one-third of an inch thick. You may have to slit a slightly deeper opening in the loin to make room for the garlic and olives. Cut the olives in small chunks and put them, along with the garlic and rosemary, into the opening. Add a bit of pepper but no salt unless your olives are especially bland. Roll and tie the loin firmly at one-inch intervals; then rub it well with salt and pepper. Put the roast and all the bones into a long, narrow baking dish about three inches deep and place it in the preheated oven until it turns a biscuit brown—about 30 minutes. Heat the stock and wine together (ideally this should be a veal stock because a strongly flavored beef bouillon overwhelms the lovely flavors of the pork and wine) and pour it around the roast. Were you using truffles instead of olives, their juice would be added now. Cover the baking dish, **reduce the oven temperature to 325°,** and cook the roast gently for another 2½ hours, basting two or three times. Should the loin be tender in only 2 hours, don't feel that you have to go on baking it; it will only dry out.

While it is still in its trussing strings, cool the roast to room temperature; then wrap it closely in foil to seal in the flavors and moisture. Chill it for 4 hours or more. Strain the stock and stir in the Madeira; then chill it until the fat forms a hard cake. Lift off the fat in one piece, if possible, and mop up any stray bits with a damp paper towel. You can clarify the meat jelly according to directions on page 167 (Braised Shoulder of Pork) or you can skip this extra process. I seldom bother (unless I intend to serve a jellied consommé) because the beautifying removes too much flavor. Further to that, I am such a skinflint that I make a little jar of *rillettes* out of the meat picked from the roasted bones and pounded up with the fat from the broth and a bit more salt and pepper. This is delicious spread on thin, hot toast for hors d'oeuvres. The fat is also great for frying bread and potatoes or making croutons. Naturally all these byproducts are better if the roast is truffled, but it's still excellent if done with only a bit of garlic and rosemary or thyme.

To serve, remove the strings, slice thinly, reassemble on a chilled platter, and surround with the jelly broken up with a fork and some kind of greenery—parsley or watercress.

NOTE: Rosemary should be bought frequently in very small quantities, as it deteriorates quickly.

BRAZILIAN ROAST PORK AND BLACK BEANS

Feijoada is the *pot-au-feu* of Brazil. It is a rich orchestration of meats, vegetables, fruits, and spices in hot and cold, crisp and soft counterpoint. This recipe comprises only two elements of it, but you can put a little more Latin spin on the meal by serving it with rice and a salad of fresh orange slices and raw onion rings. The onion rings have less lethal fumes if soaked for an hour in ice water.

Serves 4–6

1 recipe Black Beans, page 46
1 pork loin roast, about 4 lbs.

1 clove garlic, slivered

The Glaze

salt and pepper
¾ cup orange juice
¼ cup thick honey

½ tsp. ground ginger
¼ tsp. ground cloves

Prepare the black beans. Have the butcher remove the chinebone and crack the bones between the chops so that carving is simplified. **Preheat oven to 450°.** Make some tiny incisions on the underside of the loin and stick the slivers of garlic in. Rub the roast well with salt and pepper after trimming off any excess fat, which should be about one-third of an inch thick. Put the roast on a rack in a shallow pan and brown it (or you can brown it in a heavy skillet) for about 20 minutes. **Reduce the heat to 325°,** pour a cup of water in the roasting pan, cover loosely with foil, and cook the meat for approximately 1 hour longer. Boil together the orange juice, honey, ginger, and cloves until it thickens enough to cling to the meat. Uncover the roast and brush the top and ends well with the glaze. Continue roasting another half hour, glazing twice more during this time. The total roasting time is 1 hour and 50 minutes, but the pork may require less or more time, depending on its age and quality. The loin is particularly susceptible to dryness and we have a tragic tendency to believe that pork can't be cooked too long. It can; and often it is roasted to a juiceless stringiness. Put it in a warm place for 30 minutes before carving. Serve it with the black beans, white rice, and the orange and onion salad, which is not a salad at all but a side dish.

STUFFED PORK CHOPS

Pork loin fluctuates a good deal in price, not only from season to season, but from store to store. A supermarket near me sells center-cut chops for 89¢ a pound the same day a telephone-order snob grocery two blocks away is getting $1.59 for the same meat. You must have the very best thick loin chops for stuffing, so naturally this is a dish to make when the price is right. In western Pennsylvania, stuffed pork chops are to be found on the table of every class, from blue collar to school tie.

Serves 2

2 center-cut loin pork chops, 1½ inches thick
4 Tbsp. butter
¼ cup minced scallions or onion
2 Tbsp. chopped parsley

¼ tsp. dried thyme
1½ cups soft bread crumbs made from day-old bread
salt and pepper
1 egg, beaten

Have the fat trimmed to a quarter-inch rim and ask the butcher to make a pocket without splitting open the whole chop—this is done with a small curved knife, or a small straight boning knife. Melt 2 tablespoons of the butter and sauté the onions or scallions until limp but not browned. Stir in the parsley, thyme, and ¾ cup of the soft bread crumbs, and season to taste with salt and pepper. Stuff the chops with this and skewer them or sew them closed. Coat each chop in beaten egg and then in the rest of the bread crumbs, pressing them into the meat. Leave them to dry 15 minutes. **Preheat the oven to 325°.**

Brown the breaded chops in the remaining 2 tablespoons butter; then lay them on a rack in a baking pan. Bake, uncovered, for 1 hour, or until tender. If they begin to look dry, baste with a little melted butter. Buttered parsnips and cabbage salad go with this wintry meal.

RAGOÛT DE PORC

Although a stew made of fresh pork is a rarity in American cooking, there are several diverting ones in both French and Mexican cookery. Boned pork shoulder is the stuff of all of them, but it is used with utterly different results. This French stew has a rich, gamy, rather Burgundian flavor, which it owes to being marinated in red wine. The Mexican *tinga*, next recipe, is a curious combination of well-done pork, briefly cooked tomatoes, and a raw avocado garnish.

3 lbs. fresh pork shoulder, cut in 2-inch cubes

2 cups dry red wine (California jug wine that is making some effort to be a Bordeaux)

2 carrots, sliced

2 medium onions, sliced

2 cloves garlic, crushed

1 bay leaf

plenty of freshly milled coarse black pepper

¼ tsp. dried thyme (or more)

10 juniper berries, crushed in a mortar (or ¼ cup gin)

1 tsp. salt

salad oil

1 Tbsp. flour

2 Tbsp. tomato paste

salt

cornstarch mixed with a little water, if necessary

An earthenware casserole with a lid is ideal both for marinating and cooking this dish (the Mexican one too), but if you haven't one, a 3-quart bean pot is a cheap, attractive substitute. You can cook the stew in any heavy pot, but the marinating must be done in china, earthenware, or stoneware.

Trim away as much fat as possible because this cut has considerable marbling within the meat. Boil all the remaining ingredients together *except* the tomato paste, salt, salad oil, and flour. Cool the marinade, and pour it over the pork, mixing all the ingredients together. Cover and store in the icebox for 3 days, stirring the meat once or twice a day. (You may leave it 4 or 5 days if you wish.)

Preheat oven to 325°. Dry the meat and brown it in some oil, sprinkle it with 1 tablespoon of flour, and stir-fry a couple of minutes. Pour in the marinade with all the vegetables, herbs, and spices. Add enough water to cover the meat completely, stir in the tomato paste, bring the stew to a simmer, and season to taste with salt. Set the casserole on the lower shelf of the preheated oven. Braise for 3 hours, or until you can cut the meat with a spoon. The sauce should be a mahogany brown and as thick as heavy cream. If it isn't, stir a little cornstarch mixed with cold water into the ragout and simmer briefly. Serve with boiled or mashed potatoes sprinkled with parsley.

TINGA POBLANA

Elisabeth Lambert Ortiz is the English wife of a Mexican diplomat, and it is to her we owe the only good Mexican cookery book in the English language. Her desire to learn Mexican cuisine, or to cook at all, was regarded as an embarrassing aberration by her husband's family. Because all the cooking was done by illiterate peasants, there were few written recipes. Mrs. Ortiz harassed old market women, her mother-in-law's cook, her own maid, and anyone who would talk to her about food until she acquired enough knowledge to write *The Complete Book of Mexican Cooking,* a splendid compendium of recipes, techniques, and gastronomic history of Mexico. Her book contains many *tingas, adobos, guisos,* and *moles,* which are all stews of one sort or another made with pork. If you are one of those unfortunate souls who thinks Mexican cookery begins and ends with chile, I urge you to try this unusual stew.

I realize that in some places avocados are expensive (not in my neighborhood, where they sometimes go four-for-a-dollar), but this flourish isn't absolutely essential.

Serves 6

2 Tbsp. lard or salad oil
3 lbs. boneless pork [shoulder], cut in 2-inch cubes
salt
2 *chorizo* sausages, skinned and sliced [about 6 inches of pepperoni, a hot Italian dry sausage, is a possible substitute]
1 onion, finely chopped (about 1 cup)
1 clove garlic, chopped (minced)
1 pound (about 3 medium) tomatoes, peeled, seeded, and chopped, or 1½ lb. can of

best quality, whole tomatoes, drained and seeded
½ tsp. oregano
2 canned *chipotle* chiles, chopped [small brick-red, very hot pickled peppers]
pinch of sugar (optional) [I opt out]
freshly ground pepper
12 new potatoes, freshly cooked and peeled [I don't peel]
1 avocado, peeled and sliced [marinated in a little lemon juice to prevent darkening and sharpen flavor]

"Heat the lard in a large, heavy skillet, and brown the pork. Transfer the pork to a flameproof casserole with a lid; barely cover with water; season with salt; and cook, covered, over a moderate heat until the meat is tender when pierced with a fork—about 2 hours. Strain off the stock, leaving the pork in the casserole, and set it aside.

"In the fat remaining in the skillet, fry the sausages, and add to the casserole. Then fry the onion and garlic until limp. Add the tomatoes, oregano, chiles, and sugar to the pan, and cook, stirring, for about 5 minutes. Stir in about 1 cup of the reserved stock. The sauce should be quite thick. Season to taste with salt and pepper. Add the potatoes to the casserole, and pour the sauce over all. Cook, uncovered, over very low heat for about 15 minutes. Garnish with sliced avocado."

PORK LIVER PÂTÉ

Pâtés would never have become so popular in France if they were not thrifty, sensible, delicious solutions to what to do with some of the less desirable parts of a beast, embellished with odd bits of expensive cuts. Pâtés can be made of just about any kind of meat or fowl, they keep well (in French farmhouses they are put up in wide-mouthed canning jars, sealed with a layer of fresh pork fat that preserves the pâté without refrigeration for up to a year), can be simple or elaborate, cheap or expensive, and are in general *a good thing*. Pork liver is preferred for this and many other pâtés. It will not be improved by using expensive calf's or baby beef liver. It would be improved by truffles, but then what wouldn't?

1 lb. fresh bacon or pork fat-back, or 1 lb. salt pork fat-back
2 lbs. pork liver
½ cup heavy cream
2 oz. brandy (*fines* are cheaper than cognac)
½ pig's foot
¼ lb. bacon, sliced (approximately)
2 cloves garlic
1 small onion
1 Tbsp. freshly milled coarse black pepper
¼ tsp. *each*: mace, cloves, allspice—ground
2 tsp. salt
¼ tsp. thyme
1 bay leaf
4 oz. dry white wine
½ cup water
1 small white onion, sliced (½ cup)
¼ cup sliced carrots

Fresh bacon, that is, unsmoked bacon, isn't always easy to find, but that is the number-one choice for this pâté. Next in order is the fresh pork fatback, which the butcher may be able to cut off a loin of pork. (Or make this pâté when you are cooking a loin of pork.) If salt pork is the best you can do, it must be washed thoroughly in cold water, then left to soak overnight in cold water. The bacon, which will line the terrine, must also be soaked in cold water for about an hour to remove some of the smoky taste, but not all.

Preheat oven to 325°.

Cube the pork liver, then purée it in the blender, using the cream and brandy to keep the blender from clogging. You could also use eggs for this purpose. Purée the garlic and onion along with the liver. Grind or mince the pork fat finely and add it to the liver mixture. Put this in a bowl with the pepper, mace, cloves, allspice, salt, and thyme and mix it thoroughly. Line a bread tin, Pyrex meatloaf pan, or something similar with the sliced bacon, leaving long ends to overlap across the top. Pour in the pâté mixture and overlap the bacon strips, sealing it up. Lay the bay leaf, carrots, pig's foot, and onion on top; pour on the wine and water mixed. Cover the terrine tightly with two thicknesses of foil and set it in a baking pan filled with enough hot water to come two-thirds up the side of the terrine. Bake the pâté in the oven for 3 hours, adding more boiling water if necessary. Remove the pig's foot, vegetables, and bay leaf, and cool. Cover and chill in the refrigerator. Unmold on a platter and serve with kosher dill gherkins and good bread.

NOTE: The pig's foot, vegetables, water, and wine are to make an automatic jelly surrounding the pâté—usually this is done by pouring melted aspic around the pâté after it is chilled. If you don't care for the jelly, just skip those last ingredients, but open the foil to brown the pâté in the last 15 minutes.

HOMEMADE SAUSAGE

This is better and cheaper than any commercially made sausage you can buy—you also have the satisfaction of knowing exactly what you're eating. Some commercial meat packers pad their sausages with cereals, extra fat, and some parts of the pig one would rather not dwell on. Divide the sausage into family-size packets and freeze it immediately—fresh sausage does not keep well.

2 lbs. fresh pork shoulder	½ tsp. dried thyme (you may prefer sage—I don't)
1 Tbsp. salt	freshly milled coarse black pepper
1 tsp. hot Hungarian rose paprika (or 2 tsp. Italian crushed red pepper flakes, which makes a rather hot sausage)	2 Tbsp. parsley, finely minced
	2 cloves garlic, crushed

In New York City, the butchers will not grind pork for you, but in some cities they will. A plain hand grinder is an inexpensive and essential kitchen tool to have anyway. Somehow, get the pork ground once, or twice if you like a closer-textured sausage. Put the pork in a bowl with all the remaining ingredients and mix very thoroughly with your hands—a spoon will take all day and won't do the job properly. Shape it into small flat patties (if you make them too thick, the outside will be too hard and crusty before the interior is cooked). Fry them slowly over medium-low heat, adding no fat to the skillet, which should be a black iron spider. Very little fat should accumulate, but pour it off if it does. Ten minutes should be long enough to cook them.

TOAD-IN-THE-HOLE

Mrs. Beeton describes this English favorite as "a homely but savoury dish," although her recipe transforms this working-class meal into a genteel pie of steak and kidneys. It is actually sausages embedded in Yorkshire pudding, or, in a pinch, mashed potatoes. It's a dish that always brings to mind Paul West's wild, half-crazed, comic *Alley Jaggers*, a "poor yob what plasters walls" in a Midlands village—perhaps because West has suffused the novel with more food images than the *Larousse Gastronomique*.

Serves 2–3

1 lb. pure pork link sausages, preferably large ones	2 eggs, beaten well
	1 cup milk
¼ cup beef dripping (or clarified butter)	1 cup flour
	¼ tsp. salt

Preheat oven to 450°.

Prick the sausages and simmer them in water to cover for about 5 minutes. Pour the beef dripping or butter into a pie pan and set it in the oven to heat—do not let it burn. Beat the eggs in a blender or electric mixer; then gradually add the other ingredients. Beat until the batter is very smooth. Take the pie pan out and pour in a thin layer of batter. Lay the drained sausages on top of this and pour on the remainder of the batter. Bake at 450° for 10 minutes, then **reduce heat to 350°** and continue baking for another 20 minutes, when the pudding should be puffed, golden, and crisp. Serve at once.

FARMER'S DINNER

In 1891 the Kickapoo Indian Remedies salesmen were handing out a "Family Cook Book" heavily larded with testimonials to their products' efficacy. Their Sagwa Tonic (Blood, Liver, Stomach & Kidney Renovator) cured Melancholy and Malaria alike. While the "miraculous cures" and lurid descriptions of diseases are hilarious, the recipes are quite sound and sober. The author laces her instructions with such maxims as "It is not what a man earns, but what his wife saves that makes him wealthy." Accordingly, this recipe, with my comments in brackets:

"Cut a fine piece of salt pork [streak of lean] into slices one-fourth of an inch thick; put into the spider [black iron skillet], cover it well with cold water, and let it come slowly to a boil; then drain it. Into a well-beaten egg stir gradually two even spoonfuls of flour, dip the pork on both sides into this; lay the slices into a dry warm spider [it should be lightly greased is what the writer means], cook slowly until brown on both sides; dish up on a platter. Pour away the fat until there is about a tablespoonful left with the settlings of the pork; put in a pint of milk and a spoonful of flour stirred smooth in a little cold milk—dust in a little pepper and salt. Boil five minutes, stirring constantly; pour this over the slices of pork. Serve with fine mealy potatoes. Fried apples are also a good addition, and you have a dinner relished by most people and a change from the usual fried pork."

Printed on the opposite page from the recipe were several letters; this is my favorite:

Snatched from Death

"Some years ago while in Texas, I was badly affected with dyspepsia, which gradually diseased my mind until life was unbearable. In fact, a number of doctors informed me I could live only a short time. I returned home and consulted all the physicians here, and was confronted with the same answer: 'You are as good as a dead man.' At my sister's, one day, I came across a bottle of Kickapoo Indian Sagwa. I commenced to take this, and continued until I had taken six bottles, when I found I was completely cured. That was in 1887, and since then have had no recurrence of the disease. When I first began taking Indian Sagwa I weighed 112 pounds and when I stopped taking it, I weighed 147 pounds.

CHARLES A. SIBLEY
New Harmony, Ind."

BRAISED HAM

Braising allows a partly cooked ("tenderized" in supermarket parlance) ham an opportunity to pick up some much-needed flavor, supplied by wine, vegetables, and herbs. Old American and English cookbooks recommend simmering the ham in cider—but they were discussing country-cured aged ham and strong, hard cider, which has nothing to do with the pasteurized apple juice we now call "cider." But if you *can* buy some unsweetened, unpasteurized cider from a farmer, keep it in a cool place for two weeks, when it will start to effervesce slightly. Then you can drink it and cook ham in it. Allow half a pound of ham, bone in, per person.

1 whole or half "tenderized" ham (average weight of a whole ham is about 10–12 lbs.)
2–3 carrots, sliced
2 large onions, sliced
2 Tbsp. oil or butter
3 cups dry white or Rosé California jug wine (or the same amount of hard cider)
1 bouquet garni: 2 sprigs parsley, 1 bay leaf, ½ tsp. thyme, ½ tsp. rosemary, all tied in a cheesecloth bag
water
1 Tbsp. cracked black pepper

These amounts are for a half ham; more wine, cider, or water will be necessary for a whole one. However, the vegetables and the bouquet can remain the same.

Preheat oven to 300°. Wash the ham in cold water and dry it. Gently simmer the carrots and onions in the oil until the onion is limp. Lay the ham, skin side down, on top of the vegetables, add the bouquet, the wine, and enough water to come halfway up the sides of the ham. Add rather a lot of cracked pepper, at least 1 tablespoon. Bring everything to the simmer, cover the pan and braise in the preheated oven for approximately 20 minutes to the pound. Baste occasionally and turn the ham over halfway through its cooking time. The iliac bone near the shank can be pulled out easily when the ham is done, or test the ham with a sharp kitchen fork for tenderness. Let the ham cool in its cooking liquid. After this, skin it and trim the fat smoothly. You may serve it as it is, carved in thin slices, or you may score the fat, cover it with your favorite glaze, and bake it until it is browned and heated through. Personally I think ham is tastier and certainly a lot easier to carve at room temperature or slightly chilled.

Another classic way of finishing a ham is to skin it when it's cooled, cover it with a mixture of fine soft crumbs and ground parsley, **bake it in the oven at 350°** until the coating is golden, and then cool again to room temperature before carving.

You can use the cooking liquid for a soup (bean, for instance), or make a sauce for the ham as follows: strain the braising liquid, skim off the fat, reduce the liquid to 2½ cups. Mix together a little cornstarch and sherry, port, or Madeira. Stir in enough of it to make the sauce the texture of very heavy cream. Add to this ¼ cup of heavy cream, taste for seasoning, and serve as a sauce for warm ham.

Ham prepared in this way is excellent in any recipe calling for cooked ham; in soufflés and omelets, ham mousse, scalloped ham and potatoes, sliced ham in cheese sauce, ham lightly warmed in butter to serve with eggs, or just plain cold slices to serve with potato salad.

JAMBON PERSILLÉ

Ham is to Easter what turkey is to Thanksgiving in most households. And so it is in Burgundy, famous for its hams and its monasteries, among other things, and the mustard of its capital city, Dijon. This glittering pink-and-green aspic of ham and parsley is a Burgundian Easter specialty. It would make a spectacular summer dish for a large buffet party—or, for that matter, a winter buffet.

½ **ham (about 6 lbs.) cooked according to the recipe for Braised Ham, page 179, made with white wine**
1 **whole calf's foot**
1 **lb. cracked veal bones**
1 **cup fresh, bright green parsley, minced**
1 **Tbsp. white wine vinegar (tarragon-flavored if possible)**

Add the calf's foot and the veal bones to the braising pan to add flavor and gelatinous properties to the broth. If you can't get these two items (the calf's foot is the more important), use 1 envelope of plain un-flavored gelatine for each pint of stock to stiffen the aspic.

When the ham is done, skin it, cut away all the fat and gristle, and discard the bone. Pull the meat to shreds, put it in a wooden bowl, and pound it with a wooden potato masher. Reduce the broth to 4 cups, strain it through damp cheesecloth laid in a sieve over a bowl, and put it into the freezer until the fat congeals. Remove the fat carefully and wipe the surface of the jellied broth with a damp paper towel. Bring the broth to a simmer and either clarify it (as directed on page 167) or not as you wish. The elegance of the dish is increased if the colors are distinct, so clarifying is worthwhile here.

If you are using the gelatine, soften it first in a little cold water; then stir it into the hot clarified broth to dissolve it completely. Stir in 1 tablespoon of white wine vinegar. Cool this to lukewarm; then stir in the minced parsley. Chill a plain, round-bottomed, 3-quart bowl (dishes with crevices are much harder to unmold) and line it with some of the half-set parsley aspic. Chill it. Mix the remaining parsley aspic with the pounded ham and turn it into the aspic-lined bowl and chill very thoroughly. It's a good idea to make this two or three days in advance, most certainly at least one day before it is to be served. To unmold, loosen the edges of the Jambon Persillé with a thin sharp knife, cover it with a big, round flat plate, and invert the whole thing. Cover the bottom and sides of the bowl with towels wrung out in very hot water for a few seconds until the jellied ham drops out onto the plate. If you have some other way of detaching an aspic from its mold, by all means use the one you're accustomed to. Cut in thin wedges, this will serve about 15 people. Watercress and hard-cooked eggs tinted in beet juice are a nice garnish for the Jambon Persillé, a time-consuming but very festive dish for special occasions.

12

VEGETABLES

I sometimes think that fresh vegetables may, like the blotting paper wiped out by the ballpoint pen, become an anachronism in my own lifetime. Frozen-food plants (freezeries?) and the distribution economics of the country have nearly succeeded in making fresh vegetables a luxury to everyone but the farmers who grow them. However, *in-season* vegetables are something we all get a shot at, if we can just remember what they're supposed to look—and taste— like from year to year. Frozen produce is eerily bright-hued, although some of it is excellent and perhaps fresher than the "fresh" vegetables that often are lugged halfway (or *all* the way) across the country to market. Freezeries and canneries are usually built very near the produce they process.

Fresh vegetables will never, ever, look like the Technicolor wonders in women's magazines. Those are really pieces of pop sculpture —leftovers from a Claes Oldenburg show. For example, cooked fresh peas are really sort of a dull grayish-green, not the color of an Antonioni lawn. Although frozen peas are still that firefly green, they have improved enormously. Canned peas can be excellent if one buys the youngest and tiniest kind (English tinned peas are tinted a revolting green that bleeds into other foods). Since there are rarely more than three or four vegetables in peak season at once (except in August, when it still makes little difference to New York greengrocers, who get all of their stuff from as far away as possible when Long Island is bulging with exquisite produce), we must use canned and frozen vegetables or die of boredom.

The United States Department of Agriculture grades are pretty obvious: Grade A is that manufacturer's very best, in terms of taste, color, and tenderness. Grade B means they're still good quality but older vegetables. Grade C means they're older and uneven in color and flavor. They are also the cheapest, but, unless they're going to be used in a soup or some kind of puréed dish, are probably so unpalatable there's more waste than thrift involved. "Packed under continuous inspection of the U.S.D.A." is the bottom, and assures you of nothing except that it isn't poisoned.

Now the catch about all these grades is, and I quote from the Government's own pamphlet, "Use of the U.S. grade standards and inspection service is *voluntary*, and *paid for* by the user" (italics mine). According to my own personal survey, few of the top food processors give a hoot for the U.S.D.A. grades. They rely on their own "brand-name" image to woo the customer. Of course they must protect those "brand names" with food that is of the highest quality —and the highest price. Where the U.S.D.A. grades can be useful is in purchasing unadvertised chain-store house brands, which are often very good buys. In the Grade A category, the big chains offer canned fruits and vegetables of a quality comparable to most of the more expensive "name" brands.

Frozen-food processors apparently give even less than a hoot about U.S.D.A. grading. Despite the fact that almost none of them have any famous "brand names" (most consumers would falter after naming Birds Eye), I have yet to see a U.S.D.A. grade on *any* frozen product. I suppose it's rather a lot to expect private enterprise to both *volunteer* and *pay for* a critical appraisal of their products. Consumers should demand that the Government make grading free and mandatory.

The only thing that *is* mandatory is inspection for wholesomeness, and this isn't up to the U.S.D.A. It is the responsibility of the Food and Drug Administration, whose reputation is sliding faster than Warren G. Harding's, after the recent "additives and preservatives" squabbles and turnabouts, to say nothing of the spectacular botulism-in-the-vichysoisse caper that killed one and sickened several people before the maker shut down its ironically named Bon Vivant plant in New Jersey. (Simmering food for 30 minutes destroys the toxins of botulism, which are unfortunately odorless and invisible, but not the bacteria.) Do not buy severely dented cans—even if they're marked to 5¢ apiece—or cans with bulging ends or seams, an almost certain sign of spoilage.

Frozen vegetables are often left lying in supermarket corridors long enough to soften or even thaw completely before they are stacked in their proper bins. This is probably no health hazard, but the refreezing certainly affects the color and flavor of frozen food. If the packages look a bit frowsy or stained, or are stuck together, they've probably been thawed and refrozen. Naturally, you wouldn't buy squashy packets, which are clearly either coming from or going to the freezing point. If you have room to store them, the large transparent bags of loose-frozen vegetables are not only cheaper, but you can pour out just the required amount easily, and if they're not loose in the bag, it's easy to tell they've been thawed and refrozen.

But no one needs to be told how to *cook* canned and frozen vegetables, so this chapter deals almost exclusively with fresh, in-season vegetables or combination dishes that will make a meal-in-one.

ASPARAGUS

Neither canned nor frozen asparagus is *ever* any bargain, nor is it much good. But fresh asparagus during April and May can drop to as little as 29¢ a pound. The big, fat expensive stalks are half woody waste and to my mind not nearly so good as the long, slender (⅝-inch) green asparagus with an almost entirely edible stalk—if you peel it part way.

This aristocrat of veges was esteemed by the ancient Greeks and Romans, and their way of eating it—with the fingers—is still the custom in France. It's the best way too; forks ruin the flavor. Asparagus soup, soufflé, gratin, hollandaise, béarnaise; cold with mayonnaise or vinaigrette or, simplest of all, fresh and glistening with butter beside a plump, yellow omelet.

TO BOIL ASPARAGUS

While one of those enamelware French oblong asparagus-cookers is indeed a nice thing to have (you can boil corn on the cob and any other vegetable in it too), an old-fashioned speckled enamel oval roaster will do as well. Asparagus may be cooked in a wide skillet (though not iron) and there are those who advocate the inverted double-boiler technique: the stalks are tied in serving bunches and stood on their ends in boiling water, leaving about two inches of tip exposed to steam only. But if you peel the stalks up three inches they will cook in the same length of time as the tips anyway. With the exception of the double-boiler method, do this:

Peel the stalks after snapping off the woody section. Tie the asparagus in serving bundles with soft string, which enables you to remove it quickly when it reaches the just tender stage.

Bring to a boil enough salted water to cover the asparagus by one inch. Lay the bunches in gently, and after the water returns to a boil, reduce the heat so that the water bubbles slowly and cook, uncovered, until crisp-tender. This usually takes only about 5 minutes but it could take 10. Test by balancing (not piercing) one stalk (which is left free for this purpose) on a long fork. When it just begins to droop very slightly, it's done. If it flops over lamentably, it's overdone and you had better make soup out of this batch.

Have ready a long platter with a clean white napkin or towel on it. Lift out the asparagus by its strings and lay each bundle on the cloth. If you're serving asparagus as a first course, transfer each bundle to a hot plate, quickly remove the strings, and get it to the table right away with hollandaise, mock hollandaise, sauce mousseline, or just melted butter and lemon. If you're going to serve it cold, untie all the strings and cool the asparagus quickly before chilling covered with plastic wrap. Fresh hot asparagus with a little piece of salty ham seems to me a lovely meal in spring—just as in August one of my favorite feasts is a mound of fresh buttered corn on the cob accompanied by nothing except sliced ripe tomatoes.

ASPARAGUS GRATIN

I can imagine the consternation of some readers upon discovering this entry in a book devoted to "cheap food." As a side dish, it *is* a luxury; as a main course, it is a satisfying, nutritious, delicious, and inexpensive meal. Just pretend it's Lent, or that you're a vegetarian, and remember that you don't *need* meat every day. Vegetarian meals needn't be dull, although some of their evangelists do their utmost to make it seem that way. You might appease the meat maniac with a bitey salad of fresh spinach in vinaigrette dressing with a bit of bacon crumbled over it.

Serves 2

1½ lbs. fresh green asparagus
1½ cups sauce Mornay (see recipe, page 34)
  3 Tbsp. soft bread crumbs
  2 Tbsp. butter

Preheat oven to 400°. Prepare and cook the asparagus as in the preceding recipe for plain boiled asparagus. Butter a long, shallow oven-to-table casserole; lay the asparagus (strings removed, of course) in it, and pour over the hot sauce Mornay. Sprinkle the crumbs over the top and dot with the butter, divided in tiny bits. Bake until hot and bubbly, about 10 minutes. If the top isn't a golden color, run the dish briefly under a broiler flame, watching closely.

GREEN BEANS IN BUTTER

Green, French, string, or snap beans are all the same thing—to begin with. Pale green, slender, crisp, and dewy fresh, few vegetables are more appetizing. But they are seldom cooked properly anywhere but in France, and alas, New York's French restaurants appear to have forgotten all they ever knew about the business of cooking vegetables. The French method (open boiling in lots of water) is heresy to American home economists, who I daresay are accurate in claiming that this dissipates half the vitamins. They may be right, but half the vitamins is better than none and at least the vegetables aren't left on the plate cooked the French way. *Les haricots vertes* alone can lure me to Paris, even if the Sacré-Coeur were replaced by a supermarket. By serving the beans as a first, or separate, course, you will give them their due attention and save money, too, since you can then serve a smaller meat course or a soufflé.

Serves 4

1 lb. slender, fresh green beans   salt and pepper
3 quarts boiling water   hard-cooked egg yolk (optional)
2 tsp. salt   parsley (optional)
2–3 Tbsp. butter or margarine

Wash and pick over the beans and snap off the tips. I have not bought any beans in years that had strings, but if yours do, pull them off. Leave the beans whole, but if any are thicker than a third of an inch in diameter, slit them about halfway up the length so that they will cook in the same time as the others. Drop them into the boiling water, add the salt, and boil slowly, uncovered, until the beans are crisp-tender. This could be 5, 10, or 15 minutes if the beans are old (in which case, you should not have bought them). Bite one to test.

When they are just right, immediately drain in a colander and plunge the colander into a waiting basin of ice water to cool the beans instantly. They will keep their texture and bright green color even though you do not use them right away. Empty them onto a clean, dry towel. You may complete the recipe to this point several hours before serving. Heat the butter in a heavy skillet, toss in the beans, and keep them moving by shaking the pan until they are hot through. Salt and pepper to taste and serve at once. The beans are splendid as is, but if you want to gussy them up, sieve a little hard-cooked egg yolk over them and sprinkle with chopped parsley. Some people dress beans in a sauce béchamel, but I don't.

VARIATION: Green Beans Vinaigrette

Cook the beans as above. Chill covered in plastic wrap until serving time. Mix gently with vinaigrette dressing, chopped scallions or chives, and some tiny bits of peeled, seeded tomato. Do *not* pour the vinaigrette onto the warm beans; they will absorb it and become flabby. Good with baked Virginia ham and various cold buffet dishes.

FRESH GREEN BEANS SZECHUAN

The Szechuan province of China is noted for a cuisine spiced with dried red peppers and hot oil, but this dish is not. At my favorite Szechuan restaurant, the waiter staggers out with a half bushel of beans for one order. You might serve this (real) Chinese vegetable with my Fake Chinese Meal (see page 58)—or just with a bowl of fried rice.

Serves 3

   1 lb. fresh, thin green beans
   1 pork chop, ½ inch thick
1–2 Tbsp. peanut oil
   1 Tbsp. soy sauce

Cook the green beans according to the preceding recipe for Green Beans in Butter, *except* boil them for 5 minutes only.

Grind up the pork chop, fat and all. Heat the oil in a wok or very roomy skillet and brown the ground pork quickly over a high flame. Scoop out the pork with a slotted spoon and set aside. In the remaining oil, toss the half-cooked green beans and stir-fry (keep them moving with chopsticks or the handle of a wooden spoon) until the outside is slightly crisp and the interior just tender. Toss in the reserved ground pork and stir into the beans with the soy sauce. Turn onto a hot platter and serve at once.

BROWNED BRUSSELS SPROUTS

When I think of all the vegetables I hated as a child—and the list was endless—Brussels sprouts came in around third. (Rutabagas, which I still despise, were Number One.) I was converted when a friend showed me how to make sprouts this way: parboiled almost tender, cooled, and then butter-fried to a crisp, black-brown crustiness.

Serves 3

1 package frozen Brussels sprouts (baby, if possible)
  salt
2 Tbsp. clarified butter (or ½ butter, ½ oil)
  freshly milled black pepper

Partially thaw the sprouts; then drop them into 2 cups of salted boiling water. Simmer, uncovered, until barely tender—do not overcook, as there will be further cooking. Drain in a colander and lower the colander into a bowl of ice water for 30 seconds or so. Drain the sprouts on paper towels. Heat the clarified butter (the milky residue in unclarified butter burns too easily) sizzling hot before adding the cold, dry Brussels sprouts. Shake the skillet every few minutes so that the sprouts are browned and crisp on all sides; this should require about 5 minutes over medium-high flame. Pepper the vegetable well and serve with beef, pork, lamb, or turkey.

BEETS AND BORSCHT

Richard Gehman, a novelist, journalist, and raconteur I have mentioned elsewhere, claims he ate beet slices, baked by a street seller, called the *Dasht Faroosht* in Teheran. His anecdote is a lot better than the beets, I'll bet. Gehman has precisely captured my own feelings on this subject: "The truth is, beets are not much good. People say they are, but they are wrong. Borscht is abominable." I can only add that the French theatrical slang word corresponding to our "turkey" is "navet," which translates: turnip—the next thing to beets.

Anybody who wants to can buy them in cans for practically nothing. I've had home-canned beets and beets just ripped out of the garden soil —and I cannot see that one is any better than the other. Beets are edible if wine vinegar and pickling spices are added to their liquid and they are left to steep for a day or two. The liquid is good for coloring hard-boiled eggs at Easter time, and if the eggs are left in the beet juice and vinegar very long they can be used for playing jacks.

SOUTHERN FRIED CABBAGE

In nearly every French province, cabbage is the mainstay of the peasants, who live chiefly on this vegetable, even though it has little nourishment, is windy, and spreads an evil odor.
      —Alexander Dumas, *Le Grand Dictionnaire de Cuisine*

Cabbage is the mainstay of the proletariat in all the cooler regions of the world, and, as Dumas admits, was venerated by the ancients. Pickled cabbage (sauerkraut) was invented by the Chinese thousands of years ago, and to this day the common diet of the poorer Korean peasant is rice and *kim chee*, a spicy, hot pickled cabbage that "spreads an evil odor" all right. Dumas may have been right about the food value of cabbage cooked, as it was in the mid-nineteenth century, for hours on end. This method is neither windy nor foul-smelling, and it fair bulges with nutrients (vitamin A, calcium, and ascorbic acid).

Serves 4

1 small head green cabbage, shredded
3 Tbsp. bacon fat (or more)
2 tsp. red pepper flakes
  salt to taste

Wash and shred, do not grate, the cabbage. Cut the cabbage in quarters; then make thin slices across the cut sides of the cabbage, discarding the white core and any tough ribs. Heat the bacon fat in an iron Dutch oven, toss in the cabbage, and stir until it is all glistening. Lower the heat, add the pepper flakes, and continue cooking and turning the cabbage until it is barely tender—about 10 minutes.

ALSATIAN CHOUCROUTE GARNI

Alsace is a province of rich farms, fields of hops, vineyards, crotchety political autonomists, and a culture spread-eagled between French and German. Choucroute Garni, the regional specialty (not counting *pâté de foie gras*), expresses this. It may start out as pickled cabbage but it doesn't end up just sauerkraut. Never a sauerkraut fancier (in the South no one had the vaguest notion of what to do with it), I was smitten with *choucroute* and it has become one of my favorite dishes. In Strasbourg, which is famous for its enormous variety of beautifully designed and delicious *charcuterie*, the dish is laden with weisswurst, bratwurst, *Ripchen*, *Landjäger*, and sometimes ham and slices of smoked salt pork. It may be as elaborately or as simply garnished as means dictate. Oh, yes—it is also garnished with *les quenelles de foie* (liver dumplings), which I have never learned to make. In fact my history with all kinds of dumplings is dismal—but if you can produce the little cloudlike mouthfuls, serve them with this dish. Boiled potatoes are traditional as the bland foil for all this richness. If you have no German neighborhood to buy in, the dish is probably not worth trying with endless substitutions.

Serves 6

2–3 lbs. sauerkraut (from a barrel or in plastic bags—never canned)

¼ lb. smoked bacon jowl (*Speck* in German)

1 medium onion, peeled and stuck with 2 cloves

1 bouquet garni: 2 cloves garlic, mashed, 1 bay leaf, 10 juniper berries, mashed (or ¼ cup gin), sprig of parsley, pinch of dried thyme, tied in a cheesecloth bag

2 cups dry white wine

freshly ground black pepper

1 garlic sausage (a *Landjäger*, smoked Hungarian paprika sausage, garlic salami, or any hard, garlicky, well-smoked sausage that won't disintegrate)

water to cover

The Garnish

Weisswurst, a small white veal and pork sausage

Bratwurst: a fat, pinkish-gray pork sausage

Kassler Ripchen: salted (and sometimes smoked) pork loin, cut in chops (it is sold precooked)

Knockwurst: fat frankfurters (never so in Alsace, but an acceptable substitute)

Frankfurters: good ones, and for size contrast, cocktail franks, boiled

Loin of pork, roasted, carved in chops, and placed in a circle around the *choucroute*

Small Boston butt picnic ham, simmered 30 minutes to the pound and sliced thinly to decorate the *choucroute*

Two or three of the above suggestions, contrasting the flavors and shapes as much as possible, should be enough.

Preheat oven to 325°. Put the sauerkraut into a colander and wash it in cold water, pulling it apart with your fingers until it is fluffy and most of the saltiness is gone. Cut the jowl bacon into thin slices and line a heavy nonmetallic casserole with half of the bacon. Put the washed and drained sauerkraut on top of the bacon and bury the bouquet in the middle along with the garlic sausage and onion. Pour on the wine and enough water to cover the ingredients. Seal with foil and a cover. Bring to a simmer topstove, then set into the preheated oven for 3 hours. Be careful not to let the *choucroute* cook dry. Add more boiling water if necessary from time to time. When the *choucroute* is done, it should have absorbed all but about half a cup of its cooking liquid. Prepare all the meats separately, cook some boiled potatoes, and heat the dinner plates and a large platter. Arrange the drained *choucroute* in the middle and dispose the various meats and sausages around it. It must be served very hot, so keep the platter in the oven until people are seated at the table.

STUFFED CABBAGE

Chou farci sounds absolutely elfin—like the name of some langorous, throaty chanteuse. The sight of the words "stuffed cabbage," however, always used to dull my eye and set my liver aflame. To my great surprise, I discovered that I'd been snubbing a very fine dish. There are lots of ways to stuff a *chou*—Russian, German, Balkan, probably Scandinavian, for all I know—but this is the most delicate recipe I've tried.

1 firm, fresh head green cabbage
1 cup onions, chopped
1 Tbsp. butter or oil
1 lb. lean ground pork shoulder
1 tsp. salt
1 tsp. freshly milled pepper
½ tsp. thyme
  pinch of sage
1 cup coarsely crumbled dry
  bread

1 Tbsp. parsley, chopped
1 egg, beaten
2 slices thick bacon or washed
  salt pork
1 onion stuck with 2 cloves
1 carrot
1 cup V-8 (or any mixed vegetable) juice
2 cups water or beef stock

Preheat oven to 300°.

Wash cabbage and discard any unsightly leaves. Parboil 10 minutes in salted water, plunge it into cold water, then invert and drain well in a colander. Meanwhile, prepare the stuffing. Sauté the onions and ground pork in a little butter or oil until onions are tender. Drain off fat and add salt, pepper, thyme, sage, bread crumbs, and parsley. Bind the stuffing with the beaten egg. Carefully spread the cabbage apart so that you can cut out a core large enough to accommodate half the stuffing. Fill this cavity; then put a thin layer of stuffing between the leaves until it is all used. Reshape the cabbage and tie it firmly in a washed cheesecloth bag.

Lay the bacon in a heavy casserole of about the same size as the cabbage, which is set on the bacon. Add the onion, carrot, vegetable juice, and water. Bring to a simmer topstove; then cover and braise slowly in the oven for about 2 hours. Add more water if necessary. When it is done, remove the cabbage to a hot shallow bowl and discard the cheesecloth. Strain the cooking liquid, skim the fat from it, and reduce it to 1 cup. Pour this over the stuffed cabbage and serve.

STUFFED EGGPLANT

Despite its beauty of form and gentle nature, this bland vegetable polarizes people quicker than a discussion about dope addicts on welfare. Small eggplants (why, oh, why didn't we go along with the English in calling this by its French name, *aubergine?*) are better than big ones, but unless you garden, you will never get the baby eggplants—about three inches long—required for many French and Middle Eastern recipes. Invariably overgrown but attractive, eggplants are available year around now in our markets.

Serves 2

2 small (5-inch-long) eggplants,
    or 1 large one
salt
2 Tbsp. olive oil
1 onion, chopped
2 cloves garlic, minced
½ lb. ground lamb or beef
1–2 Tbsp. curry powder

salt and pepper to taste
½ cup cooked white rice
¼ cup soft bread crumbs
2 Tbsp. parsley, chopped
olive oil
½ cup tomato juice mixed with
½ cup water or broth

Slice the eggplants in half lengthwise and make diagonal slashes in the flesh. Sprinkle the cut side with salt and lay the eggplant on a rack to drain for 30 minutes. Prepare the stuffing by scooping out the eggplant with a small melon ball cutter or getting it out the best way you can and dicing it. Leave a firm rim of flesh in the shells—about a quarter of an inch.

Preheat oven to 350°. Heat the olive oil in a skillet and fry the onion, garlic, and lamb or beef together 5 or 10 minutes, stirring often. Add the eggplant pulp and cook until the vegetables are tender and some of their moisture has evaporated. Add the curry powder and rice and season to taste with salt and more pepper than usual. Pile the stuffing into the shells and top with the bread crumbs mixed with parsley. Drizzle a bit of oil over the top. Oil a baking dish and place the stuffed eggplants in it close together, so they won't be misshapen. Pour the tomato juice mixed with water or chicken stock around the base of the eggplants and bake 30 or 40 minutes, when the tops should be browned and the shells tender but firm enough to hold their shape. Spoon some of the cooking liquid over the top of the stuffed eggplants and serve.

FRENCH-FRIED EGGPLANT

This simple preparation was my first favorable impression of eggplant, a vegetable then as mysterious and exotic to me as cardoons and salsify. Italian P.O.W.'s awaiting the end of the war in some kind of political limbo cooked for the mess at a military hospital where I struggled with my summer job. Unauthorized crashers were always trying to sidle into our mess hall, the envy of the airbase.

1 firm, blemishless eggplant of about 1 lb.
salt and ice water
flour, salt, pepper, and thyme
deep fat for frying

Pare the eggplant and cut it into thin sticks. Soak them in salted ice water for one hour; then drain and dry in towels. Shake them in a bag with seasoned flour (salt, pepper, and thyme), shake off excess flour, put the eggplant sticks into a wire basket, and lower it into deep, boiling fat or oil. In a few minutes shake gently so the pieces won't stick together. When they are crisp and pale gold in about 5 minutes, drain on paper toweling and serve very hot.

VARIATION: Plain Fried Eggplant
Slice the eggplant, unpeeled, in rounds about one-quarter inch thick. Soak them in salted ice water for an hour. Drain, dry, and dredge in seasoned flour. Heat some olive oil or bacon fat (plain salad oil is too insipid) in a heavy skillet and fry the eggplant rounds a few at a time, browning them lightly on each side, about 5 minutes. Don't overcook. Salt and pepper the slices and serve with lemon wedges.

SAVOURY ONIONS

> There is in every cook's opinion,
> No savoury dish without an onion;
> But lest your kissing should be spoiled
> The onion must be thoroughly boiled.
> —DEAN JONATHAN SWIFT (1667–1745)

Raw leeks and wild onions sustained the Celts before the potato was known—the leek is the national symbol of Wales—and the ancient Egyptians elected the onion one of their many gods. (Those poor old polytheistic Egyptians have been accused of worshiping just about everything from cats to garlic; Cheops is supposed to have paid off the construction crew on his pyramid in garlic.) The onion is surely at least a culinary god, such is its influence over all our cookery. But this is one of the few states in which the onion is eaten for itself alone.

8 medium-small onions, or 4
  large flat Bermudas
⅛ lb. butter, melted
  salt and pepper

grating of nutmeg
¼ cup hot beef bouillon
¼ cup grated Parmesan cheese
  (optional)

Preheat oven to 325°.

Skin the onions by dropping them into boiling water for 1 minute and then plunging them into cold water so that the skins will slip off easily. Pierce an "x" in the root end of the onion. Brown the onions in 2 tablespoons of the butter; then set them close together in a heavy casserole, pour the remaining butter over them, and season with salt, pepper, and nutmeg. Pour the bouillon around the base of the onions, cover, and bake until tender—25 to 45 minutes, depending on the size of the onions. Sprinkle with cheese.

OKRA GUMBO

Gombo or *gombaut* migrated to the West Indies aboard slave ships and then to New Orleans and Charleston under the same circumstances. The exotic little green pods became a fixture in Southern cooking and were called okra because that's as near as the English tongue could come to the vegetable's native West African name, *nkruma.* (*Gombaut* is how it sounded to the French.) Anyway, okra and gumbo would be redundant except for this quirk: although Creole cooks invented the term gumbo, in New Orleans a gumbo does not necessarily contain okra but may be a kind of game or poultry stew thickened with filé powder, a thickening agent made from ground, dried sassafras leaves. Fortunately, you won't need any for this recipe.

1 large onion, chopped
1 clove garlic, minced
2 Tbsp. olive oil
1 medium can stewed tomatoes
  (or 3 fresh, ripe tomatoes,
  chopped, with juice)
1 dried red chile pod, minced
  and soaked in hot water
1 bay leaf

1 sprig fresh thyme (or ½ tsp.
  dried)
½ cup diced, cooked ham
1 cup fresh or frozen field peas
  (optional)
  salt and freshly milled pepper
½ lb. small, fresh okra (or 1
  package frozen sliced okra,
  thawed)

Sauté the onion and garlic in the olive oil. Add the tomatoes and their juices, the chile pod, bay leaf, thyme, ham, and salt and pepper (and, if you like them, the field peas). Simmer gently for about 1 hour.

Slice the tops off the okra and blanch it in boiling water for about 2 minutes; then plunge into cold water and drain thoroughly. This preliminary blanching checks the gluiness of okra. Slice up the okra into quarter-inch rounds, and when you're sure the field peas or anything else you put into the basic gumbo is done, throw in the okra. Simmer just crisp-tender —about 5 minutes for the frozen product, and usually no more than 10 for fresh okra. (Traditionally, okra was stewed for an hour, which gave it that objectionable stickiness.) Gumbo is a soupy sort of thing and is best served in shallow soup plates over a big spoonful of perfectly cooked white rice. Pickled hot peppers or some kind of pepper sauce is usually served on the side.

NOTE: This is just the basic gumbo, except for the field peas, which are my own idiosyncrasy and would never be put into a classy Creole gumbo. Instead, you would find delicious little soft-shelled crabs or sweet Gulf shrimp (shelled raw and thrown into the gumbo about 2 minutes before it is done), or a tender young chicken, cut up and browned along with the onions and garlic before being added to the other ingredients. In my *Picayune Creole Cookbook*, one gumbo recipe starts, "Take four dozen fresh oysters. . . ." Nowadays you'd have to add, "and run."

CREAMED SPINACH

Although this is a simple thing everyone probably knows how to make, I feel I must include a recipe because it is suggested elsewhere in the book as a background to other foods. And I have another reason: in my last book, the printer managed to interleave the recipe with four unrelated pages and I'd like to clear up those baffling instructions. Creamed spinach is an agreeable side dish with almost any meat or fish; it is the bed for a number of poached-egg dishes, and is one of the many fillings for French crepes served with some kind of sauce.

Makes about 3 cups

2 packages frozen chopped spinach
3 Tbsp. butter
¼ cup minced onion
2 Tbsp. flour

1 cup boiling milk
salt, pepper, and nutmeg to taste
grated Parmesan cheese (optional)

The spinach should be barely cooked and this is easier to control if the spinach if first thawed. If you haven't time, watch it carefully and as soon as all the spinach is loose and bubbling, it is done enough. Drain and press out most of the liquid. Leave it to cool. Heat the butter in a small, heavy saucepan and melt the onion in it without browning. Stir in the flour and cook, stirring constantly, 1 minute; then dump in the boiling milk and whisk smooth over low heat. Return spinach to sauce and season with salt, pepper, and nutmeg. Turn it into a hot serving dish and sprinkle with a very little cheese.

POTATOES

Columbus, Sir Walter Raleigh, and Francis Drake are variously credited with bringing "batatas" from the New World. Maybe they did, but they were not the white potatoes that are second only to wheat as the world's most important crop. According to the botanist Alex D. Hawkes, the conquistadores packed a few tubers along with the Inca treasures they took back to Spain from Peru early in the sixteenth century.

The "earth apples" were shunned as suspiciously as the "love apple" (tomato) and were thought to be poisonous or, at the very least, unwholesome. For some time they were planted merely as an ornamental curiosity. Even though the European peasantry subsisted on a dismal diet of gruels and hardtack, they did not take to potatoes. The Germans were the first to give in—actually the peasantry was *ordered* to plant potatoes by Frederik Willem to avert famine in the late seventeenth century. At the time, the English were adamant meat-eaters, and God knows what the Scotch, Irish, and Welsh were eating besides leeks and seaweed. Potatoes were not planted in Ireland until the mid-eighteenth century.

Although there are now more potato recipes in the French cuisine than in any other, the Gallic nose was turned up at the lowly tuber until the late eighteenth century. Parmentier, a French army veterinary surgeon, learned to like potatoes as a prisoner of war in Prussia. When he returned home, his experiments with the white-and-blue-flowered vines convinced Louis XVI they were good for more than trailing on garden walls. The king planted a field in Paris, fenced it in, and set a guard over it. The psychology worked, of course, and when one sees "Parmentier" suffixing a French dish, it indicates that potatoes are in or around it.

TRUFFADO

"Auvergnats show strong Celtic characteristics—for instance they are players of the bagpipes," writes Waverly Root in his classic book *The Food of France*. They are also potato-eaters, and *truffado* is the most typical dish of the Auvergne. There are "many differences of opinion about how to prepare it" (also Celtic). Of the many examples Root gives, I found I'd been making one of them (untitled) for many years, Truffado Mont d'Or, and from his description, I've made another quite different Truffado. Both are composed of potatoes and cheese, plain dishes that have warmed the tough Auvergne mountaineers for generations.

Serves 4

Truffado I

4 large old "boiling" potatoes	½ cup Swiss (Gruyère) or pale
3 slices thick-sliced bacon	cheddar cheese, cut in very
2 small cloves garlic, minced	small dice
⅔ cup onions, sliced thinly	chopped parsley

Preheat oven to 350°.

Peel the potatoes. Cut them in half and then in half-rounds an eighth inch thick. Soak in cold salted water. Slowly fry the bacon in a deep heavy earthenware or enameled iron casserole. Remove and drain on paper towels. Sauté the garlic and onions in the remaining bacon fat. Drain, dry, and add the sliced potatoes, turning them gently until they are lightly browned. Cover and bake in the oven until the potatoes are tender. Uncover and add the diced cheese. When it is half melted, take the casserole from the oven, crumble the bacon over the top, and sprinkle with parsley. Serve in its baking dish along with an astringent green salad.

Truffado Mont d'Or

This is really only mashed potatoes with cheese beaten into them and a few other little touches.

4 large old "boiling" potatoes	1 clove garlic, crushed through
salt	press
2 Tbsp. butter	½ cup grated Swiss or pale sharp
2 eggs, beaten	cheddar (coon cheese is very
¼ tsp. grated nutmeg	good)
¼ tsp. white pepper	3 Tbsp. additional grated cheese

Peel and quarter the potatoes. Boil them in just enough salted water to cover until just tender. Too much water and too much boiling make slushy potatoes. Drain them, put them back into the dry pot, and shake them over low heat to evaporate any remaining moisture. Mash them smoothly with the butter; then beat in the eggs, nutmeg, pepper, garlic, and the ½ cup of grated cheese. Taste and add more seasoning if necessary. Top with the 3 tablespoons of cheese and bake in a moderate oven until the potatoes are hot and the top lightly browned.

VARIATION: You could mix tiny cubes of fried slab bacon into the potatoes before baking, or some fragments of leftover ham.

RÖSTI

One of the clearest images that remains with me from a long ago reading of *Heidi* is that of the old man kneeling before the fireplace toasting cheese for his grandchild. How could you toast *cheese* on a fork, I wondered? Why didn't it run up his sleeve or string down to the hearth? The *Times, The New York Times,* has brought me the news at last: it's what the Beautiful People are eating in Gstaad, Davos, or wherever they're skiing this year. Toasted cheese and Rösti, no less. In German-speaking cantons, Rösti (pronounced *roysh*-tee) is a beloved but ordinary dish in Swiss family cooking. It's very good hot or warm, as a snack or as part of a meal.

Serves 4

    4 medium baking potatoes, baked or steamed
    ¼ cup butter
    3 or 4 minced scallions
      salt and freshly milled black pepper

Bake or steam the potatoes in their jackets to retain the maximum undiluted potato flavor. (A colander set over a pot of boiling water with a cover to trap the steam makes an adequate "steamer.") Cool and peel them, then cut them in matchsticks. Melt the butter in a heavy skillet and when it clears, add the potatoes, sprinkle with scallions, and season. Lower the heat a bit and cook slowly until the bottom forms a browned crust. With the help of a wide spatula, slide the potatoes onto a cookie sheet. Smear the skillet with butter and invert it over the unbrowned side of the potatoes. Now invert the cookie sheet over the skillet and fry until the other side of the potato cake is browned and firm. Slide onto a plate, cut in wedges, and serve.

Oh, yes, the toasted cheese. First you will need a fireplace with some good hot embers glowing in it. Then you will require a patient, leathery-faced old person with strong legs to squat in front of it. Give him a poker with a huge hunk of Gruyère stabbed onto the end of it and have him turn it slowly in front of the red-hot embers until it begins to run. Then the old gentleman snaps open the widest blade on his Swiss army knife and scrapes the cheese onto your outstretched slab of Rösti. That's the *Heidi* (or ski station) technique I extrapolated from the newspaper account. You could, of course, shred some Gruyère (that's Swiss for Swiss cheese), strew it over the finished Rösti, and run it under a hot broiler until the cheese melts.

STUFFED POTATOES WITH KIDNEYS

Klein aber fein was a platter I often ate in a terrace restaurant in Wiesbaden, Germany. It means "small but good" and it was a variety of vegetables, a big helping of whipped potatoes, and a silver-dollar-sized beefsteak. The amount of meat in this is a mere *schmecht* too, so choose a couple of nonstarchy vegetables to serve with it. This is a main course.

Serves 2

2 medium-sized Idaho or russet baking potatoes	¼ to ½ cup hot milk
salt and pepper	2 Tbsp. chopped parsley
2 Tbsp. butter	4 lamb kidneys (2 pairs)
	4 strips bacon

Wash, dry, oil, and prick the potatoes before baking them in a moderate oven until done. Split them lengthwise, scoop out the pulp, and put it through a food mill or ricer. Beat in the butter and enough hot milk to make a soft, smooth purée. Season to taste with the salt and pepper and stir in the parsley. Pile the whipped potatoes back into the shells. Wash, dry, and sear the kidneys in butter or bacon fat. Half cook the bacon and wrap one strip around each kidney. Push one kidney down halfway into the center of each stuffed potato. Put them in a pan and bake in a **preheated 350°** oven until the kidneys are medium-rare, or just a bit pink in the center, about 20 minutes. Make a tiny incision in the middle of a kidney to inspect the color. Overdone kidneys are rubbery.

FRIED GREEN TOMATOES

Green tomatoes may seem an unpromising subject, but now that the Burpee seed people have developed a hybrid tomato plant that will grow on a window sill, anyone can have them. Several good things came out of wondering what to do with fall's last tomatoes before frost killed the vine. (Many home gardeners give them away.) Hot green-tomato relish and pickled tomatoes are two of them, and this nostalgic old Southern favorite. The tomatoes should be fairly large and bright green, but not rock hard. This was a breakfast dish, but in a modern meal is more appropriate for a plain supper.

Serves 2

4 slices thick-sliced bacon
2 medium-large green tomatoes
  (or half-ripe tomatoes)
1 egg, beaten with 1 tsp. water

flour
salt and pepper
2–3 scallions, minced
¼ cup cream

Slowly fry the bacon in a heavy skillet until semi-crisp. This kind of bacon will have a burnt flavor and unchewable lean streaks if you try to cook it completely crisp. Drain the bacon on paper towels and keep it warm. Reserve the fat. Slice the tomatoes vertically from bottom to blossom end (this keeps the seeds in) about a quarter inch thick. Discard the two outer slices. Dip the slices first in egg, then in flour, then fry over medium heat in the bacon fat, adding salt and pepper as necessary. Turn once so that both sides are golden brown and crisp. Put the slices on a hot platter, pour off any remaining fat, deglaze the pan with the cream, and pour it over the tomatoes. Scatter the scallions on top and put the bacon around the tomatoes.

PAN-BROILED CHERRY TOMATOES

Pungent with garlic, basil, parsley, and olive oil, these tiny tomatoes are one of the loveliest, and easiest, garnishes I know for steak and roast red meats, or as an accompaniment to something rather bland, such as macaroni and cheese. Because they're rather overpowering, I don't think they should be served with fish or chicken. Allow 4 or 5 cherry tomatoes per person, depending on their size—the tomatoes, not the people.

16–20 deep red, ripe cherry to-   ½ tsp. dried basil, crushed
matoes (about 1 inch in di-   ½ tsp. salt
ameter).   freshly milled black pepper
¼ cup olive oil   2 Tbsp. parsley, finely chopped
2 cloves garlic, crushed

If the tomatoes aren't fully ripe, the dish is a dud. Since tomatoes are seldom sold ripe in city markets, buy them a day or two ahead and keep them in a brown paper bag on a dark shelf away from cold drafts. They will ripen to a deep red with an intense tomato flavor.

Wash the tomatoes in cold water very gently and let them drip dry. *Five minutes* before you are ready to serve your meal, heat the olive oil in a heavy skillet large enough to hold all the tomatoes in a single layer without crowding. Crush the garlic through a press into the oil. Add the basil and stir all this around over very low heat until you can smell the basil releasing its perfume. Add the tomatoes all at once, sprinkle them with salt and pepper, and cook over medium heat, shaking the pan constantly to coat and cook all sides evenly. Four or 5 minutes is enough—overcooking bursts the skins—and then you have yourself a pizzaiola sauce. Sprinkle with parsley and serve.

TOMATOES GRATIN

When you're desperate for a nonstarchy vegetable to eke out a measly meal—say there's a snowstorm; it's Yom Kippur on the Upper West Side of Manhattan—the makings for this dish are usually in the cupboard.

Serves 2–3

1 small (2-inch) onion, thinly   big pinch dried basil
sliced   pinch of celery seed
1 clove garlic, minced   salt and pepper
1½ Tbsp. olive oil   3 slices bread
1 medium can Italian plum   handful of parsley
tomatoes   1–2 additional Tbsp. olive oil

Preheat oven to 400°.

Sauté the onion and garlic in the olive oil until limp and lightly browned. Add the tomatoes plus their juices, the basil, and celery seed to the skillet. Stir and cook until the tomatoes break up somewhat and about half the juice evaporates. Season with salt and pepper. Trim the crusts from the bread, break it in chunks, and put it into the blender with the parsley. Pour the tomatoes into a small oven-to-table dish and sprinkle the parslied crumbs evenly over them. Drizzle on the olive oil and bake on the top shelf of the oven for 20 minutes. The top should be very lightly browned—if it isn't, run it under the broiler a couple of seconds.

VEGETABLE FRITTERS

The Japanese have their tempura, the Italians their *fritto misto*, the French their *beignets*, and we've got fritters. They're all pretty much the same though the batters and vegetable choices may vary. Almost any cooked vegetable can be turned into a fritter, or some, like onion rings, small green beans, and green pepper strips can be cooked from the raw state. Small whole okra pods, sticks of zucchini, cubes of eggplant, flowerets of cauliflower or broccoli, mushrooms, and celery are some of the vegetables to use for fritters. They should not be overcooked to begin with, and should be cut into rather large bite-size (two-bite size) pieces. You can also fry fish, shellfish, and chicken in the following batter.

Beer Batter
1 cup flour	¼ tsp. salt
¾ cup water	pinch of sugar
3 Tbsp. beer	1 egg white
1 Tbsp. oil	oil for deep frying

Put all ingredients except egg white in a blender and beat smooth on low speed. Cover and let stand 1 hour or more at room temperature. Just before using, beat the egg white stiff and fold it into the batter. Dip whatever vegetables you have chosen into the batter and fry quickly in deep hot salad oil (peanut oil is best). Drain on paper towels and serve very hot. These fritters do not bear waiting, and since they are done in about 3 minutes, it is a good idea to keep two woks or skillets of oil going if you can manage it.

ZUCCHINI AND SUMMER SQUASH SAUTÉ

In summer, when these green and yellow squashes are plentiful and cheap, there is no lovelier vegetable to serve with fish. You can also make a simplified *ratatouille* of them by adding some ripe tomatoes and eggplant. Summer squash, sometimes called yellow gooseneck, is, like zucchini, best when it is about six inches long. The older it gets, the more seedy it becomes, but if it is *too* small, the flavor is almost nonexistent.

Serves 4

1 lb. zucchini
1 lb. yellow summer squash
1 large mild onion, sliced thinly
2 cloves garlic, minced

3–4 Tbsp. olive oil
salt and red pepper flakes to
taste

Wash and dry the two squashes with towels, making sure all the sand is rubbed off. Slice both in eighth-inch rounds. In a deep heavy casserole, heat the oil very hot and add the two squashes, the onion, and garlic. Sauté over fairly high heat, watching carefully and turning often with a wide spatula. The vegetables should brown lightly but not burn and they mustn't become mushy. When they are just transparent and tender, season with salt and pepper flakes and transfer immediately to a serving dish. Zucchini and summer squash are watery vegetables and if left in the casserole will continue cooking and become somewhat mushy—though some people prefer them that way. If you decide to make a *ratatouille*, add the tomatoes and eggplant when the other vegetables are half cooked; it may be served hot or cold.

SFORMATO

This is Italian but you will probably not have heard of it unless you happen to *be* Italian. It's never served in restaurants but is strictly *casa cucina*. Sformato, which may be made with a number of different vegetables, is a cheap and simple cross between a soufflé and a steamed pudding. Because it doesn't rise much, it isn't as tyrannical as a conventional French soufflé and will suffer a little waiting.

If you have some meat to go with it, the amount below will serve 8 people, if not, 4 people who are otherwise padded with some salad or soup. (Chicken livers sautéed with onions and mushrooms in a little Madeira sauce provide a bit of meat and a sauce for the Sformato.)

2 packages frozen chopped
  spinach

¼ cup chopped onion
2 Tbsp. butter

2 Tbsp. flour	salt, pepper, and nutmeg
1 cup hot milk	3 egg yolks, beaten
⅓ cup grated Parmesan cheese	3 egg whites, beaten stiff

This may be baked in the oven or steamed on top of the stove. In either case you will need a large round pan at least three inches wider than your soufflé dish, which should be of about 1½- to 2-quart capacity. Both need covers, which can be made from double thicknesses of foil. Any straight-sided round or oval baking dish will serve to bake the Sformato in.

Cook the spinach according to package directions and drain, cool, and press out excess juices with the back of a spoon. Purée in a blender with the onion, adding a bit of milk if the machine clogs. If you haven't a blender, mince the two vegetables together as finely as you can.

Melt the butter in a heavy saucepan, stir in the flour, add the hot milk, and beat the sauce smooth with a wire whisk. Over very low heat, stir in the cheese and season with salt, pepper, and nutmeg to taste. Cool slightly, then beat in the egg yolks, the spinach and onion mixture, and, when tepid, fold in the beaten egg white very gently. Do not over-mix.

Scrape the mixture into a buttered baking dish and cover with foil and the dish cover. Set it in a pan containing enough hot water to extend two inches up the sides of the baking dish. Cover the whole thing with two thicknesses of foil and steam for 1 hour on the top of the stove or in the oven at 350°. Add boiling water to maintain depth.

This is supposed to be unmolded onto a hot platter and is often masked with a mushroom or cheese sauce. If unmolding things jars you, just serve it from the dish and pass the sauce separately, if you have one.

NOTE: Slices of ham or roast meat look very nice arranged in a circle around the unmolded Sformato. Peas, broccoli, or cauliflower may be substituted for the spinach. Unfortunately, frozen cauliflower is lousy and fresh cauliflower a luxury.

13

DESSERTS

A. J. Liebling in *Between Meals* describes a dessert served at Maillabuau's in Paris, 1927: "The omelette au kirsch was the sole dessert he ever permitted to be served, he said. He was against sweets on principle, since they were 'not French,' but the *omelette* was light and healthy. It contained about two dozen eggs."

M. Maillabuau's comment is as amusingly preposterous as an omelette made with two dozen eggs. French desserts are peerless; the restaurateur happened to have been a chef, not a *patissier*. I am not against desserts on principle; it's just that my passion for them cooled at the end of my adolescence. The art of the pastry chef is a very special one and requires a long apprenticeship. Besides that, it's a gift; being a crack sauce-maker doesn't guarantee you'll ever succeed with puff paste.

When I want something elegant for a dinner party, I bus over to the Patisserie Dumas on Lexington Avenue, knowing there will be wonders to choose from. But when I'm out of pocket, or out of range of this quality shop, I serve mousses, soufflés, or some kind of rather naïve pudding or fruit dessert that is simple to make.

If you seek fancy baking, I advise you to look into the superior works of Julia Child and Simone Beck, or Paula Peck's book *The Art of Fine Baking*. The selection of *bonne femme* desserts in Elizabeth David's *French Provincial Cooking* have a wholesome charm and delicacy. Of course they are made with the best quality butter, cream, eggs, and fruits. There aren't many truly cheap desserts worth eating. Considering the waistline and wallet, it's preferable to have finer desserts less often.

BIRTHDAY, WEDDING, AND WAKE CAKE

I once bought a birthday cake from a bakery for one of my children. She greeted it with a pinched expression. (It may run in the family—my grandmother never got over the idea of store-bought bread.) So for special occasions, this is the painless milestone cake I've been using for all ages. Put liqueurs in the frosting for grownups and put chocolate or orange flavor in it for kids. It looks and tastes like honest-to-God home-made poundcake if you bake it in a big fancy tube pan or spring mold (the easiest of all cake pans, because the sides can be lifted off the bottom and there is almost no possibility of sticking).

Serves about 20 (1½-inch wedges)

2 boxes Dromedary poundcake mix
   nutmeg
   grated rind of half a lemon (or more)

Preheat oven to 325°.

Grease the cake pan with unsalted shortening (Crisco or something like that) and be sure to cover every cranny. Sift in a little flour (package directions omit this old-fashioned step with rueful results) and shake it all around the pan to coat the bottom and sides with a thin film of flour. Bang the pan around the edges in three or four places and dump out the excess flour.

Follow the package directions, *but remember you are doubling* every added ingredient on the box. Add the eggs one at a time, instead of all at once. Grate in a little nutmeg, about ¼ teaspoon. Grate in the lemon rind (squeeze in some of the juice too, if you're a lemon fancier). Add the salad oil now.

You could also add at this point some finely chopped or broken nuts, some grated orange rind and a bit of juice, or a few tablespoons of cognac or bourbon, depending on the age and condition of the celebrant.

The cake is twice as big but takes more than twice the baking time in-dicated on the package—I can't explain it. Bake the cake (and don't open the oven door for at least 45 minutes) for about 1½ hours, or until a broomstraw or metal skewer comes out clean. Cool in the pan for 30 minutes; then turn it out onto a rack. When the cake is quite cold, slather on your favorite frosting. The cake looks great bare, but then it isn't really a birthday cake. I prefer it plain, the center filled with sweetened whipped cream and the base outlined in fresh strawberries.

PUMPKIN CHIFFON PIE

Traditional pumpkin pie has never been one of my favorites, but the inexorable demand for it at Thanksgiving and Christmas led me to this invention. Delicate and creamy, this pumpkin pie lies lightly on the overburdened holiday stomach.

1 8-inch baked pie shell	½ cup brown sugar
1 envelope unflavored gelatine	½ tsp. each: cinnamon, nutmeg, and ginger
¼ cup cold water	
3 egg yolks	4 egg whites
½ cup evaporated milk or cream	¼ cup white sugar
	whipped cream
1¼ cups canned puréed pumpkin	

Soften the gelatine in the cold water. Beat the egg yolks well in the top of a double boiler. Stir in the evaporated milk or cream and the pumpkin, brown sugar, and spices, mixing well. Cook, stirring over hot water, until smooth and thickened. Add gelatine and stir until dissolved. *Cool to tepid.* This is important; otherwise the hot custard will collapse the egg whites. Whip the egg whites to a fairly stiff meringue; then beat in the white sugar with a whisk or electric mixer. Spoon one third of the meringue over the pumpkin custard and fold it in with a rubber spatula to lighten it. Scrape the remaining meringue *on top of the custard* and gently fold in with the rubber spatula, using an over-and-under motion to avoid breaking down the air bubbles in the egg whites. Turn into the baked pie shell and chill well. Serve with whipped cream.

KEY LIME PIE

New York grocers continue to sell limes as if they were exotic curiosities. Why, I don't know, because they grow as plentifully in Florida as lemons and travel just as well. This vivid green citrus is useful for many more things than decorating a gin and tonic. In Mexico, the Caribbean, and Florida it is used as a marinating agent for fish and shellfish and otherwise interchangeably with lemons. Even though the price is weirdly inflated, this pie requires only 2 large juicy limes.

1 9-inch baked pie shell
1 cup sugar
3 Tbsp. cornstarch
½ tsp. salt
2¼ cups boiling water
3 eggs, separated

6 Tbsp. lime juice
3 Tbsp. lime zest (grated rind)
meringue or rum-flavored whipped cream

Combine the sugar, cornstarch, and salt in the top of a double boiler (or use a very heavy saucepan over very low heat). Pour in the boiling water, beating constantly with a wire whisk. When it is smooth and thickened, cover and cook over barely simmering water for 10 minutes. Off heat, beat in the egg yolks one by one, replace the double boiler over the simmering water and cook, stirring constantly, for 5 minutes. Off heat, whisk in the lime juice and lime zest, cool slightly, and pour into baked pie shell. Traditionally, this is covered with a meringue made from the remaining egg whites and a little sugar, then browned briefly in the oven and chilled. I prefer it simply chilled, then served with a dollop of rum-flavored whipped cream, very lightly sweetened.

CAROLINA FRIED PIES

I survived the rigors of boarding-school fare chiefly on bi-weekly supplements from my Aunt Helen. These pies arrived crisp and tart with fillings of stewed apricots or apples. (Those were the days when the mails were fast and dried apricots were cheap.) Mincemeat, prunes, or any kind of dried fruit will do, but apricot fried pies are my *madeleines*.

Makes about 1 dozen

6–8 oz. dried apricots
　water
　sugar to taste
1 recipe pastry (see Empanadas recipe, page 118)
　oil for deep-frying

Wash the fruit; then cover it with cold water and simmer gently until the apricots are tender, 30–40 minutes. Add sugar to taste and cook a few minutes longer until the fruit is a thick compote. Cool.

Cut the pastry in six-inch rounds. Put a spoonful of the apricots in the center of each. Moisten the edges with ice water, fold the circle in half, and crimp the edges securely together. Deep-fry in fresh flavorless oil until golden and crisp—about 5 minutes. Drain on paper towels. Some people like the pies sprinkled with a light drift of confectioner's sugar, but I have always found the texture unpleasantly chalky. Serve warm or at room temperature. Never put them in the icebox; they keep well in a tin box for several days.

RHUBARB COBBLER

"From an old and resourceful Arizona housekeeper, a natural cook, and one always ready to rise to the occasion . . . even on an isolated ranch." The following is adapted from her recipe printed in Emma Paddock Telford's *Good Housekeeper's Cookbook*, 1908.

Serves 6

6 cups rhubarb, cut in 1-inch pieces
1½ cups sugar
½ cup water

2–3 Tbsp. cornstarch mixed to a thin paste with cold water
2 Tbsp. butter, melted
Short Biscuit topping (recipe follows)

Combine the fruit, sugar, and water in a heavy pan. Heat slowly until the rhubarb juices begin to flow. Raise heat slightly and simmer until the rhubarb is tender (this will depend on how young and fresh the rhubarb is). Stir often to prevent scorching. When the fruit is very soft, add the cornstarch paste in a slow thin stream, stirring rapidly. Use only enough to make a fairly thick, smooth sauce—you don't want the sort of rigid paste found in commercial cherry pies. Pour the rhubarb into a shallow round baking dish of about 2-quart capacity. Cool it 5 minutes; then pour a thin film of melted butter over the surface. Make the biscuit.

Short Biscuit (a basic recipe)

2 cups sifted all-purpose flour
3 tsp. baking powder
¾ tsp. salt
2 Tbsp. sugar

6 Tbsp. butter or shortening
1 egg, beaten well
¼ cup milk (approximately)

Preheat oven to 450°.

Sift the dry ingredients together into a large bowl. Work in the shortening with your fingertips until you have a very coarse meal. Add the egg and just enough milk to form a soft dough, which should clean the bowl. On a lightly floured pastry cloth, roll or pat the dough to a half-inch thickness. Cut it into two-inch rounds and lay lightly on top of the rhubarb. (There is a brand of refrigerator "flaky" biscuits, packaged in a tube, that might be used if you cut them a little smaller.)

Bake about 12 minutes, until light brown. Serve warm. Whipped cream does this no harm. Another kind of stewed fruit can be substituted for the rhubarb if you don't care for it.

NOTE: The basic short-biscuit recipe makes too much dough for the Rhubarb Cobbler. However, the excess may be cut in small rounds, placed on a greased cookie sheet, and baked as above. They make a delicious shortcake with any kind of fresh or cooked fruits and berries. Chicken and mushroom shortcake is another possibility if the sugar is omitted from the dough.

VARIATION: The original recipe was made with dumplings simmered on top of the rhubarb. But as I have admitted, dumplings defeat me. Anyone with the fabled fine-light-hand-with-a-dumpling can simplify the cobbler even further.

BRANDIED PEACHES AND CREAM

Every August my grandmother used to fill squadrons of Mason jars with her famous peach butter. Unfortunately, the recipe existed only in her head, but I watched closely enough to be able to almost duplicate it years later. Luscious, tree-ripened peaches are sold for a song at roadside stands on the East End of Long Island late in the summer and surely in many other regions as well. I realize that few modern cooks share my enthusiasm for canning and preserving, so this will be a very abbreviated recipe intended to be used within two weeks.

Makes 2 pints

Brandied Peach Butter

8 large, ripe, firm peaches	½ lemon
1½ cups sugar	1 stick cinnamon
⅓ cup brandy, bourbon, or Calvados	

Skin peaches (drop each into boiling water about 20 seconds, remove with slotted spoon, and with the point of a small knife pull the skins off quickly). Drop them into cold water acidulated with the juice of the lemon to prevent the fruit from darkening. Stone and chop the peaches. Cook them in their own juice about 10 minutes, stirring often. Add no water.

Mash to a coarse purée (it should be slightly lumpy) in a blender or with an old-fashioned potato masher. Return to a heavy enamel-lined saucepan, stir in sugar and cinnamon stick, and cook over medium-high heat, stirring constantly for about 5 minutes. Reduce heat to medium-low and cook, stirring frequently, about 30 minutes longer, or until a bit dropped on a cold plate holds its shape and only a fine ring of liquid forms on the perimeter. Remove the cinnamon stick. Stir in the brandy or bourbon and pour at once into clean hot jars, sealing them tightly. When the peach butter has cooled to room temperature, wipe the jars clean and store in a cool, dark place. The alcohol and sugar prevents spoilage and the peach butter doesn't need refrigeration. For long preservation, the jars are sealed first with a layer of melted parafin.

Now for the Peaches and Cream: soften some good quality peach ice cream, spoon it into glass dessert dishes, and cover it with a big spoonful of Brandied Peach Butter.

Other things you can make with Brandied Peach Butter:
Make a peach mousse by adding the Peach Butter to any good standard recipe for vanilla mousse.
Spread it between thin slices of plain poundcake, fried in butter.
Fill small meringue shells (homemade or bought from a French bakery) and top with whipped cream—a variation on the classic *meringue Chantilly*.
Sandwich it between buttered hot Short Biscuits, serve with thick unwhipped cream.
Eat it on toast.
Peach Bombe: Line a 1-quart melon mold with softened vanilla ice cream, leaving space for ¾ cup peach butter in the center. Cover with plastic wrap and freeze. Unmold and slice at the table.

APPLE CRISP

Those who don't like apples should pass on by, because that's about all there is to this very simple dish. We have a great variety of apples to choose from and they are nearly always cheap. At least the cooking varieties are, and I've never cared for those enormous red or golden "Delicious" apples for any purpose. Any tart, hard apple will be best for this recipe: Winesaps, Jonathans, or green pie apples.

Serves 4

2 lbs. hard, tart apples
4 Tbsp. butter (not margarine)
½ cup light brown sugar
¼ cup bourbon or brandy

½ cup dry bread crumbs
1 tsp. cinnamon
1 Tbsp. butter, broken in tiny pieces

Preheat oven to 400°.

Peel and core the apples (dropping them into acidulated water to prevent discoloration). Slice them about a quarter inch thick. Melt the butter in a skillet and when it is bubbling, add the apple slices. Sauté them gently until they are transparent and tender, turning carefully with a spatula from time to time. Sift the sugar and fold it in. Heat the bourbon in a ladle, set it alight, and pour it over the apples. When the flames subside, transfer the apples to a small gratin dish. Mix the bread crumbs with the cinnamon and sprinkle it in an even thin layer over the top. Dot with butter. Bake in the oven just long enough to brown the top lightly. Serve hot with or without cream.

BANANA FOOL

Flummerys, trifles, slumps, and fools were some of the soft, custardy desserts popular in colonial America. Those unflattering names and the dishes themselves originated in England. Except for trifle, they may have disappeared from English cookery, but they've remained popular in the South, especially in Virginia. The cook's fancy is all that determines what goes into them, and this one was tailored to the taste of an English friend as his seventy-fifth "birthday cake."

Serves 6–8

approximately 3 dozen small Italian ladyfingers
½ cup rum mixed with ½ cup water
2 packages vanilla pudding (not the instant kind)

10–12 dried apricots, chopped coarsely
¼ cup cognac
¼ cup water
3 Tbsp. sugar (or to taste)
1½ ripe large bananas
2 Tbsp. lemon juice

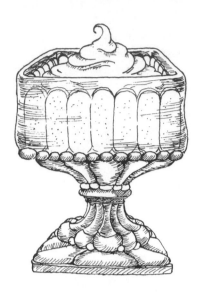

Banana Fool

Make this in a clear glass bowl or footed compote with straight sides, about three inches deep and of about 2-quart capacity.

Bake the ladyfingers in **a 400° oven** for 5 minutes—they're usually a bit too soft and spongy. Cool them and dip them quickly into the mixed rum and water. Split them (they come that way normally) and line the sides and bottom of the glass bowl, arranging the rounded side against the glass.

Make the vanilla pudding according to the package directions and cool it. Cook the apricots in the cognac, water, and sugar, which they should absorb in about 10 minutes. Slice the bananas and turn them in the lemon juice to keep them from discoloring. Mix the cooled (tepid) pudding, the apricots, and the bananas (drained of the lemon juice) together. Fill the ladyfinger-lined bowl with this and chill until serving time. Rich though it is, this dessert is not cloyingly sweet; the apricots, rum, and cognac offset that problem. If you wish to serve the Banana Fool with whipped cream, leave the cream unsweetened.

VARIATION: Raspberry Charlotte. Line a charlotte mold with the ladyfingers prepared as above, but use kirsch and not rum. Soften 1 quart of raspberry sherbet. Make a purée of fresh or frozen unsweetened raspberries. Put half the sherbet in the mold, smoothing it down. Spread the raspberry purée over this. Cover with remaining sherbet. Cover tightly and freeze until half an hour before serving time. Transfer to the refrigerator to soften slightly; then cut into wedges with a silver knife dipped in hot water after each slice.

VIRGINIA CHOCOLATE-PECAN MOUSSE

No candidate for the Weight-Watcher's magazine, this is a superhigh for dessert heads. Chocolate is the all-time front-runner in popularity polls and seems to have delighted everyone who's ever tasted it—from the South American Indians to present-day Japanese. Rich desserts are a hallmark of Southern cookery, and this one is adapted from a recipe in *Virginia Cookery—Past and Present,* a collection of recipes donated by women from all over the state to the Olivet Episcopal Church Fund in Alexandria.

Serves 4

2 envelopes plain gelatine	⅛ tsp. salt
2 Tbsp. very strong cold coffee (espresso)	pinch of cream of tartar
¼ cup boiling water	½ cup sugar
3 squares semisweet baking chocolate	1 tsp. vanilla extract
4 eggs, separated	½ cup chopped pecans
	whipped cream flavored with brandy (optional)

Soften gelatine in the cold coffee; then pour on boiling water and stir to dissolve. Melt the chocolate in the top of a double boiler, add the gelatine mixture, and beat in the egg yolks over hot but not boiling water. Cook about 3 minutes, stirring constantly. Cool. Beat the egg whites stiff with the salt and cream of tartar; then beat in the sugar. Add the vanilla and chopped pecans to the cooled chocolate mixture and scrape this into a large bowl. Put the stiff meringue on top of the chocolate base and carefully fold it in with a rubber spatula. Don't attempt to do this with an electric mixer, no matter what the maker claims for his machine. Mixers break down the air bubbles too much and the mousse will turn out dense and sodden. Select a mold (see Salmon Mousse recipe, page 86, for instructions on unmolding) just large enough to hold the mixture and rinse it with cold water. Shake out water. Turn the mousse into the mold and chill it for at least 6 hours. Unmold and serve with whipped cream or not.

THE POOR AUTHOR'S PUDDING

Eliza Acton gave this name to a simple bread pudding in *Modern Cookery for Private Families*, 1845. Her publisher, rejecting her poetry, told her to go home and write a cookbook. Miss Acton never married and had no Women's Liberation Movement to turn to. So she went home and wrote the first intelligent, careful, specific, and well-written cookbook in England. (There was no one to compare with her until Elizabeth David came along more than a century later.) I often cook from this book and found that Miss Acton's bread pudding was very similar to mine, so I borrowed the name. There cannot be any dessert simpler to make than this, and everybody adores it.

Serves 4

6 slices firm home-style bread, trimmed
butter (not margarine—the flavor won't do)
2 cups milk
½ cup sugar, minus 1 Tbsp.
2 oz. of any kind of liqueur

(Cointreau, Grand Marnier, kirsch) or brandy
1 tsp. vanilla extract
3 eggs
any kind of stewed fruit sauce (optional)

Preheat the oven to 350°.

Butter the bread rather heavily and cut it in one-inch squares. Scald the milk with the sugar, liqueur, and vanilla extract. Beat the eggs until very light and, still whisking, pour the scalding milk over them in a medium stream. Put the bread in a small deep 1-quart baking dish and pour the thin custard over it. Bake about 25 or 30 minutes. It should be lightly browned and puffed up. Unfortunately it falls instantly, but don't overcook it thinking you can change this. The pudding is done enough when a silver knife comes out of the center with just a little custard on it. Let the pudding settle 5 or 10 minutes and serve warm. Most people (all ages) prefer this pudding with no sauce.

QUEEN OF PUDDING

This very old English dessert I first had in an Irish nursing home, where I was luxuriously recovering from a skirmish with a headstrong Irish stallion. All the food was wonderfully and delicately prepared, served on different sets of porcelain at each of my four daily meals. Ireland has many excellent restaurants with a number of Swiss or French-trained chefs. Much of the food is the sort of thing the English used to do well about a hundred years ago, but seem to have forgotten. Queen of Pudding, for instance.

Serves 6–8

4 eggs, separated
¾ cup sugar (reserve 4 Tbsp. for meringue)
1 quart milk, tepid

1 pint soft bread crumbs (see note)
grated rind of 1 lemon
red currant jelly

Preheat oven to 350°.

Beat egg yolks light with sugar; blend in milk and crumbs and then the lemon zest. Pour into a buttered 2-quart soufflé dish. Bake for about 25 minutes. It will be very slightly underdone. Cool 10 minutes; then spread the top of the pudding with currant jelly. Whip the egg whites to a soft meringue (firm but not dry); then whip in the 4 tablespoons of sugar. Swirl it over the pudding, sealing it completely. Brown lightly in the oven on the top rack position. Serve warm.

NOTE: Soft bread crumbs are easily made in a blender on medium speed. Use trimmed day-old white bread.

PÂTE À CHOUX

This cream-puff paste has nothing whatever to do with the very difficult puff paste (*pâté feuilletée*). It is simple to make and is useful to know because the *panade* is the basis of other nonsweet dishes (various meat or vegetable fritters, *gnocchi* and *quenelles*, for instance). The puffs are usually filled with a plain but rich-tasting pastry cream, sometimes with whipped cream or ice cream (I don't really care for the ice-cream idea—it makes the puffs terribly heavy). They may also be served as a first course filled with creamed chicken, veal and mushrooms, or a mixture of the three with a little ham added. The recipe below is for the sweet puffs—for non-dessert puffs, omit the sugar and increase the salt to 1 teaspoon. This is a classic recipe that varies only minutely from book to book.

Makes about 12 large puffs (3-inch diameter) or about 3 dozen small puffs

1 cup water
¾ stick of unsalted butter or margarine
pinch of salt

1 tsp. sugar
1 cup sifted flour
4 large eggs

Preheat oven to 425°.

Use a heavy-bottomed saucepan—copper-bottomed stainless steel is good because it has the thickness where you want it and isn't too heavy to handle. Bring the water, butter, salt, and sugar to a boil. Remove from heat and dump in the flour all at once. Beat vigorously with a wooden spoon until the mixture forms a ball and cleans the saucepan. If it doesn't, return to low heat and continue beating until it forms a ball. Remove from heat and give it a couple of stirs so the dough won't be so hot it will cook the eggs. Make a well in the center and beat in the eggs one at a time, blending well before adding another. Now you should have a pliant, shiny, yellow *panade*. Immediately pipe the warm dough onto an *ungreased* cookie sheet, using a pastry bag with a one-inch opening, making mounds about one inch high and of one and a half inches diameter. They should be two inches apart. Bake in the preheated oven 35 to 40 minutes. Remove from oven, slit to allow steam to escape or, if there seems to be a lot of doughy, uncooked center (there is always *some*), scrape it out, replace the tops, and return the puffs to an unlit warm oven for 20 minutes to dry out. The drying out in the oven must be done no matter whether you make large or small puffs and whether or not the centers are scraped. Small puffs take about 30 minutes to bake at 425°. Cool on a rack away from drafts.

The *panade* must be warm to rise to maximum. If you only need half this amount, refrigerate or freeze the rest. Warm it to tepid in a heavy saucepan before using it.

NOTE: If you haven't a pastry bag (not one of those dreadful little tin cylinders, which are useless), take up spoonfuls of the *panade*, using a round or oval soup spoon, and place them two inches apart on the baking sheet. For small puffs, use a teaspoon.

VARIATION: Another simple dessert made from the *panade* is Beignets Soufflés. Flavor the warm *panade* with orange or vanilla extract. Take up a teaspoonful and use another teaspoon to push it off into deep hot oil. Fry for about 5 minutes until brown and about double in size. Drain on paper towels. Serve warm with a fruit or custard sauce.

CRÈME PÂTISSIÈRE

This pastry cream is one of the mainstays of French pastry-makers: it goes into *mille feuilles* and cream puffs, and forms the bottom layer of open fruit tarts and hundreds of other desserts. It has a lavish texture and subtle flavor that packaged dehydrated puddings, good though they are, will never duplicate.

Makes about 2½ cups

6 egg yolks (freeze the whites for another use)
6 Tbsp. flour
⅓ cup sugar
2 cups milk
1½ tsp. vanilla extract

Beat the egg yolks until light; then beat in the flour and sugar gradually. Scald the milk and pour it in a stream into the egg mixture, whisking rapidly. When it is smooth, put it into the top of a double boiler and cook it over barely bubbling water, stirring constantly. It is done when it is quite thick and absolutely smooth, but it should not be allowed to boil. Beat in the vanilla extract, or you might want to flavor it with a liqueur or some melted semisweet chocolate.

Press a layer of plastic wrap down onto the surface of the pastry cream to prevent a skin forming. When it is tepid, fill the cold cream-puff shells and chill until serving time.

CLOVELLY TOAST

This isn't really a dessert, but a treat for the after-school maw that has to be appeased until dinnertime. It is from *The Memphis Cookbook*.

Slice bread into one-inch-thick slices, trim crusts; fry until crisp in plenty of butter. Sprinkle with cinnamon, powdered cloves, and sugar mixed together, and serve hot.

Hats off to Mrs. Hubert K. Reese of the Memphis Junior League!

14

THE BITTER END

Here are some dishes to make when the string is really out. They may not become family favorites, but who can say? I know a guy who's still daft about grits with sorghum, the mainstay of his dirt-farmer childhood. Some of these dishes are cheap because they're unfamiliar, therefore unpopular, in this country; others are just superb ways to wring the most food value out of a dollar or less (at this writing). Short of stealing saltines and catchup from cafeterias, these recipes are about as economical as you can get.

A.J.MUSTE MEMORIAL SUPPER (Fish Heads and Rice)

Fasting is cheaper than this dish, but almost nothing else is. Go to your fish dealer (preferably one you've built up a friendly relationship with) and buy one small cheap fillet of anything. Ask for some *large* (small ones haven't enough flesh) fish heads and trimmings to make a soup. This should melt the hardest heart and anyway fish dealers are often compassionate artists who worry a lot about the decline of fish-eating. Yours will probably give you some great, meaty trimmings left over from the rich folks' fillets.

Serves 2

1 fresh fillet of any kind of fish	water
2 large fish heads	1 tsp. salt
about 2 lbs. fish trimmings (if you're lucky)	½ tsp. pepper
	2 onions

220

1 bay leaf
3 sprigs fresh thyme (or ½ tsp. dried)
1 small can stewed tomatoes

1 cup raw long-grain white rice
1 Tbsp. bacon dripping
2 Tbsp. parsley, chopped (optional)

Wash all the fish under cold running water. Put the heads and trimmings into an aluminum or enamel pot. Cover with about one inch of cold water and add 1 onion, the salt and pepper, the bay leaf, and the thyme. Bring to a boil, skim, and reduce heat, and simmer about 15 minutes, or until the fish can be flaked with a fork. Add the little fillet during the last 5 minutes of cooking time.

Strain the fish into a colander set over a large bowl. Pick out all the fish from the bones and heads and reserve. Return the fish broth to the pot, add the canned tomatoes, and boil rapidly until it has reduced to 2 cups. Meanwhile, chop up the remaining onion and fry it gently in a little bacon dripping in a large, heavy skillet with cover. Stir in the rice and pour in the boiling broth. Stir once around with a fork, reduce heat to very low, cover, and cook, undisturbed, for 20 minutes. Check to see if all liquid is absorbed; if not, continue cooking about 5 minutes longer with the lid askew. Just before serving stir in the reserved fish bits and flakes, re-cover for a minute or two to heat through, and sprinkle with chopped parsley. You can omit the tomatoes and parsley if things are really tough.

This dish should be served with a glass of cold water and a prayer for peace.

STONE-BROKE HASH

This is simple to make, very filling, and deeply satisfying. It's a casserole I make about once a month no matter how near or far the wolf is from the door.

Serves 4

1 12-oz. can corned beef
1 large onion, chopped
2 Tbsp. margarine
1 Tbsp. flour
1 cup milk

2 medium-sized "boiling" (old) potatoes
salt and pepper
parsley

Preheat oven to 400°.

Peel the potatoes, cut them in half-inch dice, and put them on to boil in enough salted water to cover. They should be done in about 10 minutes. Don't overcook. While the potatoes simmer, chop the onion and sauté it gently in the margarine until soft but not browned. Add the flour and cook, stirring, over low heat about 1 minute. Pour in the milk, turn up the heat to medium, and stir rapidly with a wooden spoon or wire whip to prevent lumps forming. When the sauce starts to boil, reduce the heat to a very low simmer. Drain the potatoes well and shake them over low heat to dry. Dump the can of corned beef into the cream sauce and break it up thoroughly with a fork. Gently fold in the potatoes, mashing them as little as possible. Taste and add as much salt and pepper as you like. Add a couple of tablespoons of chopped parsley if you have any. Pour into an earthenware or Pyrex casserole and set it in the oven on the middle rack for about 10 minutes, or until the top browns nicely.

SPAGHETTI CON AGLIO ED OLIO

Most of us are brought up to think of spaghetti as something that supports a blob of thick red sauce in which there may or may not be some meat. Italians, however, appreciate their pasta for itself alone, and this is a simple and popular way they serve it.

Serves 2

1 clove garlic, mashed	½ lb. thin (#9) spaghetti
2–3 Tbsp. olive oil	pepper

Heat the oil in a small skillet and cook the garlic gently until the kitchen smells very good. Throw away the garlic. Cook the spaghetti in a large pot of boiling salted water until just tender (*al dente*). Drain, but do not rinse, the spaghetti; then toss with the warm oil and serve in hot bowls. If you have it, a handful of chopped fresh parsley can't hurt.

JANSON'S TEMPTATION

Nobody knows who Janson was, but undoubtedly he must have come from a deprived Visigoth background if this dish is what he dreamed of. The classic Swedish recipe calls for real cream, somewhat of a luxury these days in our country, but over-all the dish is still cheap and very filling.

2 large "boiling" potatoes, cut in matchsticks

2 medium onions, thinly sliced

1 small can flat anchovy fillets

1 cup heavy cream (evaporated milk, in a pinch)

2 Tbsp. butter

pepper and salt

Preheat oven to 350°.

After peeling the potatoes, to prevent darkening put them in cold water as you slice them into matchsticks. Drain and dry them. Butter a small baking dish and arrange half the potatoes in it. Dribble a bit of the anchovy oil over the potatoes; then add the onions, the anchovies distributed evenly over the dish, and last, the remaining potatoes. Pour on the cream, dot with butter, sprinkle with pepper and a very little salt (remember, the anchovies). Cover tightly with aluminum foil and bake 45 minutes. Uncover and continue baking 15 minutes longer, turning down the oven heat if the cream is evaporating too quickly. The potatoes should be tender and absorb most of the cream.

MARROWBONE, BROTH, AND TOAST

Marrowbones are the cheapest thing you will find on any meat counter and a friendly butcher will often give them away. They are beef shinbones sawed into approximately one-and-a-half-inch lengths so that the marrow can be extracted after poaching and spread on bread or toast. It looks just terrible, but is considered a great delicacy by the French; you will agree if you can overcome your initial shock at its unloveliness. Oysters don't win any beauty prizes either. Marrow is rich and nutritious.

Serves 2

about 8 pieces marrowbone

1 can undiluted beef bouillon

1 soup can water

4 thick slices toasted home-style bread

kosher salt (if possible) and pepper

It is more elegant to pry the marrow from the bones before cooking it, but this can be tricky so I generally cook it in the bone when it's a just-folks snack. If you'd like to pry it out, use a narrow strong knife, and then slice it in neat rounds about a half inch thick.

Bring the bouillon and water to a simmer and add the marrow slices or the whole bones. Slices will be done (translucent) in about 3 minutes —in the bone, it will take a bit longer. When the marrow is done, spread it thinly on hot toast, sprinkle with salt and pepper, and eat it right away. Discard the bones, skim off any fat that may have accumulated, and drink the broth right up.

RICE AND BEANS

People who were raised on this basic food develop a craving for it that persists no matter to what dizzying heights they rise in business and commerce. All the way from South America to the Mason-Dixon Line, variations of rice and beans are a way of life. This is a combination I like, but you can fool around with it endlessly, depending on your preferences and/or economic condition.

Serves 4

½ cup smoked bacon, diced
1 large onion, chopped
2 cloves garlic, minced
1 can or 3 ripe tomatoes, peeled
1 cup (or more) chicken broth
pinch of basil
1 tsp. salt

1 Tbsp. tomato paste
1 cup converted rice
2 cups cooked beans: red or white kidney beans, garbanzos, pinto beans, California pink beans, black beans
2 Tbsp. parsley, chopped

Fry the bacon slowly in a heavy skillet until nearly done. Add onions and garlic, and sauté until soft. Chop the tomatoes and squeeze as much juice as possible out of them into a bowl. Add enough chicken broth to make 2 cups of liquid. Put the tomatoes, basil, salt, and tomato-and-chicken broth into the skillet with the vegetables and bacon. Stir in tomato paste and bring to a boil. Add rice and cooked beans. Cover and cook over low heat until liquid has evaporated, and rice is tender, about 20 minutes. Turn into a hot serving dish and sprinkle with parsley.

CANNELLINI WITH TUNA

Normally this is served as a first course, but it is not so heavy or monotonous that it can't be a whole meal . . . especially if you're in no position to be picky. Cannellini are white kidney beans usually found in the Italian-foods section of most supermarkets.

1 can cannellini (about 1½ cups)
1 can white, chunk-style tuna
2 scallions, minced
¼ cup olive oil

salt and pepper
1 lemon
1 Tbsp. fresh parsley, chopped
2 hard-boiled eggs (optional)

Drain and rinse the beans in cold water. Drain well, then combine beans, minced scallions, and olive oil. Do this very gently with your hands to avoid mashing the beans—the canned ones are very soft. Arrange on a platter, sprinkle with salt, pepper, and parsley, and garnish with chunks of tuna, lemon wedges, and the eggs, cut in half, if used. Do not chill—the flavor is much better at room temperature.

SHINBONE STEW

Although the basic preparation is rather long, this delicious peasant soup can keep you alive and healthy for several days. Its composition is so optional you're bound to find most of the things you need at a good price. Scout the produce section for damaged vegetables being sold cheaply.

Basic Ingredients

2 slices thick bacon, cut in squares
1½ lbs. shin of beef
2 medium onions
1 clove garlic
1 can stewed tomatoes
1 cup water
1 can beef bouillon plus 1 can water

2 carrots, sliced in thin rounds
2 medium potatoes, diced
1 small turnip, peeled and cubed
½ tsp. dried basil
¼ tsp. dried thyme
2 cups shredded green cabbage

Optional Ingredients

handful snap beans
1 package frozen speckled butter beans
1 package frozen green lima beans
1 can garbanzos (chick-peas)

1 can kidney beans
1 cup cooked dried beans (navy, pea, or marrow)
½ cup any kind of pasta (except spaghetti), e.g., shells, elbow macaroni, orzo, cavetelli

Choose one kind of beans and one kind of pasta from the optional ingredients and cook them in the soup for the length of time indicated on their packages. Precooked dried beans (including the canned garbanzos) should be added about 1 hour before the soup is done. I do urge you to stick to the basic ingredients (yes, even the turnip—I know they're out of style, but a little bit gives a rich, decisive flavor to the stew). You can stretch the stew and alter its character from day to day by adding new ingredients, but don't cook it to a sludge.

Fry the bacon slowly in a big, heavy iron pot that you have some kind of lid for. (A Dutch oven or enamel-coated iron casserole is perfect.) When nearly crisp, remove and drain on paper toweling. Dry the shin-bone and brown it in remaining fat. Peel and chop the onions and garlic and sauté in the same pot. Add the tomatoes, water, bouillon, carrots, potatoes, turnip, basil, and thyme. Stir it up and bring everything to a boil; then turn heat very low and simmer until the soup meat is very tender—about 1½ hours. Take the meat out, discard bone and fat, cut into chunks, and return it to pot. You don't have to pay too much attention to it, but stir it occasionally and just keep it burbling gently. Add the cabbage and cook for half an hour longer. You must time your optional ingredients to be done when the cabbage is done. Season with salt and pepper to taste and serve in big soup plates. When I haven't used pasta, I sometimes put a spoonful of cooked rice in the bottom of the soup plate before ladling on the stew.

COLCANNON

Irish cookery may not be the *dernier cri* in refinement, but filling it is. Colcannon is a mound of fluffy mashed potatoes and buttered, chopped greens with a well of melted butter in the center to dip each forkful into. Kale is the traditional vegetable, but since it isn't popular at my table, I substitute spinach. Shredded cabbage, cooked to the crisp-tender stage, is another possibility.

The Irish are rather fond of burying rings, coins, buttons, and suchlike in breads and puddings, and they put them in Colcannon on Halloween to foretell the future. The ring and coin are obvious and I seem to recall that the button means you're doomed to sewing them on for yourself for-ever—if you're tempted by this sort of whimsy.

4 large "boiling" potatoes	5–6 scallions, minced
1 lb. bag of washed spinach (or package of frozen spinach)	½–¾ cup boiling milk
	4 Tbsp. melted butter
2 Tbsp. butter	salt and pepper to taste

Peel and dice the potatoes and drop them in salted boiling water. (Or make 2 envelopes of dehydrated mashed potatoes according to the package directions.) Wash the spinach and remove stems (fold the leaf in half, grasp the stem, and pull toward the leaf). Put the spinach into a pot with just the water that clings to the leaves, cover, and cook over brisk heat until the spinach wilts—about 4 minutes. Drain, press out juices lightly, and chop coarsely. Mince the scallions. When the potatoes are tender (about 15 minutes) drain, return to saucepan, and shake over low heat to evaporate moisture. Put them through a food mill or a ricer and beat in the 2 tablespoons of butter and enough of the hot milk to fluff up the potatoes nicely. Don't make them too runny. Beat in the chopped spinach and scallions and season to taste with salt and pepper. Reheat over low heat, stirring constantly. Heap into tall mounds on hot plates. Make a well in the center of each mound for the melted butter.

BRAISED CHICKEN HEARTS

The only thing I know about this for sure is that it's cheap. A trusted friend tells me her children (middle-aged teen-agers) bleat for it, and this is her recipe. It has been tested many times, though not by me. Chicken parts like this average around 49¢ a pound and are bulging with vitamins and minerals.

2 Tbsp. butter	1 Tbsp. paprika
2 medium onions, chopped	1 cup water
2 cloves garlic, minced	¼ cup white wine, vermouth, or sherry (optional)
½ lb. fresh mushrooms, sliced (optional)	salt and pepper
1 lb. chicken hearts	2 Tbsp. chopped parsley

Sauté the onions and garlic in the butter until soft and transparent. If using mushrooms, add them and sauté lightly. Wash and dry the chicken hearts, remove any bits of chicken fat that cling, and stir into the pan. Brown lightly. Add the paprika, water, and wine, bring to a boil, and salt and pepper to taste. Lower heat to a simmer, cover, and stew for about 1½ hours, stirring occasionally. Add a bit of water if the sauce is cooking away too quickly. Serve over hot, fluffy white rice and scatter the parsley on top. The ragout is also served with kasha or buttered noodles.

RYE BREAD SOUP

Mrs. Beeton, in her *Book of Household Management*, gives a "Useful Soup for Benevolent Purposes" she apparently inflicted on the poorer inhabitants of her village in the winter of 1858. It cost the benefactress 1½ pence per quart. This comes to a little more than that—the extravagance of a half bottle of beer pushes up the price recklessly. But this is much better than Mrs. Beeton's charity soup.

Serves 2

4 slices rye bread with seeds
3 Tbsp. butter or olive oil
1 large onion, sliced
1½ pints water
½ bottle of beer

salt, pepper, pinch of nutmeg or mace, ground clove to taste
1 hard-boiled egg

Trim the bread of crust and cut it in dice. Fry the bread cubes and onions in the butter until the onions are tender and lightly browned. Heat the water and beer, mixed, to boiling and pour over the bread and onions. Save the other half to drink with your soup. Season with salt, pepper, and spices and simmer 1 hour. Purée in a blender or food mill, then reheat. Float slices of hard-boiled egg on top of each serving.

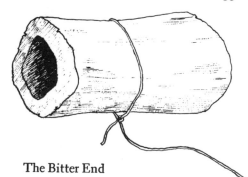

The Bitter End

INDEX

Coq au vin, 95–96
Corn, from cob, 15; chowder, 15
Cornbread stuffing, 102–103
Cottage cheese salad, 19
Country Captain, 96–97
Cream puffs, 217–19
Cream sauces, 30–35; thick, 31, 32; thin, 31
Crème pâtissière, 218–19
Creole fish gumbo, 16
Creole sauce, 36–37
Creuset ware, xi, xiv, 79
Cucumber and tomato salad, 15
Cucumber sauce, 83
Curry, cucumber sauce for, 83; egg, 70; Jamaican "goat," 142–43, 153; lamb, 153; lamb kidneys, 159–60; lentil salad, 28; lentil soup, 12–13; veal, 142

David, Elizabeth, *French Country Cooking*, 52; *French Provincial Cooking*, 169, 206
Deep-fat frying, xix–xx
Degreasing: of chicken stock, 105; of gravy and sauces, 35–36
Desperation soup, 18–19
Dizi, 157–58
Dressing, Salad. *See* Salad dressing
Duchess potatoes, 129
Duck cassoulet, 48–49
Duckling, domestic, 94; roast, 113–14; use of fat, xx
Dumas, Alexandre, *Le Grand Dictionnaire de Cuisine*, 90, 189

Egg cream, 74
Egg sauce, 44
Egg-liaison sauces, 37–44
Eggplant, french-fried, 193–94; stuffed, 192–93
Eggs: baked en cocotte, 65; curried, 70; Florentine, 64; fried, 63; grading of, 61–62; hot buttered, for storing, 62–63; how to buy, 61–62;

poached, 63–64; in Purgatory, 72; refrigeration of, 62; sauce, 44; scrambled, 65–66; storage of, 62–63; stuffed Mornay, 73–74
Empanadas, 118–20
Equipment, kitchen. *See* Kitchen equipment

Fake Chinese Meal, 57–58
Farmer, Fannie, *Boston Cooking-School Cook Book*, 87
Farmer's dinner, 178
Feijoada, 171
Filet of Sole à la Bonne Femme, 81–82
Fish: cold with dilled sour cream, 83–84; Creole soup, 16; fillets in cream sauce, 81–82; heads and rice, 220–221; frozen, 76; how to buy, 76, 79; stock, 32. *See also* individual Fish listings
Fisher, M. F. K., *How to Cook a Wolf*, 72
Flounder, 75; fillets in cream sauce, 81–82; grilled, 76–78; how to buy, 79; roe, sautéed, 79–80
Food of France, The, Waverly Root, 39, 89, 198
French dressing, 21–22; egg sauce, 44
French Country Cooking, Elizabeth David, 52
French Provincial Cooking, Elizabeth David, 169, 206
Fried bread, 64, 91, 170
Frijoles negros, 46–47; soup, 11
Fritto misto. *See* Vegetable fritters
Fruit, 208–15; pies, 209–10; tarts, 219. *See also* individual listings
Frying fat, xix–xx, 35–36

Galantine, 106–108
Garbanzo soup, 13–14
Garlic sauce, 40–41
Gehman, Richard, *The Haphazard Gourmet*, 3, 188

London broil, 122–23
Louisiana bean soup, 12
Lucas, Dione, xiv

Macaroni: and cheese, 55–56; and sausages, 54–55; and tuna salad, 29
Margarine, xviii–xix
Marrowbone(s), 131; broth and toast, 223–24
Maruzzelle and sausages, 54–55
Mastering the Art of French Cooking, Simone Beck, Louisette Bertholle, and Julia Child, 141, 206
Mayonnaise, 37–39; commercial, 30–31; garlic, 40–41; reconstituted when curdled, 38–39; verte, 39
Meat jelly, 124–25
Meatballs Stroganoff, 121–22
Meatloaf, 120–21
Memphis Cookbook, The, 219
Mexican ingredients, where to buy, 47
Mille feuilles, 218
Modern Cookery for Private Families, Eliza Acton, 4, 127, 216
Mornay sauce, 34
Mousse: Chocolate-pecan, 215; salmon, 86; to unmold, 87
Mussels: and potato salad, 25–26; Dumas, 90–91
Mutton and chick-pea stew, 157–58

Okra gumbo, 195–96
Omelet(s), 66–68, 67 (*illus.*); Bauernfrühstück, 68; Mediterranean, 71; soufflé, 69
Onion(s), boiled, 194–95; soup, hot and cold, 10–11
Oriental Cook Book, editors of *Sunset,* 58
Ortiz, Elisabeth Lambert, *The Complete Book of Mexican Cooking,* 174
Ossi buchi, 140

Paris broil, 122–23
Parisienne sauce, 32–34

Parsley soup, 8
Pasta, 54–60
Pâté, pork liver, 175–76
Pâte à choux, 217–18
Peach butter, brandied, 211–12
Peaches, brandied, and cream, 211–12
Peck, Paula, *The Art of Fine Baking,* 206
Picadillo, 118–19
Pies, 208–10; apricot, 209–10; Key lime, 208–209; pumpkin chiffon, 208
Pig roast en sanglier, 168–69
Pig's feet, 155
Pilaf, 53
Piperade, 72–73
Poor author's pudding, 216
Pork: chops, 58, 172; grading, 161–165; fat for cooking, 170; how to buy, 161–62; liver pâté, 175–76; loin with ripe olives, 169–70; ragout, 172–73; roast with black beans, 171; shoulder, braised, 166–67; Tinga poblana, 173–75. *See also* Salt pork; Sausage
Potatoes, 197–200; with anchovy paste, 222–23; baked, 199–200; and cheese, 198–99; Duchess, 129; and greens, 226–27; and leek soup, 7–9; rösti, 199; stuffed with kidneys, 200; Truffado, 198–99. *See also* Potato Salad
Potato salad: French, 25; mashed, 26; and mussels, 25
Pot-au-feu, 4–7; chicken, 105
Pots: buying, xi, xiv, xvi; Chinese, 59; fish, 76; French stock pot, 5; soup, 5; steamers, 199
Poultry, grading, 92–93, 95. *See also* individual listings
Princess Pamela's Soul Food Cookbook, Princess Pamela, 162
Pudding: bread, 216; queen of, 216–17
Puff pastry, frozen, 143
Pumpkin chiffon pie, 208

Stir-frying, 59
Stock: chicken, 98, 105; clarifying, 167–68; meat, 167–68; tongue, 12, 133; turkey or goose, 35
Stockfisch, 89–90
Stone-broke hash, 221–22
Stoves, electric or gas, xv
String beans. *See* Green beans
Stuffing, 101; cornbread, 102–103
Suet, beef, xix
Summer soup, savoury, 9–10
Summer squash and zucchini sauté, 203–204
Suprêmes, sautéed, 97–100; with Chinese mushrooms, 100–101

Tempura, chicken, 110–11. *See also* Vegetable fritters
Tinga poblana, 173–74
Toad-in-the-hole, 177
Tomato Creole sauce, 36–37
Tomatoes: green fried, 201; gratin, 202–203; pan-broiled cherry, 201–202
Tongue: smoked, 132–33; stock, 131
Tortillas, 58
Truffado: I, 198; II, 198–99
Truffle, substitute, 169
Tuna: and macaroni salad, 29; mold, 86
Turkey, 93–94; roast, 112–13; self-basting, 94
Turtle beans and rice, 46–47
"TV supper" (poached eggs), 64

Uova in purgatorio, 72
U.S.D.A. grading systems. *See* Grading

Veal, 134–46; à la Bonne Femme, 141–42; blanquette, 135–36; curried (Jamaican "curry goat"), 142–43; grading, 135; and ham and mushroom bouchées, 143–45; how to buy, 134–35; kidneys (rognons de veau), 144–46; Ossi buchi, 140; roast, 141–42; sauté Marengo, 137–38; shanks, 140; stuffed breast, 138–140
Vegetable salads: Argenteuil, 28–29; bean, tomato, and olive, 23; spinach, mushroom, and bacon, 23–24
Vegetable shortenings, hydrogenated, xix
Vegetables: fresh, 182; fritters, 203; frozen, 184; grading, 183; how to buy, 182–84; leftover, with vinaigrette dressing, 7. *See also* individual listings
Velouté sauce, 31–32; Parisienne, 32–34
Vichyssoise, 7–9
Vinaigrette dressing, 21–22
Vinegar, hot, 111
Virginia chocolate-pecan mousse, 215
Virginia Cookery Past and Present, Olivet Episcopal Church Fund, 215

Watercress soup, 8
Whisks, 37
White beans: in cassoulet, 47–49; and lamb-neck casserole, 50–51; and roast lamb, 148–52; soup, 11–12; and tuna (cannellini), 224–25

Yorkshire pudding, 131

Zucchini: and lamb ragoût, 154; soup, 9–10; and summer squash sauté, 203–204